Does the New Testament Imitate Homer?

DENNIS R. MacDONALD

Does the New Testament Imitate Homer?

FOUR CASES FROM THE ACTS OF THE APOSTLES

Yale University Press
New Haven and London

Published with assistance from the
Louis Stern Memorial Fund.

Set in Sabon type by Keystone Typesetting, Inc.
Printed in the United States of America by Sheridan Books.

Library of Congress Cataloging-in-Publication Data

MacDonald, Dennis Ronald, 1946–
Does the New Testament imitate Homer? : four cases from the Acts of the Apostles /
Dennis R. MacDonald.
     p.   cm.
Includes bibliographical references and index.
ISBN 0-300-09770-0 (alk. paper)

1. Bible. N.T. Acts—Extra-canonical parallels. 2. Greek literature—Relation to the
New Testament. 3. Homer. Iliad. I. Title.
BS2625.52.M33 2003
226.6′066—dc21
2003049688

A catalog record for this book is available from the British Library.

The paper in this book meets the guidelines for permanence and durability of the
Committee on Production Guidelines for Book Longevity of the Council on Library
Resources.

10 9 8 7 6 5 4 3 2 1

For Gordon, Wynne, Don, and
Treehouse

Contents

Acknowledgments

At the risk of being trite, I must acknowledge that this book would have been impossible without the encouragement, efforts, abilities, and support of my students, comrades, family, and friends. Several passages are stronger for the insights of students at the Claremont School of Theology and the Claremont Graduate University, especially Ruben Dupertuis, Brett Provance, Michael Schufer, Syng Won Suh, Mariano Tomaszewski, and Young Cho, each of whom has made significant contributions to my understanding of mimesis or its application to particular texts. Michael also checked the Appendix of Greek and Latin texts for accuracy. Brett and more recently Leslie Hayes have ably administered the Institute for Antiquity and Christianity and thus freed me to pursue my research and writing with increased intensity. Olga Morales and Judy Little have provided secretarial assistance with class and care. As was the case with my previous book on Homer and the New Testament, the staff at Yale University Press has been professional, competent, and solicitous. Their reader, whoever he or she may be, made brilliant suggestions concerning improvements. A grant from the National Endowment for the Humanities allowed me to complete the manuscript earlier than otherwise would have been possible.

Amy Furth, my wife, with immeasurable grace encouraged my other passion: ancient religious literature. It is to her father, Gordon Furth, her sister Wynne

Furth, and her brother-in-law Donald Brenneis that I have dedicated this book in gratitude for their friendship and support. I also have dedicated it to Treehouse, their home in Marin County, where I have spent many productive and memorable days hiking, reading, writing, and ruminating about Homer and the New Testament.

Does the New Testament Imitate Homer?

Introduction

"Who would claim that the writing of prose is not reliant on the Homeric poems?"[1] This rhetorical question by a teacher of rhetoric requires a negative answer: no ancient intellectual would have doubted that the *Iliad* and the *Odyssey* informed the composition of prose, including potentially the stories of the New Testament. In *The Homeric Epics and the Gospel of Mark* I argued that the author of the earliest Gospel used the *Odyssey* as his primary literary model for chapters 1–14; he used the *Iliad*, especially the death of Hector and the ransom of his corpse, as his model for chapters 15–16.[2] I am gratified by many responses to the book, but it also has generated skepticism, criticism, and occasional hostility. It is to answer my critics that I have undertaken this book, which compares four extensive passages in the Acts of the Apostles with the *Iliad*.

From the outset I knew that my reading of Mark would meet resistance not only from those who read the Gospels as historically reliable but also from critically trained scholars. Most modern treatments of the Gospels and Acts view their authors as redactors, or editors, of preexisting traditions and written sources. These practitioners of form criticism divide texts into constituent units and categorize them by genre, such as parables, proverbs, prayers, prophecies, or legends of various types, like miracle stories and epiphanies. They then seek to reconstruct the geographical, linguistic, or theological environments that created and transmitted them before their articulation in the text. Many scholars would go so far as to ascribe nearly all narratives in the Gospels and Acts to historical memory or at least to tradition. Others would grant more originality to these works, but few consider literary imitation as a dominating compositional activity.

But early Christian authors not only fiddled with traditions and sources; they created stories after pagan literary models, sometimes without Jewish or Christian traditions to inform them. That is, they wrote as they had been taught in school: through μίμησις or *imitatio*.[3] A contemporary of the evangelists wrote: "There can be no doubt that in art no small portion of our task [as teachers of rhetoric] lies in *imitatio*, since . . . it is expedient to follow whatever has been invented with success."[4] A historian of rhetoric claims that "Rhetorical *mimesis* or imitation . . . became such a major interest of teachers of rhetoric that in later Hellenistic times it tended to overshadow everything else."[5] No targets for imitation were more popular than the *Iliad* and the *Odyssey*, even for the writing of prose. Whereas a form critic compares a narrative in the New Testament to other tales of the same genre as a collectivity, a "mimesis critic" will compare it with earlier texts, one or more of which might have served the author as a model. Of course, literary imitation cannot account for all stories in the Gospels and Acts, but it can account for an impressive number of them.

It is one thing to acknowledge the significance of mimesis for ancient narratives in general but quite another to recognize an imitation in a specific text. Students learned to disguise their dependence to avoid charges of pedantry or plagiarism, but mimesis often is difficult to recognize even when authors advertise their works as imitations. Today we read these texts with a cultural competence radically different from those for whom they were written; ancient readers could detect allusions invisible to all but the best-trained classicists. Even though the detection of mimesis is difficult, it is one of the most valuable contributions a critic can make for understanding a text. To be sure, one may profitably read a mimetic text for its own sake, but awareness of its model or models allows one to interpret it more comprehensively, more dialogically.[6]

I have designed six criteria for spotting literary imitation in ancient texts, not just in the New Testament and not just of classical poetry. I crafted the criteria to reflect descriptions of mimetic practices in Greek and Roman authors, but they apply to all types of direct literary influence.

The first two criteria assess the cultural significance of the proposed model. Accessibility, criterion one, pertains to the dating of the proposed model relative to the imitation and its physical distribution and popularity in education, art, and literature. Obviously no author can imitate a text that he or she has not read, so the more widespread the circulation and popularity of the model, the stronger the case that the author used it. Less obvious but no less important is the accessibility

of the model to the intended readers. Ancient narratives often paraded themselves as rewritings of earlier ones to invite comparison; this strategy worked only
if their readers knew the models well enough to get the point.

If an ancient Greek reader knew only one work of literature, it probably was
the *Iliad*.[7] One catalogue of manuscripts from Greco-Roman Egypt lists over six
hundred for Homer, and most of these pertain to the *Iliad*.[8] After Homer the
next best preserved authors were Demosthenes with eighty-three, Euripides with
seventy-seven, and Hesiod with seventy-two. In other words, two texts survive of
Homer for every text by these three authors combined. One of Luke's contemporaries spoke of Homer's popularity like this: "From the earliest age, children
beginning their studies are nursed on Homer's teaching. One might say that while
we were still in swathing bands we sucked from his epics as from fresh milk. He
assists the beginner and later the adult in his prime. In no stage of life, from
boyhood to old age, do we ever cease to drink from him."[9] Reading was not the
only access to the epics. Homeridae and rhapsodes were trained actors who
memorized and performed the epics publicly, and visual artists repeatedly depicted Homeric scenes on coins, gems, sculpture, and vases of all sorts.[10] Homer
was a cultural inevitability.

His influence even spanned the gap between archaic Greek and imperial Latin.
According to a preeminent classicist, Lucan's comparison of Pompey to Agamemnon "shows that the imitation of Homer by Roman epic poets is not only an
intertextual and aesthetic phenomenon, but it also was grounded in the significance of Homer for the daily life of Romans. Homeric forms of speech, situations, and maxims were perceived not only by the Greeks but also by educated
Romans as models for specific types of situations, forms, and codes of conduct
and were applied in real life for actual events."[11]

Any claim that an author in the first century C.E. imitated the epics thus would
satisfy the first criterion, accessibility. My critics concede the point, though with a
caveat. The qualification usually goes like this. Even though the Homeric epics
were ubiquitous in the Greco-Roman world, they were not common in the circles
that produced the New Testament. When Mark, for example, alluded to other
texts, they were Jewish, and he often identified them as such by introductory
formulae (e.g., "as it is written . . .") or other markers. The cultural world of the
earliest Gospel was Jewish, not Greek.

This objection fails on three counts. First, Jews were by no means immune to
Homeric influence. If someone learned to read Greek in school, he or she would
have been exposed to the epics. Long before Mark, Hellenistic Jewish poets
imitated Homer to prosify biblical themes; the historian Artapanus imitated the
Iliad to narrate a story about Moses; and the Book of Tobit (probably composed
in Aramaic!) almost certainly imitated the first four books of the *Odyssey*.[12] The

historian Josephus frequently imitated Homer when narrating Jewish themes.[13] To say that someone was Jewish says nothing whatever about his or her knowledge of Homer. Second, in all likelihood neither the author of Mark nor his intended readers were ethnic Jews, for he had to translate simple Aramaic words and basic Jewish practices for this audience, and did not always do so accurately. One can account for the Jewish concerns in the Gospel from memories of Jesus' Galilean environment and familiarity with biblical texts. Third, even though I agree wholeheartedly that the Gospels and Acts display enormous debts to Jewish literature and culture, such debts do not exclude other influences. Indeed, a common practice in ancient mimesis was the use of multiple literary models, intertextual eclecticism. Mark and Luke, I submit, borrowed from both the Jewish Bible and the Greek epic.

Analogy, the second criterion, asks if other ancient authors imitated the same proposed model. Surviving school exercises often document the popularity of a Homeric passage for literary education. The first two books of the *Iliad* clearly were the most popular, but most other books are attested as well.[14] The writings of rhetoricians, literary critics, and historians refer to imitations, but the most important witnesses are the ancient narratives themselves, including dramas, histories, later epics, and novels. I will argue that the Acts of the Apostles imitates four famous passages from the *Iliad* that also informed imitations in the *Odyssey,* Aeschylus, Sophocles, Aristophanes, Herodotus, Plato, Xenophon of Athens, Apollonius of Rhodes, Chariton, Xenophon of Ephesus, Lucan, Vergil, Ovid, Seneca, Silius Italicus, Statius, Philostratus, Lucian, Heliodorus, Nonnus, and Pseudo-Callisthenes.

Critics of my approach raise two objections to this criterion of analogy. First, most Homeric imitations appear in works produced by highly cultured authors; this cannot be said for Mark. To some extent this comment is fair, but Homeric imitation was by no means restricted to high culture. Such imitations often appear in works that occupy the same cultural register as the Gospels and Acts, such as Chariton's *Chaereas and Callirhoe,* the Book of Tobit, Xenophon's *Ephesiaca,* Philostratus's *Life of Apollonius of Tyana,* Josephus's *Jewish War* and *Antiquities,* and the apocryphal *Acts of Andrew.*

A second objection to my use of analogous imitations is potentially more damaging. The popularity of Homeric scenes in Greco-Roman literature allows that Mark or Luke may not have imitated Homer directly, but indirectly through one of his imitators. Homer not only had mimetic children; he had grandchildren as well. For this reason one must analyze narratives in the New Testament not only with Homer but also with derivative writings in mind. We shall see, however, that the parallels between Acts and the *Iliad* are more compelling than those between Acts and any Homeric imitator. The next three criteria are designed to test for this very thing: density, order, and distinctive traits.

The criterion of density assesses the number or volume of similarities between two works. The more parallels one can identify, the more convincing is the case for imitation. This third criterion may seem intuitive, but its application is tricky insofar as it is by no means transparent what constitutes a parallel. Ancient imitators borrowed whatever they needed from their literary antecedents, including vocabulary, grammar, names, settings, characterizations, and especially motifs. In some cases the similarities are obvious, while others are subtle and elusive.

Ironically, even opposites occasionally function as parallels. Many literary imitations parody, transvalue, or otherwise rival their models, and to do so they transform motifs, spinning them with new meanings. My book on Mark argued that the Gerasene demoniac resembles Homer's Polyphemus. In the epic, when the ogre asks Odysseus his name, he responds by saying "Nobody is my name," a ruse that later allows him to escape. A similar motif appears in Mark, but now it is Jesus who asks for the name, and the demoniac responds, "Legion is my name." Both works use the motif of requesting a name but Mark transforms it: the hero asks for the name of the caveman, who replies with a name indicating multiplicity. Nobody has become Legion. Obviously one cannot make a case for mimesis solely on the basis of such disagreements, but these transforms are necessary for an author to resignify his tale. I will indicate such transformed motifs with the symbol ≠.

The fourth criterion examines the relative sequencing of motifs in the two works. If parallels appear in the same order, the case strengthens for imitation; conversely, if the parallels are random, the case is less compelling. Three of the four texts that I compare with the *Iliad* are narratives, and in each case the two works not only share several parallels, they do so in impressively similar sequences. One example, however, is a speech, and here Luke rearranged the motifs into an elegant chiasmus, or ring composition. By taking into account this new structure, one can recognize similarities in the sequence of the motifs with that of the model.

Density of parallels and similar sequencing may not be sufficient of themselves to demonstrate literary dependence insofar as stories of the same genre display similarities with no genetic relationship between them at all. Proving mimesis often requires satisfaction of the fifth criterion: distinctive traits. Authors often announced the relationship of their works to their models by supplying unusual features as mimetic flags. The flag might be a significant name or a telling word, phrase, literary context, or motif. Distinctive traits also may appear in texts that disguise dependence, but in such cases they may be clumsily assimilated details. In either case, if one finds in the model and its putative imitation characteristics uncharacteristic of the genre as a collectivity, one may suspect mimesis.

Because this criterion is the most important for binding two texts together, it also generates disagreement. For example, if one attaches significance to a name, another reader might suggest that the name was historical and that the similarities with the model are accidental. If one argues for a distinctive motif or phrase, someone else can almost always, by looking hard enough, find the same motif elsewhere in ancient literature. Some scholars thus restrict distinctive traits to words or phrases that are nearly unique to the proposed model and copy, an approach that has been called "philological fundamentalism."[15] Although this approach might be the most scientific, few ancient imitations can clear so high a bar, and they should not have to. To be distinctive, a motif need not be unique; it need only be unusual for the literary genre and context in which it appears. At its best, the argument for distinctive traits is cumulative. Even though one might find other examples of an isolated unusual trait shared by the proposed model and imitation, one is less likely to find constellations of such traits elsewhere. In each case to be studied in this book, at least three distinctive features bind it to the parallel scene in the *Iliad*. It is such distinctive traits that decisively tilt the balance against form criticism toward mimesis.

These last three criteria—density, order, and distinctive traits—provide the glue for holding the model and the imitation together hermeneutically. The sixth and final criterion assesses the strategic differences between the two texts: interpretability. As often as not, ancient authors borrowed from their models to rival them, whether in style, philosophical adequacy, persuasiveness, religious perspective, or whatever. Such emulations (Greek: ζῆλοι; Latin: *aemulationes*) were most effective when readers recognized the targeted model, so authors often advertised their dependence. For example, Vergil blatantly imitated the Homeric epics in the *Aeneid* but took up the Trojan cause, not the Greek. I have argued that Mark openly imitated Homeric epic to depict Jesus as superior to Odysseus and Hector, and Jesus' God as superior to the Olympians. Emulation applies also to the four passages in Acts, where Luke substitutes his own values for Homer's.

Critics of my work have complained that my criterion of interpretability is a rubber hammer too weak to nail down mimesis, but the category must remain flexible. There exists no way of limiting or taming the variety of benefits a reader may derive from reading a text as sophisticated as Acts against its targeted models. By mixing Homer's stories with Luke's one creates alchemical reactions that are impossible to control. It is like watching a parody of a film classic: only amnesia of the original limits the discovery of transformations of plot, characterization, or dialog. Some of the changes will be transparent, others more subtle, and others so cryptic that the viewer may never know what the screenwriter or director intended. Even so, the viewer gains a new appreciation of the work simply by being aware of the object of the parody.

I created these criteria as carefully as I could in hopes of a measure of objectivity. They seek to formalize the observations classicists and biblical critics make when arguing for literary imitation, even though scholars seldom discuss their criteria explicitly. My criteria may be flawed, and, if so, I welcome alternatives, but I refuse to be a mimetic agnostic. I refuse to believe that the discovery of literary imitation is impossible. Witnesses to ancient education and composition show that mimesis was rampant and that emulation was a strategic weapon in cultural interaction. The difficulty of recognizing these clashes is no reason to give up doing so. No matter how precise and demanding the criteria, they will never replace imagination and playfulness. Comparing literary works is an art, not a science. I trust that my criteria will help train the eye to detect imitation, but they will never be tests to prove it.

If any author of the New Testament was capable of imitating Homeric epic it was the author of Luke-Acts. He quotes Aratus's *Phaenomena* in Acts 17:28, and Euripides' *Bacchae* in 26:14, and his vocabulary, style, and compositional techniques display an impressive level of literary education. The same year that I published my book on Mark, Marianne Palmer Bonz published *The Past as Legacy: Luke-Acts and Ancient Epic,* in which she argues that Luke-Acts is neither a history nor a historical novel but a prose epic modeled after not the *Iliad* but Vergil's *Aeneid*.[16] "Luke has endeavored to interpret the underlying meaning of the whole of Christian history—and in a manner surprisingly analogous to Virgil's interpretation of the meaning of Roman history."[17] Although Vergil was not the first author to do so, he linked the creation of the Roman people to Aeneas and other Trojans who had fled the city. Furthermore, by composing an epic transparently modeled after Homer's *Odyssey* for the first six books and the *Iliad* for the last six, the poet gave Rome an epic of its own. "Just as Virgil had created his foundational epic for the Roman people by appropriating and transforming Homer, so also did Luke create his foundational epic for the early Christian community primarily by appropriating and transforming the sacred traditions of Israel's past as narrated in the Bible of the diasporan Jewish communities, the Septuagint."[18] Bonz also shows that the *Aeneid* and Luke-Acts share several dominating concerns and techniques: a mission in the form of a journey that leads to the formation of a new people in Italy, ambiguous prophecies, dramatic reversal of fortunes, insistence on moral rectitude, and an apology for the universal benefits of the mission. One of her most important observations has to do with the catalytic role of heavenly messengers in both works: "Luke's use of supernatural beings as a narrative device employed at critical junctures to shape the direction and further movement of the plot finds its closest parallel in Greek and Roman epic. Originally introduced by Homer, supernatural interaction with the central characters of the narrative remained a signature characteristic of the epic genre."[19]

Bonz also analyzes imitations of the *Aeneid* in four later Latin epics, and by so doing demonstrates both the popularity of the *Aeneid* and its inadequacy for addressing Roman political crises in the first century, especially the decadence and ineptitude of the Julio-Claudians. Lucan distanced the rule of Augustus from the divine will in *Bellum civile;* Statius's *Thebaid* more pointedly opposed Vergil's enthusiasm for Augustus and applied the benefits of heaven to the Flavians instead; in his *Argonautica* Valerius Flaccus revised Vergil's optimism and made Domitian's Rome once again the "center of universal saving history"; Silius Italicus's *Punica* mythologized Rome, depicting its rulers as gods and its destiny as cosmic.[20] According to Bonz, Luke "decided to recast his community's sacred traditions in a style and manner that would make the Christian claim a powerful and appealing rival to the ubiquitous and potentially seductive salvation claims of imperial Rome."[21]

> Luke-Acts presents a rival vision of empire [viz. the kingdom of God], with a rival deity issuing an alternative plan for universal human salvation. Furthermore, Luke-Acts names a very different sort of hero as the primary instrument for the implementation of that plan, a different concept of the chosen people, and a very different means by which conquest leads to inevitable victory. . . . The divine plan ultimately calls for the eternal reign of the risen Jesus over a universally chosen community of believers.[22]

Bonz has made a compelling case for viewing Luke-Acts as a prose epic, but her proposal must clear a high hurdle: the *Aeneid* was composed in Latin, not Greek. Although it is possible that an educated man like Luke could read Latin, if he did, he was unusual. Indeed, if one could demonstrate that he had imitated the *Aeneid,* he would be the only Greek author to have done so before Quintus Smyrnaeus in the third century.[23] To bridge this linguistic gap, Bonz proposes that Luke knew a Greek paraphrase of the *Aeneid,* perhaps the one produced by an imperial slave, C. Iulius Polybius, who also rewrote Homer in Latin prose. According to Seneca, Polybius's paraphrases made both authors *celebrati.*[24] If Luke did know of a Greek prose paraphrase, it would not only explain how he had access to the Latin epic, it could explain why Luke imitated it in prose.

That Luke might have known a Greek paraphrase of the *Aeneid* certainly is possible, but it is also unnecessary. Bonz recognizes that the similarities between Luke-Acts and the *Aeneid* are seldom "one-for-one" or "direct analogies," but common literary strategies, themes, and plot devices, many of which may be found in Greek epics as well.[25] None of the parallels Bonz identifies requires direct access to the epic or even to a paraphrase. All Luke needed to know was that the Latin epic existed, that it linked the Roman *gens* to the Trojan War through a rewriting of Homeric epic, that it was foundational to the identity of the Roman Empire in general and the Julio-Claudian line in particular, and that it employed tropes, characterizations, and plot devices typical of epic in general, whether Greek or Latin.

Though few Greeks in the East could read the *Aeneid* in Latin, many of them knew of its existence and significance to the empire. "What makes the reception of Virgil unique among Roman poets is the pervasive quality of his influence, which is visible both at the level of popular culture and of official ideology. This broader effect is almost entirely linked to Virgil's authorship of the *Aeneid*. . . . Verses and characters from his poetry appear in wall-paintings and graffiti, mosaics and sarcophagi, even the occasional spoon, in locations ranging from Somerset [England] to Harlicarnassus [Asia Minor]."[26] Johannes Irmscher argues that Greek-speakers not only were familiar with Vergil, they held his works in high regard.[27]

For example, early in the first century C.E. an Egyptian Jew writing in Greek retold Aeneas's escape from Troy and journey over "the land and frightful sea" to "set up the mighty city of the Latins." Even after his death, "the nations of men will not forget him. For the race of this man will later rule over all as far as the rivers Euphrates and Tigris, in the midst of the land of the Assyrians, where the Parthian tarried. It will come to pass in future generations when all these things happen." The author of this eleventh *Sibylline Oracle* could have gotten this information from several sources, but he acknowledges Vergil in the next line: "There will be again [viz., after Homer] a certain elderly wise man, a bard, whom all call the wisest among men, by whose noble mind the whole world will be educated. For he will write the chief points with power and intelligence, having mastered my words and meters and phrases."[28] In this amazing text one finds a Greek-speaking, Egyptian Jew calling Vergil a poet who will educate "the whole world." Even allowing for its obvious hyperbole, this statement is noteworthy. The author surely had in mind the *Aeneid*, for the lines immediately preceding had praised Aeneas for founding Rome and its vast empire.

The author need not have read the epic himself to write these lines. Luke, too, I submit, did not need to read the epic in Latin or even in a Greek paraphrase to have imitated its general strategy. Many of the literary features that link Luke-Acts with the *Aeneid* appear already in Homer, as Bonz recognizes. Luke may well have wanted to write a prose epic to rival Vergil's *Aeneid*, but when he looked for literary models for particular tales, they often came from Homer. That is, Luke not only transformed the scriptural legacy of Judaism, he occasionally transformed the epic legacy of Hellenism much as Vergil had. In fact, we shall see that both authors occasionally imitated the same Homeric models. Luke is not Vergil's direct literary offspring but his younger, admiring, but independent sibling; both are sons of Homer.

To illustrate my method, let me compare a story in Luke 7:11–16 with a story from the Greek version of 1 Kings 17:10–24. Luke's access to the story in 1 Kings is certain (criterion one). In fact, earlier in the gospel Luke mentioned this widow explicitly: "Elijah was sent to . . . a widow in Sarepta [= Zarephath]."²⁹ Criterion two, analogy, assesses if other authors targeted the same text. The Elijah-Elisha cycle influenced Mark as well as Luke-Acts. 2 Kings 4:8–37 tells a similar story of Elisha raising a dead youth, and several interpreters have argued that Jesus' raising of Jairus's daughter in Mark 5:21–24a and 35–43 was modeled after it.³⁰ Other scholars have made a similar case for the raising of Dorcas in Acts 9:36–42.³¹ If Luke used 1 Kings 17:10–24 as a model for a story about Jesus, it would find analogies elsewhere in rewritings of the Elijah-Elisha cycle.

The following columns show the extent of parallels between the two tales, and the parallels for the most part appear in the same order (criteria three and four: density and order). Throughout this book I use such columns to facilitate comparisons between the *Iliad* and Acts. To simplify matters, I compare only English translations of the texts; the Appendix presents identical columns in the original languages. All translations of ancient literature presented in this book are my own. When translations appear in parallel columns, I highlight the closest parallels but only to train the reader's eye. In many cases the similarities extend beyond my emphases. For the most part ancient mimesis involved motifs, not words or grammatical constructions, so the parallels presented here differ from comparisons of the Synoptic Gospels, for example. Rhetoricians took replication of exact wording as artless and lazy.³² Elements that appear in an order different from those in the parallel column are isolated by square brackets, as are my comments.

1 Kings 17:10–24 (LXX)	Luke 7:11–16
And he arose and *went* *up to Sarepta*	Soon afterwards he *went to* a city called *Nain*
[καὶ ἐπορεύθη εἰς Σαρεπτα]	[καὶ . . . ἐπορεύθη εἰς . . . Ναίν],³³
	and his disciples and a large crowd went with him.
and *when he came to the gate of the city,*	*As he approached the gate of the city,*
[εἰς τὸν πυλῶνα τῆς πόλεως]	[τῇ πύλῃ τῆς πόλεως]
behold [καὶ ἰδού] there was *a widow*	*behold* [καὶ ἰδού] a man who had *died*
woman [γυνὴ χήρα] gathering sticks. . . .	*was being carried out.*
[Soon after Elijah's arrival the boy took	He was his mother's only *son* [υἱός],
sick and died, and the widow blamed	and she was a *widow* [χήρα];
the prophet for his death.]	and with her was a large crowd from the city.
	When the Lord saw her, he had compassion for her
And Elijah *said to the woman,*	*and said to her,*
[καὶ εἶπεν Ηλιου πρὸς τὴν γυναῖκα]	[καὶ εἶπεν αὐτῇ]
"Give me your son [υἱόν]."	"Do not weep."

So he took him from her bosom and
carried him up into the upper chamber
where he lodged, and laid him on *his bed*.
[What follows is a prayer in which Elijah
scolds God for having slain the boy.]
He breathed into the child three times,
called on the Lord, *and said* [καὶ εἶπεν],
"O Lord my God, I beseech you,
let this child's life be restored to him."
And so it came to pass, *and the child cried*.
And he came down from the upper room
into the house
and he gave him to his mother
[καὶ ἔδωκεν αὐτὸν τῇ μητρὶ αὐτοῦ].

. . . [T]he woman *said*, "Now I know
that you are *a man of God* [θεοῦ]
and that the word of *the Lord* is
in your mouth."

Then he came forward and touched *the bier*,
and the bearers stood aside.

And he said [καὶ εἶπεν],
"Young man, I say to you, rise!"

The dead man sat up *and began to speak*,

and he gave him to his mother
[καὶ ἔδωκεν αὐτὸν τῇ μητρὶ αὐτοῦ].
Fear seized all of them;
and they glorified God [θεόν], *saying*,
"*A great prophet* has risen among us!"
and "*God* [θεός] has looked favorably
on his people!"

The parallels between the two stories clearly are dense and in the same order:

1 Kings 17:10–24

• Elijah went to Sarepta, and when he
approached the city gate, he saw a
widow. Later in the narrative the boy
took sick and died.
• Elijah commanded the widow, "Give me
your son."

• Elijah took the corpse and cried to God.
• The dead son revived and cried out.
• "And he gave him to his mother."
• The woman praised "the man of God."

Luke 7:11–16

• Jesus went to Nain, and when he approached
the city gate he saw the dead son of a widow
being carried out on a bier.

• Jesus commanded the widow, "Do not weep."

• Jesus came to the corpse and spoke to it.
• The dead son revived and spoke.
• "And he gave him to his mother."
• The crowd praised "the prophet."

Many ancient texts narrate resuscitations, but none more closely resembles this
story in Luke than this.[34] Although form critics would not rule out Luke's model-
ing the story after 1 Kings 17, they would quite rightly question any argument
based exclusively on the density and order of parallels insofar as stories of miraculous healings follow a predictable pattern: the healer's encountering the sufferer,
a description of the ailment, the healing act itself, a proof that the person was
healed, and an acclamation of the spectators. An argument for direct imitation

requires the presence of distinctive traits not found in such stories generically (criterion five).

In both stories the healer enters a walled city with a gate. This detail is not noteworthy in itself, except that Nain was not a city but a small village. If the identification of Nain with the present town of Nein is accurate, the village seems to have had a simple stone wall that could have allowed a gate, but no clear evidence of a gate survives. Luke apparently expanded the village into a *polis* with a wall and a gate because his literary model suggested it.[35] A more distinctive clue that Luke rewrote the story is the phrase "and he gave him to his mother [καὶ ἔδωκεν αὐτὸν τῇ μητρὶ αὐτοῦ]" which is identical in both tales. This phrase appears nowhere else in the Septuagint or the New Testament and is not a stock element in ancient miracle stories.

Finally, Luke's narrative improved his model; Luke not only imitated, he emulated (criterion six, interpretability). In 1 Kings it was the widow who initiated the resuscitation by berating the prophet: "You came to my house to recall my sins and kill my son." In Luke, Jesus himself initiated the resuscitation.[36] Elijah accused God of injustice and a lack of compassion: "You have done wrong in killing her son." Luke, however, does not blame God for the boy's death and says that Jesus "had compassion" for the widow.[37] Elijah could not raise the dead from his own powers but called on God to do so; Jesus himself raised the dead: "I say to you, arise!"[38] According to 1 Kings only the widow responded to the resuscitation; in Luke "a large crowd" observed the event and acclaimed Jesus as a prophet.[39] For Luke, Jesus was a prophet, but more than a prophet. One commentator rightly has concluded that

> one may account for the data . . . by the relatively straightforward explanation that Luke had before him a copy of the text to which his work shows such affinity, the LXX, or at least a part of the LXX which contained the Elijah-Elisha narrative, and that precisely as literary artist he transformed the text, dramatizing and christianizing the ancient narrative. In some ways such a conclusion is to be expected. It is hardly surprising that a *littérateur* should have used a literary method [viz. *imitatio*].[40]

In this book I similarly claim that Luke imitated the *Iliad*. I will investigate four passages from Acts that form critics confidently identify by genre and interpret in light of that identification. One case is the casting of lots to replace Judas among the Twelve, which form critics characteristically define as a legend and ascribe to a pre-Lucan Palestinian environment. But apart from a few details concerning Judas's death, Acts 1:15–26 displays unmistakable signs of Luke's own vocabulary, style, and concerns. Furthermore, it closely parallels the casting of lots that selected Ajax to fight Hector in *Iliad* 7. It would appear that Luke modeled the apostolic lottery after the lottery for Ajax, incorporating into the story several traditional details.

The second case is Acts 10:1–11:18, the corroborating visions of Cornelius and Peter. Scholars usually assign this complex and extensive narrative to local legends about the origins of the church at Caesarea. Apparently no one has noticed that it strikingly resembles two visions at the beginning of Book 2 of the *Iliad*: the famous lying dream of Zeus to Agamemnon and the vision of the serpent and the sparrows.

The third example is Peter's escape from Herod's prison (Acts 12:1–17), generally considered a rescue miracle (*Befreiungswunder*) that Luke preserved nearly intact from a Jewish-Christian source. Such prison escapes occur frequently in ancient narratives, including two other instances in Acts itself (5:17–42 and 16:16–40). Acts 12:1–17 does indeed contain narrative elements that characterize this genre, as do the other prison escapes in Acts. Even so, I will argue that Luke did not model the narrative after a generic collection of traditional motifs but after a single literary model: Hermes' rescue of Priam from the Greek camp in *Iliad* 24.

The final example is Paul's speech to the elders of Ephesus at Miletus (Acts 20:17–38). During the last fifty years a consensus has emerged that it is a farewell discourse (*Abschiedsrede*) modeled after Jewish testaments in which a dying patriarch gives final instructions and prophecies to his most intimate associates. Critics have been content to compare the speech with the genre as a plastic collection of motifs. I will argue, however, that it is an imitation of a single, famous example, not Jewish but Greek. Luke rewrote Hector's farewell to Andromache in *Iliad* 6 and expected his readers to recognize that he did so.

If Homeric influence on the Gospels and Acts is so extensive and significant, why did ancient readers not mention it? Why did classically trained Cappadocian Fathers, for example, not see it? Why in two centuries of critical scrutiny have modern scholars not recognized it? To some extent, these challenging questions are unfair insofar as many modern critical readings of the Gospels and Acts have no confirmation in the history of interpretation. Ours would be a dreary craft if we merely repeated the interpretations of the past. That said, these questions merit a more serious response.

In my book on Mark, I advanced several reasons for failures to recognize mimesis. The earliest evangelist disguised his imitations too well; the author of Matthew rewrote Mark, further obscuring the parallels with Homer; Christian tradition soon attributed Matthew to that disciple and thus viewed it as historically reliable; the differences between archaic and koine Greek frustrate philological comparisons; form critics view the evangelists as redactors of preexistent memories of Jesus largely uncorrupted by external influences; literary critics seek analogous tales in the Hebrew Bible, postbiblical Jewish texts, or contemporary Greek prose, but not in archaic pagan poetry; few modern readers are familiar with the epics, and, apart from a few classicists, none of us knows them as well as Mark's first readers. The most important cause of our mimetic amnesia is this distance between the cultural repertoire of ancient readers and our own.

After writing my book I became convinced that at least one of Mark's ancient readers did recognize his imitations of the epics: the author of Luke-Acts. Luke records an appearance of the risen Jesus to two disciples as they walked to Emmaus, and his model for this story surely was the appearance of Odysseus to Laertes at the end of the *Odyssey*.[41] Both in Mark and in Luke the Jewish authorities play a role that Homer had given to Penelope's suitors. Similarly, Luke's recasting of epic in Acts seems not to have escaped detection. Several early Christian authors wrote Acts of various apostles, the so-called apocryphal Acts, and at least one of them, the *Acts of Andrew*, imitates Homer repeatedly.[42] On the other hand, my critics are right: the majority of ancient interpretations of Mark and Luke-Acts did not view them as Homeric imitations. The case for mimesis, therefore, must be made from an assessment of the parallels themselves, not from the history of interpretation.

Finally, criticism of my methodology frequently disguises more profound objections. Among these are theological anxiety for those who want to read the Gospels and Acts as historically reliable or at least as traditional. Another cause of resistance is academic inertia; scholarly glaciers move slowly. This approach demands competence rather rare among New Testament scholars: facility with Homeric Greek, awareness of the history of Greco-Roman literature, and attention to rhetorical education. Furthermore, such is the power of regnant ways of thinking that innovative solutions to old problems simply become invisible.[43] No matter how many examples one provides to justify the new approach, no matter how compelling the arguments, no matter how fruitful the results, practitioners of more traditional methodologies may remain unconvinced. In such cases, the proponent of a new approach might be content to make resistance difficult for veterans while hoping for a more generous hearing from new recruits.

But this book should prove to the most entrenched skeptic that four passages in the New Testament not only imitate Homer, they notify their readers that they do so. Of course, even if one were convinced of imitation in these cases, one need not concede that other texts are similarly mimetic, but it would demonstrate the legitimacy of my methodology and perhaps prod others to keep the epics in mind when studying early Christian texts.

The method proposed in this book holds enormous significance for the study of early Christian narrative well beyond the four examples in Acts. In the first place, it suggests that one best reads these texts against the backdrop not of history and antecedent Christian tradition but of classical Greek literature and mythology. It requires us to refocus attention on these texts as products of a *Kulturkampf* far more extensive and focused than we have seen before. It suggests that the cultural context of early Christian narratives was as profoundly Hellenistic as it was Jewish. Finally, it suggests that exegesis of New Testament narratives should include an appreciation of cultural struggle, transformative artistry, and theological playfulness.

Does the New Testament imitate Homer? Let's see.

PART **One**

The Visions of Cornelius and Peter and Iliad *2*

lying dream to Agamemnon and Odysseus's recollection of a portent seen by the Greek army. Peter's identification of the animals in his vision with humans stands in a tradition at least as old as Homer and at least as widespread as Homeric imitations. The apostle might have converted a god-fearing centurion, and early Christians might have celebrated it in legend, but Luke needed no history, legend, or source for the creation of Acts 10:1–11:18. All he needed was *Iliad* 2.1–335.[17]

The next chapter provides a summary and new translations of the relevant Homeric passages. Chapter 3 monitors imitations of the dream and portent in ancient Greek and Latin literature. Chapter 4 compares the dream and portent with the visions of Cornelius and Peter in Acts and exposes the remarkable density of parallels between them. Here I also argue that the alleged discrepancy between Peter's vision and his interpretation is no discrepancy at all; the literal and the allegorical not only dovetail but also are mutually dependent. Furthermore, symbolic interpretations of animals as humans are firmly rooted in ancient interpretations of visions as early as Homer. Chapter 5 argues that the similarities between Acts 10–11 and *Iliad* 2 derive from literary imitation and not from a tradition or a source.

Cornelius and Peter

Of the texts from Acts to be studied in this volume, the first, 10:1–11:18, is the most significant. Whereas one might remove the other passages from Acts without collapsing the structure of the whole book, the conversion of Cornelius and his household is a pillar supporting Luke's entire literary and theological construction. By this point in the narrative the reader of Acts anticipates God's pouring the "Spirit upon all flesh" so that "everyone who calls upon the name of the Lord shall be saved."[1] The combination of two visions, one to Cornelius and another to Peter, convinces the apostle that "God does not practice favoritism, but in every nation one who fears God and acts justly is acceptable to him."[2] Just as God had poured the Spirit upon Jewish followers of Jesus at Pentecost, God poured the Spirit upon gentiles assembled at the home of Cornelius. Peter thus told Jewish believers in Jerusalem: "The Holy Spirit fell upon them just as it did upon us at the beginning."[3] This event demonstrated to the church in Jerusalem that "the gentiles received the word of God."[4] When Peter sought to justify the gentile mission in chapter 15, he harked back to the Cornelius episode: God gave the Spirit to gentiles just as to Jews at Pentecost.[5]

The literary context of Cornelius's conversion likewise witnesses to its significance. It precedes Peter's escape from prison (the final narrative devoted primarily to him) and anticipates Paul's career. Furthermore, Luke devoted an unusual amount of papyrus to the event; almost 150 lines constitute his longest unified narrative. "The importance of the story for Luke and for Luke's book is thus unmistakable. It marks the final critical stage in the extension of the Gospel and the expansion of the church. . . . Luke intended his reader to understand that he was witnessing a decisive step, perhaps the decisive step, in the expansion of Christianity into the non-Jewish world."[6]

Acts 10:1–11:18 is a coherent unit, with an unmistakable beginning and ending. Geographical references divide it into five distinct scenes: (1) the vision of Cornelius at Caesarea (10:1–8); (2) the vision of Peter at Joppa (10:9–16); (3) the summoning of Peter from Joppa (10:17–23a); (4) the meeting of Peter and Cornelius at Caesarea before a private audience (10:23b–48); and (5) the report to the church at Jerusalem (11:1–18).[7] The narrator tells the tale of Cornelius's vision in scene one, but characters within the narrative retell it four times: the centurion tells it to his emissaries (10:8), the emissaries mention it to Peter (10:22), Cornelius regales Peter with it (10:30–33), and Peter refers to it briefly in Jerusalem (11:13–14). Similarly, the narration of Peter's vision appears first in scene two, but Peter refers to it twice later: once obliquely to Cornelius (10:28) and once in detail to the Jerusalem gathering (11:5–10).

Here is the narrator's account of Cornelius's vision.

> There was a certain man in Caesarea, Cornelius by name, centurion of the cohort called Italian, pious, fearing God with his entire household, providing many alms for the people, and praying constantly to God. At about the ninth hour of the day [3 P.M.] he clearly saw in a vision an angel of God coming to him and saying, "Cornelius." When he gazed at him, he was terrified and said, "What is it, sir?" He said to him, "Your prayers and your alms have ascended to remembrance before God. So now, send men to Joppa and summon a certain Simon, called Peter. He is residing at the home of Simon, a tanner, near the sea." When the angel speaking to him had left, he called two of his servants and a pious soldier from among those who attended to him, narrated everything to them, and sent them off to Joppa.[8]

Luke's narration of the vision of Peter immediately follows.

> At about the sixth hour [noon] on the following day, while those men were traveling and nearing the city, Peter went up on the roof to pray. He became hungry and wanted to eat, and while others were making the preparations an ecstasy overtook him. He sees the sky opened and a container, descending like a huge sail, let down to the ground by four corners. In it were all types of quadrupeds, reptiles of the earth, and birds of heaven. A voice called to him: "Peter, arise, slay, and eat." But Peter said, "Never, Lord! I never ate anything profane or unclean." The voice came to him a second time: "What God has made clean, you must not make profane." The same thing happened three times, and suddenly the container was taken into the sky.[9]

At first Peter was confused about the meaning of his vision that seemed merely to abolish Jewish distinctions between clean and unclean animals, but on learning of the coincident vision to Cornelius, he understood the animals to represent humankind. The command to eat unclean animals symbolized the removal of taboos against associating with gentiles.

This apparent disparity between the vision and its interpretation has triggered speculation. The command to eat unclean animals contravenes Jewish distinctions between clean and unclean meats, but Peter's interpretation involves not what one serves on the table but with whom one eats. Many scholars thus argue that Luke inherited two originally independent sources, each of which narrated one vision. In one, an angel told Cornelius to summon Peter, and he did so. When Peter arrived, he preached, and Cornelius converted and was baptized. Here we have a simple conversion story, much like Philip's conversion of the Ethiopian eunuch in 8:26–40 that credited Peter for not requiring circumcision. At some point, the legend was recorded—perhaps at Caesarea or Jerusalem—to justify the inclusion of all believing gentiles. The second putative source consisted of Peter's vision (and perhaps his report of it in 11:1–10), the original function of which was to pronounce all foods clean, like Mark's declaration that Jesus had purified all foods (7:19). It was Luke who skillfully combined the two sources, though without entirely removing the tension between Peter's vision and his interpretation.[10]

Even though this reconstruction of the compositional history of Acts 10:1–11:18 is the most popular, it has difficulties, and rivals exist. A few scholars have attributed the entire episode to Luke.[11] Others have been willing to grant a pre-Lucan Cornelius legend, but attribute Peter's vision to Luke himself insofar as Paul seems not to have known an abolition of dietary regulations by the Judean church.[12] Still others claim that the two visions existed together at the earliest stage of tradition as coordinating visions to create "a Jewish-Christian mission legend."[13] These scholars note that twinned, confirming dreams and visions were common in antiquity.[14]

Despite these differences in reconstructions of the compositional history of the Cornelius story, a recent commentator confidently declared: "It is undoubtedly derived from a Palestinian source."[15] Few interpreters would disagree. According to most, Luke's redactional contributions consist primarily of his addition of Peter's vision with its interpretation, Peter's sermon at Caesarea, the receiving of the Spirit, and the report to Jerusalem. Luke also located the Cornelius narrative strategically between the ministries of Peter and Paul, thereby inflating a simple conversion story into the decisive turning point for the conversion of gentiles, "an etiology for the gentile mission."[16]

The following chapters, however, will argue that Luke composed these tales with attention not to Jewish-Christian sources but to the beginning of *Iliad* 2: the

2

Lying Dream and True Portent

According to the first book of the *Iliad,* in the ninth year of the Trojan War, Apollo destroyed many Greeks to punish Agamemnon, their commander, for having taken captive the daughter of Apollo's priest. To avert the plague, Agamemnon begrudgingly freed the girl and in her place took to his tent Achilles' beloved concubine Briseis. Enraged, Achilles withdrew from the war and asked his mother, Thetis, to implore Zeus to punish Agamemnon. The king of the gods thus decided to send him a "destructive dream." Hera, Zeus's wife, stiffly opposed Troy, so without telling her or any other god, the Olympian ordered Oneiros, "Dream," to tell Agamemnon that the Greek troops could "now [νῦν]" take the city. The subsequent attack would cause the death of many. The opening lines of Book 2 describe the sending of Oneiros to Agamemnon.

> Now the other gods and men, furnished with horses, slept through the night, but sweet sleep did not hold Zeus, but he was planning in his mind how to honor Achilles and destroy many soldiers near the ships of the Achaeans. The following plan seemed to him the best: to send a destructive dream to Atreides Agamemnon. He spoke winged words to him, saying, "Go up, destructive Oneiros, to the swift ships of the Achaeans, and on arriving at the hut of Agamemnon, son of Atreus, tell him everything precisely as I command you. Command him to arm the long-haired Achaeans at once, for now he can take the wide-laned city of the Trojans. No longer are the immortals who dwell on Olympus of two minds, for

Hera's pestering has bent them all to her side, and sorrows now are stuck to the Trojans." When he heard the message, Oneiros left. Quickly he arrived at the swift ships of the Achaeans and went to Atreides Agamemnon. He found him sleeping in his hut; ambrosial sleep had engulfed him.[1]

In Homeric epic, mortals do not *have* dreams; they *receive* them as messengers of the gods. Dreamers are spectators, and dreams are not abstractions or projections but actual beings, like Oneiros.[2] Oneiros identifies himself as Διὸς . . . ἄγγελος, "an angel of Zeus," usually and aptly translated "a messenger of Zeus." Greek artists sometimes depicted Oneiros as a young man with wings, similar to angels in Christian art.[3] The poet next turns to the appearance of the ἄγγελος to Agamemnon.

He stood above his head in the likeness of Nestor, son of Neleus, whom Agamemnon esteemed most among his elders. Appearing like him, the divine Oneiros spoke. "Are you sleeping, son of wise Atreus, breaker of horses? A man burdened with decisions, on whom his people rely, with so many worries, ought not sleep through the night. Now listen attentively. I am an angel to you from Zeus, who, though he is far away, cares for you greatly and takes pity on you. He ordered that you arm the long-haired Achaeans at once, for now you can take the wide-laned city of the Trojans. No longer are the immortals who dwell on Olympus of two minds, for Hera's pestering has bent them all to her side. Zeus now has stuck the Trojans with sorrows. Hold this in your thoughts, and do not let forgetfulness overcome you when honey-minded sleep releases you." And when he had spoken, he went away.

He left him pondering in his heart things that would not come to pass. He thought that he would take the city of Priam that very day—the fool—not knowing what events Zeus was intending. For he was yet to bring pains and groaning on the Trojans and Danaans in fierce battles. Agamemnon awoke from sleep, and the divine voice engulfed him.[4]

Zeus had told him that "now [νῦν] you can take the wide-laned city of the Trojans"; but the king thought "that he would take the city of Priam that very day [ἤματι κείνῳ]."[5] Agamemnon's careless exegesis of Zeus's perniciously ambiguous "now" would bring disaster. Agamemnon had reason to trust the dream. Despite his manifest flaws, he faithfully had offered prayers and sacrifices to the gods, and several portents had promised victory. The lying dream and other signs guaranteed a victory, but it would not come until many Greeks had fallen to atone for Agamemnon's hubris against Achilles.

The king then convened his council and told them the dream nearly verbatim. Nestor replied that if he had heard it from anyone other than the commander in chief he would have considered the dream a lie—which, of course, it was.[6] The council called an assembly of the entire army, but Agamemnon did not tell them his dream. On the contrary, testing their loyalty, he said that Zeus "now has planned an evil deceit and commands me to return to Argos infamous after having lost so many men."[7] The troops were free to return home.

After nine years of futile warfare, they understandably broke for the ships. To halt the flight, Odysseus reminded them that, as they were about to sail from Aulis for Troy, they had seen a divine portent that promised them success.

> We all know this well in our minds, and you all are witnesses . . . [it was as] yesterday or the day before that the ships of the Achaeans were assembling at Aulis to bring harm to Priam and the Trojans. Around a spring and at holy altars we were sacrificing perfect hecatombs to the immortals, beneath a beautiful plane-tree from which clear water flowed. There a great sign appeared: a serpent—blood-red on its back, terrible, that the Olympian [Zeus] himself brought to the light—darted from under an altar and rushed for the plane-tree, where, on the highest branch, were nestlings of a sparrow, eight helpless chicks, crouching beneath the leaves; their mother who birthed the chicks made nine. Then the serpent devoured them as they chirped pitiably, and their mother flitted around them, lamenting her beloved little ones. Coiling back, it grabbed her wing as she squawked. When the serpent had devoured the chicks and the sparrow herself, the god who had revealed it made it disappear, for the son of crooked-counseling Cronos turned it to stone. We just stood there, amazed at what had happened.[8]

According to Odysseus, the prophet Calchas then offered his interpretation: "Why are you speechless, long-haired Achaeans? All-wise Zeus has shown us a great sign—late in coming and late in fulfillment—whose fame will never perish. Just as this serpent devoured the chicks and the sparrow herself—eight and the mother who birthed them making nine—so we will fight there for as many years, but in the tenth we will take the wide-laned city."[9]

Ancient readers took the serpent as the Greek army and the sparrows as Trojans.[10] The sign thus confirmed the message of the lying dream, but what Calchas and Odysseus did not know was that before Troy would fall, many Greeks would lose their lives. Odysseus reminded the army of this portent after nine years of toil, when naturally he assumed that the city now would fall. " 'That man [Calchas] spoke thus, and now [vῦv] everything has come to pass. But come, all of you well-greaved Achaeans stay right here until we take the great city of Priam.' So he spoke, and the Argives shouted out, and round about the ships echoed terribly at the cries of the Achaeans, as they praised the speech of god-like Odysseus."[11]

Nestor reinforced Odysseus's speech by reminding the army of yet another favorable sign from Zeus as they sailed from Troy, a lightning bolt on the right side of the ships. Agamemnon readied his troops for attack, offered a bull to Zeus, and prayed that the city might fall that very day. "So he spoke, but the son of Cronos would not yet grant his prayer. He accepted the sacrifices, but he increased the miserable toil of war."[12] The dream sets the scene for irony in Books 2 to 8, for the reader knows what no mortal character knows: even though Zeus promised the Greeks a swift victory, they were doomed. Only after losing many heroes does Agamemnon recognize that the god had deceived them.[13]

The first criterion for detecting mimesis — and a necessary condition for it — is the accessibility of the proposed model. The more widely known, available, and influential the target, the stronger the case for mimesis. Conversely, if the proposed model is obscure, mimesis is less likely.

Surely Luke and his readers could have known of the second book of the *Iliad*; the epic was the most famous work in Greek antiquity and the most common mimetic target in ancient education. Pedagogical uses of the *Iliad* were not evenly distributed among the twenty-four books; Books 1 and 2 were by far the most popular. According to one reckoning, of 89 school exercises on the *Iliad* from so-called "schoolhands," or novices, 51 come from the first two books: 29 from Book 1 and 22 from Book 2. Only 11 of these texts attest to the twenty-four scrolls of the *Odyssey* combined.[14]

This distribution is similar to exercises for more advanced students. Of 977 examples, 123 are from Book 1, and 112 are from Book 2. Of texts from all stages of Greek education, over 25 percent come from the first two books of the *Iliad*. From the third or fourth century C.E. comes a damaged papyrus containing much of the first forty lines of Book 2, Zeus's lying dream.[15] The dream also is the concern of a scholion minor dating from the second century C.E.[16] A few papyri pertain directly to the sign of the serpent and the sparrows. For example, one exercise from the first century C.E. shows an advanced hand copying *Iliad* 2.299–312 before it breaks off; in other words, it contains the beginning of the portent and may well have continued to the end.[17] A teacher of rhetoric cited as an example of a chreia (a saying ascribed to a historical character) an exchange between Alexander the Great and Diogenes the Cynic that demonstrates the popularity of Book 2. Alexander stood over the sleeping philosopher and disparagingly quoted *Iliad* 2.24: "A man burdened with decisions ought not sleep through the night." To this the waking Diogenes responded by reciting the next line: "on whom his people rely, with so many worries."[18] No one was relying on Diogenes, and he had no worries, so he should be free to sleep as long as he wanted.

Agamemnon's lying dream was a notorious blemish on Homeric theology. Plato complained: "Although we praise much in Homer, we will not praise this: Zeus's sending of the dream to Agamemnon."[19] Lucian reminded his readers that the king of the gods deceived "Agamemnon, sending a false vision to him, in order that many of the Achaeans might lose their lives."[20] In another context he cites *Iliad* 2.56, Agamemnon's statement that the dream that came to him was "divine [θεῖος]." Lucian contrasts the lying dream with "a dream appearing that was truly divine [θεῖός τις ὡς ἀληθῶς ὄνειρος ἐπιστάς]."[21] According to Aristotle, the grammarian Hippias of Thasus tried to exculpate Zeus philologically, and other textual variants, scholia, and commentaries witness to the passage as a widely debated Homeric problem.[22]

One popular solution attributed the dream to Agamemnon's optimistic imagination, even though it makes no sense of Zeus's intention to punish Agamemnon. Others, like Porphyry, emphasized Agamemnon's own responsibility for interpreting "now" to mean "that very day."[23] The Neoplatonic philosopher Syrianus (fifth century C.E.) allegorized the story to avoid its scandal.[24] The late Roman author Macrobius offered the following exculpation.

> Must we say that the deity had sent him a deceitful vision? Not so, but because the Fates had already decreed such disaster for the Greeks, there was a hint concealed in the words of the dream which, if carefully heeded, could have enabled him at least to avoid calamity, and perhaps even to conquer. The divine command was to lead out the whole army, but he, thinking only of the command to fight, did not attend to the order to lead out the whole army and overlooked Achilles, who at that time was still smarting from a recent insult and had withdrawn his soldiers from battle. The king went forth to battle and sustained the defeat which was owing him, and thus absolved the deity from blame of falsehood by not following all of his commands.[25]

Such clever apologetics did not impress Christian apologists like Justin Martyr and Irenaeus, who used the dream to besmirch the god.[26] Tatian may have had this episode in mind when he told his pagan readers that "according to you Zeus is jealous and hides the dream in a plan to destroy humankind."[27] The *Acts of Andrew* seems to have contrasted a dream given by the Christian God with the lying dream of Zeus.[28]

Popular too was the portent of the serpent and the sparrows. Ovid retold it in his *Metamorphoses,* taking particular delight in the metamorphosis of the serpent into a rock.[29] Other authors focused on Calchas's calculus: 1 bird = 1 year. For example, Cicero translated the entire vision into Latin to debunk divination: what was it about the chicks that implied the lapse of years and not days or months?[30] Similarly, the Christian Origen quoted verbatim *Iliad* 2.308–21 to discredit pagan auspices: If birds know the future, why did the mother sparrow not know to put her nest where the serpent would not find it?[31]

The omen even became a trope. Tragic characters depicted themselves as the mother sparrow, helpless to save her children from danger. A poem attributed to the bucolic poet Moschus has Megara, the wife of Heracles, likening her murderous husband to a serpent that devoured her babies despite her frantic screams.[32] The novelist Heliodorus alluded to the portent to depict the helplessness of an old man whose children had been stolen by pirates: "I suppose I am rather like a bird whose nest is plundered and chicks devoured by a snake before her very eyes. . . . [S]he twitters and flutters around the sack of her home, but her pleas and the grief she feels for her young are wasted."[33] Clement of Alexandria quoted *Iliad* 2.315 when speaking of God's love for humankind: "their mother flitted around them, lamenting her little ones."[34] Similarly, Gregory of Nazianzus likened the mother of the seven Maccabean martyrs to the mother sparrow who flies about bravely but helplessly as a serpent destroys her brood.[35]

Surely *Iliad* 2 satisfies the first criterion for mimesis, accessibility. The point merits emphasis. To judge from the physical remains of school exercises and other testimonies, these Homeric stories were not only accessible, they profoundly shaped ancient literary education, prompted theological debates among pagans and Christians, and became tropes in poetry and prose. These observations anticipate the second criterion, analogy, evidence that other ancient authors imitated the same proposed model. The next chapter discusses how poets and historians recast *Iliad* 2 for their own ends. Once we have established this mimetic tradition we may better appreciate Luke's variations on the theme.

3

More Dreams and Portents

Cicero's interlocutor was right: "history is full of examples" of dreams.[1] So common was the literary dream that rhetoricians considered it a cliché, and perhaps no dream was generative of more imitations than Agamemnon's in *Iliad* 2.[2] What William Stuart Messer said of tragedy applies as well to prose.

> I am fully convinced that the different types of dreams employed in tragedy find their being in an imitation, more or less direct, of the dreams used by Homer. . . . [T]he embryo of all the various forms [of dreams] is extant in the early epic. . . . The point to be remembered is that the immediate source of the dream in tragedy is to be found *not in religion and cult,* but in the *literature,* that is, the source of the dream is a bookish, artistic source.[3]

The portent of the serpent and the sparrow, too, was a popular target for imitation, and some authors, like Luke in Acts 10–11, imitated both in the same context. For clarity I will group the imitations into three categories: (1) texts that imitate the dream only, (2) texts that imitate the portent only, and (3) texts that imitate the dream and the portent together.

Imitations of the Lying Dream

Homer's account of the dream to Agamemnon consists of three scenes with the following motifs.[4]

1. Sending the messenger
    1.1. Decision of the deity (Zeus decides to deceive Agamemnon through Oneiros)
    1.2. Instructions to the messenger
        1.2.1. Order to depart (Zeus tells Oneiros to go to Agamemnon)
        1.2.2. Command to the mortal (Oneiros is to tell the king to attack Troy)
        1.2.3. Assurance of victory (Oneiros is to promise the king victory)
    1.3. Journey of the messenger (Oneiros flies from Olympus to the Greek ships)
2. Delivering the message
    2.1. Appearance of the messenger (Oneiros, as Nestor, stands over the king)
    2.2. Rebuke (Oneiros rebukes Agamemnon for sleeping)
    2.3. Expression of divine favor (Oneiros tells him that Zeus cares for him)
    2.4. Command to the mortal (Oneiros tells him to attack Troy)
    2.5. Assurance of victory (Oneiros tells him the destruction of Troy is certain)
    2.6. Departure of the messenger (Oneiros then departs again for Olympus)
3. Responding to the message (Agamemnon acts on the basis of the dream)

Several classicists have argued that the poet of the *Odyssey* employed the dream in *Iliad* 2 as a model for several dreams in that epic, most notably those in 4.795–841 and 6.13–51.[5] This view might well be correct, insofar as the poet of the *Odyssey* almost certainly was not the same as the poet of the *Iliad* and seems to have used it as a model for his own epic.[6] Even so, literary influence is not the only reasonable explanation insofar as the dream was common coin in epic oral performance and thus would have been available to both poets independent of each other.[7] Whether oral-formulaic or mimetic, the parallels merit mention.

1. Sending the messenger. In both Odyssean passages Athena grants a dream to a woman. In the first case the goddess sends a dream to comfort Penelope; in the second she herself appears to the Phaeacian princess Nausicaa to send her to the shore to meet shipwrecked Odysseus (motif 1.1). In these passages there is no explicit instruction to a messenger (motif 1.2), but both describe a journey (motif 1.3). Athena sends a phantom to Penelope's room, and she herself goes to the bedroom of Nausicaa.[8]

2. Delivering the message. According to *Iliad* 2, "He [Oneiros] stood above his head [στῆ δ᾽ ἄρ᾽ ὑπὲρ κεφαλῆς] in the likeness of Nestor, son of Neleus, whom Agamemnon esteemed most among his elders. Appearing like him, the divine Oneiros spoke: 'Are you sleeping [εὕδεις], son of wise Atreus, breaker of horses? A man burdened with decisions, on whom his people rely, with so many worries, ought not sleep through the night.'"[9] In *Odyssey* 4 the phantom appears in the likeness of Penelope's sister, Iphthime. "She stood above her head [στῆ δ᾽ ἄρ᾽ ὑπὲρ κεφαλῆς] and spoke to her, 'Are you sleeping [εὕδεις], Penelope, though your dear heart sorrows?' "[10] Here is the description of Athena's appearance in *Odyssey* 6: "She stood above her head [στῆ δ᾽ ἄρ᾽ ὑπὲρ κεφαλῆς] and spoke to her, looking like the daughter of Dymas, renowned for ships. She was of her same age and dear to her heart. Appearing like her, gleaming-eyed Athena spoke, 'Nausicaa, how could your mother birth such a lazy child like you? Your gleaming clothes lie there neglected.' "[11] As in *Iliad* 2, both dreams thus begin with the appearance of the messenger and a rebuke (motifs 2.1 and 2.2).

In *Odyssey* 6 there is no expression of divine favor (motif 2.3)—it would be trivial in a command to wash clothing—but there is in Book 4: "The gods who live at ease do not permit you to weep or be distressed, since your son will still have his return, for he is not repugnant to the gods."[12] The poet of the *Iliad* had written, "I am an angel to you from Zeus, who, though he is far away, cares for you greatly and takes pity on you. . . . The immortals who dwell on Olympus are no longer of two minds."[13]

Oneiros commanded Agamemnon to arm his troops and assault the city (motif 2.4), for success was certain (motif 2.5). The dreams in *Odyssey* 4 and 6 also give commands and imply success. The phantom orders Penelope to stop weeping, and assures her that Telemachus will return.[14] Athena orders Nausicaa to ask her father for a wagon to transport laundry and promises to go with her.[15] The departure of the messenger (motif 2.6) likewise appears in each instance. *Iliad* 2: "And when he [Oneiros] had spoken [ὣς ἄρα φωνήσας], he went away [ἀπεβή-σετο]."[16] *Odyssey* 4: "So saying [ὣς εἰπόν]" the phantom flew away.[17] *Odyssey* 6: "So saying [ὣς εἰποῦσ᾽], gleaming-eyed Athena went off [ἀπέβη] to Olympus."[18]

3. *Responding to the message.* After Agamemnon awoke, he summoned his elders to tell them about his dream. Penelope awoke and stopped her weeping.[19] Nausicaa awoke and immediately asked her father for the wagon.[20]

Even though these parallels are striking, they need not indicate mimesis. Dream scenes were traditional before Homer, and many of the parallels cited here appear elsewhere in the epic. On the other hand, the author of the *Odyssey* almost certainly knew the *Iliad* and borrowed extensively from it. Greek tragedy, too, is replete with dreams, many of which show Homeric influence, as we have noted.[21]

Latin poets, too, found the lying dream alluring. In 65 C.E. Marcus Annaeus Lucanus died at the age of twenty-six leaving unfinished his epic on the Roman Civil War. The poem is suffused with imitations of Homer, Vergil, and other Latin poets, though Lucan skillfully avoids scenes of direct divine intervention that had become common in the ancient epic. Consequently, dreams are less frequent in

Lucan and never reveal the divine will to passive recipients; here dreams are psychological projections. In the case of Pompey's dream at the beginning of Book 7, Lucan may well be dependent on the Roman historian Livy, but the use of historical sources does not fully explain the content or function of the dream.[22] For this one must turn to Homer.

Because the gods do not appear as characters in Lucan's epic, Pompey's dream has no parallels to many motifs in *Iliad* 2, such as the sending and arrival of the dream or the communication of divine favor and commands. Even so, scholars long have recognized Lucan's debt to the lying dream.[23] Both Agamemnon and Pompey are military commanders, both have dreams at the beginning of books, both dreams are deceptive and stand in stark opposition to coming catastrophes.[24] Pompey dreamed that throngs of celebrants filled the Roman theater singing his praises for victory over Spain in 71 B.C.E. He took this as a sign that he would defeat Caesar and again celebrate in Rome, but the reader knows better. Book 7 begins with the warning that "the night deceived" him "with a false apparition [*nox . . . vana decepit imagine*]."[25] That night would be Pompey's last.

Vergil's imitation of the lying dream in *Aeneid* 7 is famous and illuminating.[26] The *Aeneid* primarily imitates the *Odyssey* for Books 1–6 and the *Iliad* for 7–12. The lying dream thus appears at the beginning of the *Iliad* section. Expatriated Trojans, under the command of Aeneas, were negotiating with local authorities their resettlement in Italy, thereby infuriating their divine nemesis, Juno (= Hera). The founding of Rome was inevitable, decreed both by fate and Jupiter, but the mother of the gods could not tolerate the resettlement of her old foes without a fight.

1. Sending the messenger. "If I cannot bend the gods above, I will raise hell below," even if it meant the destruction of soldiers on both sides (motif 1.1).[27] To this end, she summoned from Hades the ferocious Fury Allecto and ordered her to unleash her misery: "Sow the crimes of war" (motif 1.2.1).[28] "Immediately the goddess, on dark and dismal wings, took herself from there to the walls of the brave Rutulian" (motif 1.3).[29] Allecto resembles Oneiros in several respects: Oneiros was the son of Nyx, Night; Allecto was daughter of Nox.[30] Artists sometimes represented Oneiros as an angel, complete with wings; Allecto, too, was winged.[31]

2. Delivering the message. Allecto disguised herself as an old woman and appeared to Turnus as he slept (motif 2.1). (Here and in other imitations that are cited at length I underline the elements most clearly parallel to the *Iliad*. The Appendix contains parallel columns in the original languages to facilitate further analysis.) "Here *in his high palace,* in the dark of night, Turnus was *enjoying a deep sleep*. Allecto strips off her harsh appearance and dreadful limbs and *transforms herself into the look of an old woman. . . .* She becomes Calybe, the old priestess of Juno and her temple."[32] Here, as in *Iliad* 2, is a rebuke (motif 2.2), not for sleeping, as in *Iliad* 2, but for tolerating Trojans. "Before the eyes of the young man she presents herself *with these words*: 'Turnus, will you tolerate for no good reason so many hardships, including the transfer of your scepter to Dardanian colonists?'"[33] Allecto tells Turnus: "It was this [message] that the almighty daughter of Saturn clearly ordered me to tell you as you take your rest during the peaceful night" (motif 2.3).[34] Her instructions to Turnus are a transparent imitation of Oneiros's command that Agamemnon arm the Achaeans immediately (motif 2.4). "So arise and gladly prepare to *arm the young men* and march them from the gates to battle; *lead them against the Phrygians . . .* and torch their painted ships."[35] Allecto ends her orders to Turnus with, "The mighty power of the gods orders" the destruction of Trojans (motif 2.5).[36] She vanishes when Turnus awakes (motif 2.6).

    3. Responding to the message. When Allecto was finished with Turnus, "a monstrous trembling broke his sleep, and sweat pouring from his whole body soaked his bones and limbs."[37] As a result of this dream, he would lead his troops into battle where many of them, including himself, would die. Before Allecto left Turnus, she transformed herself into her own savage appearance and pulled from her hair two hissing serpents.[38]

    Toward the end of the first century c.e., Publius Papinus Statius wrote a Latin epic based on the story of the Seven against Thebes. In this case, the author had no historical sources to inform him; his primary model for the dream in Book 2 was *Iliad* 2. Even more than Lucan and Vergil, Statius conforms to the Homeric pattern.[39]

    The literary setting for the dream is this: the sons of Oedipus, Polynices and Etiocles, had agreed to share the governance of Thebes in alternating years, but at the end of the first year, Etiocles refused to cede the throne. Each brother marshaled an army for a notoriously futile civil war in which the brothers slew each other. The disaster began with a destructive dream sent by Juno.

    1. Sending the messenger. In a spat with Juno, Jupiter expressed outrage at the sons of Oedipus for insolence and hunger for power. "I will send new wars on the guilty realm and uproot the whole clan of the destructive trunk" (motif 1.1).[40] Jupiter commanded Mercury to fetch from Hades Laius, slain father of Oedipus: "Let him bring my commands to his cruel grandson" (motifs 1.2.1 and 1.2.2).[41] Mercury descended to Hades and summoned Laius; the two of them returned to the land of the living (motif 1.3). The journey of Laius to Etiocles echoes that of

Oneiros to Agamemnon. "Such was the night when Cyllenius [Mercury with Laius in tow], flying on a silent breeze, *glided up to the bed of the Echionian king* [Etiocles]. . . . He *sleeps*. Then the *old man* [Laius] did as he had been ordered."[42]

2. *Delivering the message.* Laius disguised himself as the blind seer Tiresias, clearly an imitation of Oneiros's disguise as Nestor in the *Iliad* (motif 2.1). "Lest he be seen as a false vision of the night, he put on *the shadowy appearance of the old* seer *Tiresias,* with his voice and famous woolly pelt."[43] His first words to Etiocles are a rebuke (motif 2.2): Laius "seemed to deliver fateful words. '*This is no time for you to sleep,* you sluggard, you *who rest in the dead of night unconcerned* about your brother. For some time *momentous events* have been calling you, as well as *grave matters* yet to come, you sloth!' "[44] Like Oneiros in *Iliad* 2, the ghost of Laius here puts on a disguise and rebukes the commander for sleeping when he should be looking after his duties.

In *Iliad* 2 Oneiros told Agamemnon that Zeus pitied him, even though the gods actually intended to punish him. Similarly, in the *Thebaid* Laius lies: "Out of pity the sire of the gods himself sends me to you from on high" (motif 2.3).[45] Laius then told Etiocles, "Hold on to Thebes and repel your brother, who is blind with lust to rule and brazen against you" (motif 2.4).[46] Statius does not have Laius explicitly promise victory (motif 2.5), but it is implicit in the assurance of divine favor (motif 2.3). Laius disappears much as Oneiros had (motif 2.6): "*So he spoke,* and *on leaving* . . ."[47]

3. *Responding to the message.* When Laius had left him, Etiocles, "leaped up from his bed full of terror" and prepared his troops to defend the city in a bloody civil war that ultimately would claim his own life.[48] In the *Iliad*, Agamemnon awoke and marshaled his troops for a disastrous battle.

To this point we have seen imitations of Agamemnon's dream in the *Odyssey,* Lucan, Vergil, and Statius; the end of this chapter will examine similar imitations in Herodotus and Silius Italicus, who imitate both the dream and the portent of the serpent and the sparrows. Before doing so, however, it is necessary to discuss imitations of the portent alone.

Imitations of the Serpent and the Sparrows

Chapter 2 supplied a translation of Odysseus's speech concerning the omen of the serpent and the sparrow, but a summary here may be useful. As the Greeks were about to sail from Aulis and were sacrificing hecatombs, they saw a sign. A serpent darted from beneath an altar, slithered up a tree, and ate eight nestlings, as their mother squawked and flitted about helplessly. Finally, the serpent ate her as well and immediately turned to stone. Those who saw it were befuddled, all but the prophet Calchas, who interpreted the nine sparrows as nine years of war, with victory coming in the tenth. Later interpreters went further: the serpent represented Greeks, the sparrows Trojans. On the basis of this portent, the Greek army massed for an assault.

The first imitation of the portent may have been the appearance of fighting eagles in *Odyssey* 2.146–76. "[T]he resemblance between *Iliad* 2 and *Odyssey* 2 is so striking as to imply conscious borrowing: the obvious explanation being that the Odyssean passage imitates the Iliadic."[49] Telemachus, Odysseus's son, had finished threatening violence against the suitors of Penelope, when "far-seeing Zeus sent two eagles to fly from above, from the peak of a mountain."[50] At first they flew together in apparent harmony, but when they came to the assembly, they broke into a savage fight. "Those assembled were amazed at the birds when they saw them with their eyes. Their hearts raced in fear about things that would come to pass."[51] The old seer Halitherses then interpreted the sign to mean that Odysseus "already is near, sowing murder and doom for all these men."[52] He then reminded them of a prophecy he had made twenty years before: "I said that, after enduring much suffering and losing all his comrades, he would come home in the twentieth year unrecognized by anyone. Now everything has come to pass."[53] When they saw this portent, the suitors should have abandoned their competition for Penelope's hand and land and thus avoided the predicted catastrophe. Instead, they took the vision of the fighting eagles as happenstance.

Not only do the portents of the serpent-sparrows and the two fighting eagles follow the same basic narrative pattern (sign, bafflement, interpretation, and response), they share several distinctive traits. Both portents come from Zeus, involve Odysseus, and predict destruction. In the *Iliad*, Odysseus reminded the troops that nine years earlier, just before setting sail for Troy, they had seen the portent. Calchas interpreted the nine sparrows as nine years, with the victory over Troy coming in the tenth. According to the *Odyssey*, Halitherses reminded the suitors that twenty years earlier, "when the Argives embarked for Ilium," he had predicted Odysseus's return in the twentieth year. Immediately after Odysseus recounted the interpretation of Calchas he said, "Now everything is come to pass [τὰ δὲ δὴ νῦν πάντα τελεῖται]," precisely the same six words that Halitherses used to conclude his prophetic interpretation.[54]

Aeschylus has Agamemnon narrate a portent at Aulis that differs from *Iliad* 2 but nonetheless was inspired by it. Before the army attacked Troy, two eagles viciously attacked a rabbit pregnant with young and devoured it. Calchas again is called on to provide the interpretation. The two birds are the armies of Agamemnon and Menelaus, the mother hare is Troy. The Greeks will be victorious in the end, but their savagery will infuriate Artemis, who will prolong the war, inflict harm on the Greeks, and require the sacrifice of Iphigenia.[55]

Philostratus tells how hunters slew a lioness pregnant with eight whelps. Apollonius, as the story goes, thought each of the whelps signified one month, the mother one year. His companion, however, was not convinced. "But what do the sparrows in Homer mean — the eight that the serpent devoured at Aulis, seizing their mother as the ninth? Calchas explained these as nine years."[56] By that measure, the eight whelps would represent eight years and the lioness the ninth. Apollonius countered that born chicks obviously are older than unborn lion whelps; ergo, the whelps must represent a shorter period of time. Homer didn't count chicks as years before they hatched.[57]

The epic poet Nonnus wrote: "I will make my pattern like Homer's and sing the last year of warfare, I will describe that which has the number of my seventh sparrow," viz., the seventh year.[58] Just a few lines earlier he had spoken of nestlings in a plane-tree (= Indians) about to be eaten by a serpent (= Dionysus).[59]

Scholars long have recognized Vergil's use of Homer's serpent and sparrows as a model for the death of Laocoön.[60]

> Then occurred *another sign,* greater and far more frightful, which confounded our unwary flock. Laocoön, allotted that day to be priest to Neptune, *was sacrificing at sacred altars an enormous bull.* All of a sudden — I tremble when I say it — from Tenedos over a calm sea twin *snakes* with endless coils *make their way* over the deep and together *reach the shore. Their stomachs,* erect over the path of the surge, and *their crests blood-red* rise above the waves. . . . In a straight path they rush at Laocoön. First, each *serpent* encoils the small body of one of the two boys, and each *devours the pitiable limbs* with its fangs. *As their father rushes to their aid and brings weapons, they seize him* and entwine him with their huge coils. . . . At the same time, *he lifts hideous cries to heaven.* . . . *The* pair of *serpents* slither away to the highest shrines and come to the citadel of fierce *Tritonia* [Minerva], where *they hide themselves* under her feet and the orb of her shield.[61]

Homer said that as the Greek army sacrificed bulls at Aulis, a serpent appeared, "blood-red on its back," that devoured eight chicks before their helpless and squawking mother. Finally, the serpent ate the mother as well and quickly disappeared. According to Vergil, the Trojans took the death of Laocoön and his sons as divine disapproval of his opposition to receiving the Trojan horse. Minerva (= Athena) had indeed sent the serpents against Laocoön but not because he was wrong; he was entirely correct. The goddess was manipulating the destruction of the city by having the Trojans accept the horse. Here we have not a lying dream but a lying portent. Vergil clearly modeled this passage after the vision of the serpent and the sparrows. What distinguishes this imitation from others is the absence of a symbolic meaning. The serpents do not symbolize something or someone else.

Imitations of the Dream and the Portent

Now the fun begins. A few imitations of *Iliad* 2 combine a dream with a portent. A dream is by nature private and subjective. Even when the messenger gives unambiguous commands, the dreamer has reason to suspect its reliability. A portent, however, usually occurs when the recipient is awake and may be seen by many people at once, but unlike the dream, the portent almost always is symbolic — frequently involving serpents or birds — and therefore requires interpretation, often by a seer. The combination of the unambiguous, private dream followed by a symbolic, public portent interpreted by a holy man was powerful and popular.[62]

One critic has noted that a dominant function of the dream in Greek tragedy was "to prepare the way for an omen or an oracle upon which the action may be safely based. This combination of dream and omen or of dream and oracle is found nowhere in the *Iliad* or the *Odyssey*."[63] This statement by an otherwise reliable guide to ancient literary dreams is patently wrong. As we have seen, Odysseus interpreted the earliest dream in Greek literature in light of the portent of the serpent and the sparrows.

The function of the combined dream and portent in *Iliad* 2 is not corroborative except in the mind of the Greek army. The portent at Aulis had guaranteed victory over Troy in the tenth year, the very year that Odysseus reminded the troops of it in *Iliad* 2. This as yet unfulfilled prophecy seemed to confirm the dream to Agamemnon, but the dream and the portent actually were contradictory — by deceptive divine design. Troy soon would fall, an event promised both by the dream and the portent, but the portent was truer. Troy would fall in the tenth year, but it would not fall "now" and certainly not "that very day." This disparity between the dream and the portent generates suspense for the rest of the epic: someday the Greeks would take Troy but not before many of them died as punishment for Agamemnon's insult to Achilles. Mimetic combinations of the dream and the portent usually make them unambiguously confirm each other and always fall short of Homer's sophistication.

Herodotus told how the Persian king Xerxes decided to lead his ill-fated campaign against the Greeks despite the warning of his counselor Artabanus. A deceptive dream (ὄνειρος) came to him and urged him to fight. *Iliad* 2 lies behind the tale.[64] Herodotus skillfully avoids stating that a god actually sent the dream, for he insists that he was merely recording Persian lore (ὡς λέγεται ὑπὸ Περσέων).[65] He also says that Xerxes "supposed [ἐδόκεε]" he saw the dream; Herodotus uses the same verb for the dream to Artabanus, Xerxes' counselor, who then deduced that "apparently [ὡς οἶκε]" some god must have sent it.[66] The result of the campaign would be a disastrous defeat and the death of thousands of Persians. Because Herodotus does not presume to know the mind of the divine, there are no parallels to the first cluster of motifs: *1. Sending the messenger.*

2. Delivering the message. Herodotus records four dreams, the last of which consists of a symbolic vision. In the first three, the recipient (Xerxes or Artabanus) sleeps at night and sees a man or an *oneiros* standing over him (ἄνδρα οἱ ἐπιστάντα; ὄνειρον . . . ἐπιστάν; ὄνειρον . . . ὑπερστάν) and rebuking him for not pursuing the war against Hellas. Oneiros in *Iliad* 2 "stood over the head [στῆ . . . ὑπὲρ κεφαλῆς]" of Agamemnon. In Herodotus, the three rebukes consist of questions that imitate Oneiros's question to Agamemnon, "Are you sleeping?" The first of Xerxes' dreams asks, "O Persian, are you altering your plan so as not to lead your army against Greece?" Here is the second rebuke: "O son of Darius, have you come out and renounced the campaign before the Persians and taken no account of my words as though you had heard nothing?" The dream to Artabanus asked: "Are you the one who dissuades Xerxes from battle against Greece?"[67] Each of the dreams thus begins with a rebuke in the form of a question, like the rebuke issued to Agamemnon (motifs 2.1 and 2.2). The recurrent dreams invariably ordered Xerxes and Artabanus to wage war with Greece (motif 2.4). The dreams did not explicitly promise victory (motif 2.5), but Artabanus interpreted them as propitious signs: "Since some divine impetus is at hand, and some god-sent destruction is gripping Greece—so it would appear—I reverse myself and change my opinion; you must notify the Persians of the messages from the god."[68] "It seemed to Xerxes that the one who said these things flew away" (motif 2.6).[69]

3. Responding to the message. When Xerxes awoke from his first dream, he did not heed it and, in fact, told his troops he would not ask them to fight the Greeks. But after the second dream, he was taken aback: "Xerxes, terrified at the vision, jumped up from his bed and sent a messenger to Artabanus," asking him to sleep on the throne to see if he, too, would be visited by the dream.[70] At issue was whether it was or was not θεῖος, "divine," the very word Agamemnon foolishly used of his deadly dream. When Artabanus, too, received the dream, "he leaped up with a loud cry."[71] His decision, based on the dream, sent thousands of Persians to death.

As though these three dreams were insufficient, Xerxes had yet another. Even though Xerxes was sleeping when he saw this vision (ὄψις), it may well imitate the sign of the serpent and the sparrows and its interpretation by Calchas. Xerxes saw himself crowned with an olive branch with shoots spreading throughout the world. Magicians, playing a role similar to Calchas, interpreted it to mean that all peoples would serve him.[72] The vision thus seemed to confirm the message of the dreams, and Xerxes set out at once to assemble his vast army. Just as Agamemnon did not understand the dream as insidious until after a series of military defeats, Xerxes did not question the dream until he suffered several setbacks.[73]

Late in the first century c.e., Silius Italicus wrote a Latin epic on the Punic War toward the beginning of which Hannibal pondered whether to pursue a campaign against Rome. A deceptive dream from Jupiter helped him make up his mind—with tragic consequences for Carthage. This dream, accompanied by a portent, is particularly fascinating for its history of composition. A Greek-speaking historian named Silenus had traveled with Hannibal and recorded the campaign against Rome in an account that no longer survives. A Latin-speaking historian, Coelius Antipater, used Silenus's account for his own version of the Second Punic War, but his account, too, has not survived apart from references in later authors. According to Cicero, Silenus had written that before deciding to attack Italy, Hannibal dreamed that Jupiter called him to a council of the gods. "When he arrived, Jove ordered that he wage war on Italy, giving him one of the divine council as a guide"—almost certainly Mercury. Marching to war with his Olympian companion, Hannibal looked behind him and saw a huge beast "enveloped with snakes" that destroyed every tree and house in its path. The god then told him that the serpent was the destruction of Italy.[74]

Livy's account is modestly different. Hannibal did not visit the council of the gods; instead, he dreamed he saw a godlike young man—a common description of Mercury—who told him that Jupiter had ordered him to attack Italy. As in Cicero's account, Hannibal turned around and saw "a serpent of monstrous size" that left only destruction in its path. When the general asked the meaning of the portent, the youth said it was "the devastation of Italy."[75]

Unfortunately, it is impossible to know precisely what Silenus had written, but this much is clear: Hannibal reportedly had a dream or a vision in which Zeus (= Jupiter) instructed him to attack Italy and guaranteed a victory by means of an accompanying sign that included a serpent or serpents. The parallels with *Iliad* 2 are obvious and suggest that Silenus compared Hannibal with Agamemnon and attributed his ultimate defeat to the will of Zeus.[76]

Silius seems to have recast Livy's version fully aware of its similarities to the dream and portent in *Iliad* 2, for his own embellishments display mimetic traces not present in the earlier versions.[77]

1. *Sending the Messenger.* He begins his tale with Jupiter's decision to stir up Hannibal (motif 1.1). "Then the *Father Almighty, planning* how to *trouble the Dardanian [Trojan] people* with trials, to *raise to the stars their fame* for ferocious warfare, and to resume their ancient hardships [viz. the Trojan War], precipitates the man's [Hannibal's] designs, disturbing his slothful rest and interrupting his sleep with the *sending of a terror.*"[78] One must deduce from what follows Jupiter's instructions to his messenger Mercury (motifs 1.2.2 and 1.2.3), but Mercury's journey again imitates *Iliad* 2 (motif 1.3). "And so through the

Table of Motifs

Motifs	Iliad 2	Herodotus 7	Aeneid 7	Thebaid 2	Punica 3
1. Sending the messenger					
1.1. Decision of the deity	Zeus wanted to punish Agamemnon	—	Juno wanted to punish Aeneas	Jupiter wanted to punish sons of Oedipus	Jupiter wanted to send Hannibal against Italy
1.2. Instructions					
1.2.1. Order to depart	"Go!"	—	"Sow crimes!"	"Go to Hades!"	"Send terror!"
1.2.2. Command to mortal	Take Troy	—	—	Retain the throne	Take Italy
1.2.3. Assurance of victory	Zeus takes pity (a lie)	—	—	—	—
1.3. Journey of messenger	Oneiros flew to Agamemnon	—	Allecto flew to Turnus	Mercury flew to Hades	Mercury flew to Hannibal
2. Delivering the message					
2.1. Appearance	Oneiros, as Nestor, stood over his head	1. A man stood by 2. Dream stood by 3. Dream stood over	Allecto, as old woman, came to Turnus	Laius, as Tiresias, came to Eteocles	Mercury came to Hannibal
2.2. Rebuke	"Are you sleeping?"	1. Why not fight? 2. Did you not hear? 3. Are you the one?	"Why tolerate Trojans?"	"No time to sleep!"	"It is repulsive to sleep!"

	"Zeus cares for you."		Juno gave this order	Jupiter cares for you	Jupiter gave this order
2.3. Divine favor	"Zeus cares for you."	—	Juno gave this order	Jupiter cares for you	Jupiter gave this order.
2.4. Command	Take Troy	1, 2, 3: fight Greece	Fight Trojans	Retain the throne	Take Italy
2.5. Assurance of victory	Troy's destruction is sure	—	Gods will destroy Trojans	—	"I will make you victor."
2.6. Return of messenger	Oneiros left	The dreams left	Allecto vanished	Laius and Mercury left	Mercury left
3. Responding to message	Agamemnon woke and prepared for war	Xerxes/Artabanus woke and prepared for war	Turnus woke and prepared for war	Eteocles woke and prepared for war	Hannibal woke and prepared for war
Confirming portent	Serpent and sparrows	Olive branch	Allecto appeared as herself, with attending serpents	—	Enormous serpent
Outcome	Many Greeks perished	Persians lost war	Turnus and many other soldiers died	Eteocles, Polynices, and many others died	Carthaginians lost war

cool of the night Cyllenius [Mercury], gliding on the wing, carried the orders of his father."[79]

2. *Delivering the message.* As in the *Iliad*, a rebuke (motif 2.2) immediately follows the appearance of the messenger (motif 2.1). "*Without delay he* [Mercury], *approaches the youth, who is softened by an unworried sleep,* and assaults him with bitter rebukes. '*Master of Libya, it is repulsive for a leader to squander the whole night in sleep*: wars succeed for a wakeful commander.'"[80] Mercury then tells Hannibal, "The father of the gods himself has ordered" him to lead his armies against Rome (motif 2.3).[81] "Get moving! If anything in your soul is inclined to courageous adventures, promptly make your way with me and follow my call" (motif 2.4).[82] The command to Hannibal ends with this promise: "I will establish you as victor of the high walls of Rome" (motif 2.5).[83]

At this point in the dream, where one might expect the messenger to leave and the dreamer to wake, Hannibal sees an enormous serpent leaving a path of destruction. "Terrified by this portent (for neither was he asleep nor was the power of the night at its height, for the god mixed light with the sleep by driving darkness away with his rod), he asked what the terrible pestilence was."[84] Mercury told him that he and his army were the serpent and that the devastation was the harm he would inflict on Italy and the Roman armies. Here again one finds a serpent portent confirming the message of a dream, but now it is incorporated into the dream itself, an innovation already visible in Silius's sources.

Once Mercury had interpreted the dream, he left (motif 2.6). Hannibal then acted on the basis of the dream's command and promise (motif 3). "The god and sleep *left him agitated* by these proddings. A cold sweat broke out on his body, and with a joyful dread he *turned over the promises* of the dream."[85] Hannibal reflected on the dream and the portent and their promises of victory, offered sacrifices to Zeus, Ares, and Mercury, and began to mobilize his troops. He would, indeed, inflict great harm on the Romans, but eventually he would lose the war, despite Jupiter's promises.[86]

The table on pages 40–41 lists the motifs of the dream-portent pattern as it appears in Homer, Herodotus, Vergil, Statius, and Silius. Absent are the parallels in *Odyssey* 4 and 6 insofar as it is difficult to know if they issue from mimesis of *Iliad* 2 or from the conventions of dreams in the epic tradition. Also absent is the parallel in Lucan, whose imitation of Agamemnon's lying dream takes greater liberties with the narrative pattern. It is important to remember that the parallels in Herodotus, Vergil, Statius, and Silius each derive from direct imitation of Homer, even in cases where the author knows and imitates other works as well. For example, Statius and Silius obviously knew and imitated the *Aeneid* elsewhere, but for these dreams the *Iliad* was their primary model.

In each column, Zeus, Jupiter (his Roman clone), or Juno sends a messenger to a military leader with commands to wage war. In Vergil and Statius, as in Homer, the messenger transforms his or her appearance to that of an elder (Nestor, Calybe, or Tiresias). In Homer, Statius, and Silius the messenger begins by rebuking the leader for sleeping, and each example contains a rebuke for inaction. Divine favor or assurance of victory is explicit in Homer, Vergil, Statius, and Silius, and inferred by Artabanus and Xerxes in Herodotus. In each case the leader thus awakes confident of victory, but his obedience to the command will result in a deadly debacle. The same holds true of Lucan's description of the dream to Pompey. Notice also that none of these examples is trivial: they involve the origins of the Theban civil war (the *Thebaid*), events toward the end of the Trojan War (the *Iliad*), the settlement of Trojans in Italy (the *Aeneid*), the beginning of the Persian War (Herodotus), the Roman Civil War (Lucan), and the beginning of the Second Punic War (Silius). Furthermore, in each case the dream occurs at a significant juncture in its host narrative and profoundly informs the reading of what follows.

4

The Visions of Cornelius and Peter

The visions of Cornelius and Peter conform to this venerable tradition. This chapter will investigate each of the five scenes in Acts 10:1–11:18, four of which resonate with *Iliad* 2. Chapter 5 will argue that the best explanation for the parallels is mimesis.

Scene 1: The Vision of Cornelius (10:1–8)

Luke begins his tale like this: "There was a certain man in Caesarea, Cornelius by name, centurion of the cohort called Italian, pious, fearing God with his entire household, providing many alms for the people, and praying constantly to God."[1] Later his soldiers praise his integrity by calling him "a righteous man, fearing God and attested to by the whole ethnos of the Jews."[2] Luke also refers to Cornelius's relatives, household, and companions.[3] His residence in Caesarea was large enough to accommodate a large assembly.[4]

Cornelius thus resembles Agamemnon. Both were officers of European armies in the East, both were intimately related to their families, both looked after the economic welfare of their underlings, and both were noted for piety. Agamemnon claimed never to have sailed past a shrine to Zeus without offering bulls for sacrifice.[5] Throughout the epic one finds him at prayer and worship; Cornelius, too, "prayed constantly to God."

On the other hand, one could not say that Agamemnon was righteous or that his household feared the gods. The house of Atreus was one of the most troubled in antiquity, and Agamemnon himself was no saint. He sacrificed his daughter Iphigenia to win favorable winds, and his theft of Briseis produced the rift with Achilles that led to many deaths. After the war, he brought the Trojan princess Cassandra home as his concubine, outraging his wife, Clytemnestra. Homer's Agamemnon was pious but flawed; Luke's Cornelius, on the other hand, is the picture of probity.

The name Cornelius was common among Romans, and the centurion's association with the Italian cohort — an anachronism — presents him as a quintessential gentile, not a provincial *conscriptus* who rose in the ranks.[6] In his encounter with Peter, Roman meets Jew, West meets East. Agamemnon and the other military leaders who received dreams in the imitations of *Iliad* 2 typically fought in conflicts between East and West or Europe and so-called barbarians: Greeks against Trojans (*Iliad*), Persians against Greeks (Herodotus), Trojans against Italians (Vergil), Carthaginians against Italians (Silius).

Furthermore, it is significant that the recipient of the vision was a ranked officer, as in *Iliad* 2 and its imitations. According to Cicero, Scipio Africanus had a dream of his ascendancy to military leadership and conquest, even though he was ranked "not much higher than a private soldier."[7] Commenting on this dream, Macrobius wrote:

> The critics say that dreams concerning the welfare of the state are not to be considered significant unless military or civil officers dream them, or unless many plebeians have the same dream. They cite the incident in Homer when, before the assembled Greeks, Agamemnon disclosed a dream that he had had about a forthcoming battle. Nestor, who helped the army quite as much with his prudence as all the youth with their might, by way of instilling confidence in the dream, said that in matters of general welfare they had to confide in the dream of a king, whereas they would repudiate the dream of anyone else.[8]

Unlike young Scipio, Cornelius was an officer and thus a worthier recipient of a heavenly visitor.[9]

Homer narrated Agamemnon's dream three times: once in Zeus's instruction to Oneiros, once in Oneiros's delivery of the instructions to the king, and once in Agamemnon's first-person rehearsal of it to the elders. Similarly, Luke narrates Cornelius's vision three times: once by the narrator, once by Cornelius to Peter, and once by Peter to a Jerusalem assembly. The first and second accounts parallel the second and third in Homer; there is no Lucan equivalent to *1. Sending the messenger*, Zeus's orders to Oneiros. It would be astonishing if there were, for nowhere in Luke-Acts is one privy to a heavenly council or to God's instructions to a messenger. (Imitations of Agamemnon's dream in Herodotus and Lucan likewise contain no divine deliberations.) Luke's parallels with *Iliad* 2 begin with *2. Delivering the message*.

2.1. *Appearance of the messenger.* Compare the following:

Iliad 2.17–26	Acts 10:3–4a and 30–31[10]
Quickly he [Oneiros]	About the ninth hour of the day [3 P.M.],
arrived at the swift ships of the	he clearly saw in a vision *an*
Achaeans and *went to*	*angel* [ἄγγελον] *of God*
Atreides Agamemnon.	*coming to him*
	[When Cornelius retells the tale, he says:
	Four days ago, at this very hour, at the ninth,
He found him *sleeping in his hut,* . . .	I was *praying in my house*
So he *stood* [στῆ] *above his head,*	*when suddenly a man stood* (ἔστη) *before*
in the likeness of Nestor . . .	*me* in dazzling clothes.]
[*T*]*he divine Oneiros spoke*:	and *saying:* "Cornelius."
"Are you sleeping, *son of wise Atreus* . . . ?	
A man burdened with decisions, on whom	When he gazed at him, he was terrified
his people rely, with so many worries,	and said, "What is it, sir?"
ought not sleep through the night.	
Now listen attentively, I am	
an angel [ἄγγελος] *to you from Zeus.*"	

In each column an angel from the god comes to a military leader in his home, stands before him looking like a man, and addresses him by name. The ἄγγελος stood before Cornelius (ἔστη); the ἄγγελος stood (στῆ) above the head of Agamemnon. This use of the verb ἵστημι and compounds was common in Greek imitations of the lying dream.[11]

The most striking difference between the two accounts pertains to Cornelius's wakefulness. His vision is called exactly that (ὅραμα), not a dream. He saw it clearly (εἶδεν . . . φανερῶς) not at night but in bright afternoon light.[12] Cornelius gazed intently (ἀτενίσας) at the angel, trembled, and even spoke to him. This is no dream, and for that reason there also is no *rebuke* for sloth (motif 2.2). In the *Iliad* Oneiros rebuked Agamemnon: "It is not right that" a man with his grave duties sleep the night away. Rebukes for sleeping also appear in imitations of the scene: Laius to Etiocles in Statius and Mercury to Hannibal in Silius.[13] Rebukes for sloth but not sleep appear in Herodotus and Vergil. Cornelius, on the other hand, is vigilant, "praying constantly."[14]

2.3. *Expression of divine favor.*

Iliad 2.26–27	Acts 10:4b (cf. 31)
"I am an angel to you from *Zeus,*	[The angel spoke:]
who, though he is far away, cares for you	"Your prayers and *your alms*
greatly *and takes pity* [ἐλεαίρει]	[ἐλεημοσύναι] have ascended
on you."	to remembrance before *God.*"[15]

This expression of divine approval in the *Iliad* is a cruel hoax. Zeus actually was punishing Agamemnon for having insulted Achilles. The same is true of the assurances of approval in most imitations, including Vergil, Statius, and Silius Italicus. In Acts, however, the sentiment is genuine.[16]

2.4. *Command to the mortal.* The mimetic dreams to military leaders (including Lucan's) invariably involve orders to send soldiers to their deaths. Oneiros deceived Agamemnon into sending soldiers against Troy. The dreams in Herodotus prodded Xerxes into sending troops against Greece. Allecto ordered Turnus to lead his army against Trojans. The dream of Pompey emboldened him to march against Caesar. Laius told Etiocles to arm the city against Polynices. Mercury ordered Hannibal to attack Italy. The angel's message to Cornelius, however, was irenic: "Send men to Joppa and summon a certain Simon, called Peter. He is residing at the home of Simon, a tanner, near the sea."[17] Whereas the commands in *Iliad* 2 and its imitations order military campaigns, the angel commands a friendly visit to an apostle. The vision to Cornelius thus is both true and salvific. The visitation of the angel is a genuine response to Cornelius's prayers and alms, and the command that he seek out Peter will result not only in his own salvation, but also that of his household and potentially all gentiles.

2.5. *Assurance of victory.* There is no guarantee of victory in the first or second accounts of Cornelius's vision, but when Peter retells the tale he adds that the angel had told Cornelius to send for the apostle to hear words "through which you and your house will be saved."[18] The use of the future passive here (σωθήσῃ), instead of a subjunctive or optative, assures future fulfillment. The promise implicit in the angel's command would indeed find fulfillment, unlike the divine promises in *Iliad* 2 and most of its imitators.

2.6. *Departure of the messenger; and 3. Responding to the message.*

Iliad 2.35	Acts 10:7
When [ὥς ἄρα] he *had spoken* [φωνήσας], *he went away* [ἀπεβήσετο]. [Cf. 2:70–71: "The speaker then flew off, and sweet sleep released me."] [Agamemnon then summoned his council.]	*When* [ὡς δέ] the angel who *spoke* to him *went away* [ἀπῆλθεν], he summoned [φωνήσας] two servants and a pious soldier from among those who attended to him.[19]

Scene 2: The Vision of Peter (10:9–16)

Luke alludes to the story of Peter's vision four times and gives full accounts twice: once in third-person narration (scene 2) and once on Peter's own lips to the Jerusalem assembly (scene 5). Homer told the story of the portent at Aulis only once, on the lips of Odysseus to the assembled army as a back reference, because the portent had taken place nine years earlier, before the ships left for Troy. By modestly adjusting a few phrases one can reconstruct how the poet expected his readers would understand the original event. In the following columns, the revised narrative from *Iliad* 2 appears in the left hand, and the vision of Peter in the right.

Iliad 2.303–8	Acts 10:9b–10
[And so] the ships of the Achaeans	[Peter was in Joppa, at the home of Simon
were assembling at Aulis to bring harm	the tanner, "near the sea."]
to Priam and the Trojans. Around a spring	*Peter went to the roof to pray*
and *at holy altars [they] were sacrificing*	at about the ninth hour.[20]
perfect hecatombs to the immortals,	He became hungry and wanted to eat,
beneath a beautiful plane-tree	and while others were making the
from which clear water flowed.	preparations,
There a great sign appeared.	*an ecstasy overtook him.*

Joppa was a famous seaport; it was from there that Jonah fled from God's command to prophesy to gentiles in Nineveh. Aulis, the venue for the portent in the *Iliad,* likewise was a famous port, the point of departure for the Greek army sailing for Troy. The sacrifice of hecatombs would have provisioned an enormous feast. Similarly, the preparations for Peter's meal presumably would have included slaying an animal, for the voice from heaven suggests that to satisfy his hunger Peter should sacrifice the animals himself.[21]

Not only are the two settings similar, some of their similarities distinguish them from earlier encounters with angels in both works. For example, the dream of Agamemnon and the vision of Cornelius both took place in their homes, but the portent at Aulis and Peter's vision took place outside. The apostle went to the roof, which allowed him to see the sheet descending from the sky, just as the location at the springs at Aulis allowed the Greeks to see the serpent climb the tree to eat the sparrows. Furthermore, the signs at Joppa and Aulis were symbolic, unlike the visions of Cornelius and Agamemnon, which were articulate and unambiguous.

Peter's vision, like the portent at Aulis, involved reptiles and birds:

> He sees the sky opened and a container, descending like a huge sail, let down to the ground by four corners. In it were all types of quadrupeds, reptiles of the earth, and birds of heaven.[22] A voice called to him: "Peter, arise, slay, and eat." But Peter said, "Never, Lord! I never ate anything profane or unclean." The voice came to him a second time: "What God has made clean, you must not make profane." The same thing happened three times, and suddenly the container was taken into the sky.[23]

This vision, like that in *Iliad* 2, involves reptiles and birds. The serpent devoured the sparrows (κατήσθιε and ἔφαγε); Peter was told to devour birds, reptiles, and quadrupeds in Acts (φάγε and ἔφαγον). The serpent disappears as suddenly as he had appeared; Zeus turned him to stone. The end of the vision in Acts likewise is abrupt: "suddenly the container was taken into the sky."

In both accounts, those who saw the vision were flummoxed.

Iliad 2.320	Acts 10:17a and 19a
[They] just stood there *amazed at what had happened.*	Peter *was at a loss what the vision he saw might mean.* . . . And while he was still mulling over the vision . . .

Bafflement after the sudden disappearance of the portent also characterizes some of the imitations of the portent. *Odyssey* 2: "Those assembled were amazed at the birds when they saw them with their eyes. Their hearts raced in fear about things that would come to pass."[24] Xerxes did not understand his vision and had to consult magicians. Hannibal was terrified by his vision and asked Mercury to interpret it.

Unlike these other visions, Peter's was accompanied by a command from heaven. He was to slay and eat animals from the vessel, a blatant violation of Jewish dietary regulations. In other words, Peter's bewilderment was a conflict between two divine directives: the biblical command to eat nothing unclean and the heavenly command to eat what "God has made clean." Calchas offered his interpretation of the portent almost at once, but it would take two days and eleven verses for Peter to provide his. The clue to the meaning of Peter's vision is the nearly simultaneous vision to Cornelius, which he discovers in scene three.

Scene 3: The Summoning of Peter from Joppa (10:17–23a)

Nine years separated the portent at Aulis from Agamemnon's dream, yet the two signs are temporally congruent insofar as the nine sparrows each represented one year; and Odysseus reminded the troops of the vision in the tenth. The interpretation of Calchas thus corresponded with the "now" of the dream.

Temporal correspondence between the visions of Cornelius and Peter likewise is important; indeed, the near simultaneity of the visions provides the clue to their significance. Peter's vision took place the day after Cornelius's, "while they [the emissaries] were traveling and approaching the city."[25] To bind the visions even more securely into a symbiotic unit, Luke created an episode without parallel in the epic: the summoning of Peter from Joppa, scene 3. Twice here he uses an abrupt ἰδού, "behold," to punctuate the temporal congruity of the visions. "And while Peter was at a loss concerning what the vision he saw might mean, behold [ἰδού] the men stood at the gate."[26] "And while Peter was still mulling over the vision, the Spirit said to him, 'Look [ἰδού], three men are seeking you.'"[27]

Immediately after recalling his vision to the assembly at Jerusalem, Peter adds: "behold suddenly [ἰδοὺ ἐξαυτῆς] three men stood before the house where I was."[28] The Spirit also told him to travel with them "making no distinction, because I sent them," and they insisted that an angel told Cornelius to summon him.[29] Both Peter and Cornelius are obedient but otherwise passive instruments of the divine will.

Scene 4: The Meeting of Peter and Cornelius (10:23b–48)

Luke's tale reaches its height in the fourth scene, Peter's arrival at Caesarea and his preaching to gentiles assembled there. This is the longest of the five scenes and can be subdivided as follows: 4.1. the gathering (23b–29); 4.2. Cornelius's speech (30–33); 4.3. Peter's speech (34–43); and 4.4. the outpouring of the Spirit (44–48).

4.1. The Gathering (23b–29). Peter traveled from Joppa to Caesarea and "Cornelius was waiting for them, having summoned his relatives and his intimate friends."[30] At the house, Peter found "many people assembled" and revealed for the first time his interpretation of the vision: "You yourselves are aware that it is unlawful for a Jewish man to associate with or visit a foreigner, and God showed me that no one should call any person [ἄνθρωπον] profane or unclean." The adjectives κοινός ("profane") and ἀκάθαρτος ("unclean") hark back to the vision, but there they refer to animals banned from the Jewish table. This alleged disparity between the vision and its interpretation troubled scholars into proposing that the vision came from a pre-Lucan source, but this solution is unnecessary. Luke was too sophisticated an author to let such an important matter escape his attention, and many ancient commentators saw no logical incompatibility here.[31]

At least two other solutions are possible. Several interpreters insist that neither in the tradition nor in Acts does the vision contravene the biblical division of animals into clean and unclean. They note that Luke refused to include in his gospel Mark's pericope in which Jesus declared all foods clean (7:1–23), and that he endorsed the prohibition of "things offered to idols, blood, and meats strangled" (Acts 15:20 and 29). According to this view, Peter's interpretation of the vision was the only one intended by the heavenly voice: the animals represent the diversity of humankind, all of whom God had declared clean.[32]

The second solution allows the vision two intersecting meanings, both a literal and an allegorical. Just a few verses after the heavenly voice told Peter to "slay and eat," the Spirit informed Peter that three men were seeking him and that he must go with them without a second thought, "for I have sent them."[33] At this point Peter does not know the men are gentiles or where they intend to take him, but almost at once he learns that an angel had told a Roman centurion to send for him to come "into his home."[34] Such an invitation would not only require the violation of the prohibition of a Jew visiting the home of a gentile, it would likely require him to eat unclean foods.[35] Had Peter not seen his vision, he should have declined the invitation just as he resisted the heavenly voice: "I cannot come, for I never eat anything profane or unclean." Peter remained at the home of Cornelius for several days, a duration that would have required many meals.[36] "Those of the circumcision" at Jerusalem thus objected to his conduct precisely at this point: "You went into the house of uncircumcised men and ate with them" at meals that presumably involved the eating of foods Jews would have considered unclean.[37]

According to Luke, Peter violated Jewish dietary laws because God repeatedly instructed him to do so. First, the vision told the apostle three times that whatever (ἅ) God declares clean, one must not consider unclean. Second, the Spirit commanded Peter to go with the emissaries to the home of Cornelius "making no distinction" because God had sent them. Peter's journey to Caesarea would require both lodging with a gentile and sharing foods Jews would have considered unclean. Finally, the emissaries claimed that an angel had ordered Cornelius to summon Peter. Luke here presents God as suspending the prohibition of eating unclean animals so that Cornelius could receive the apostle's message in his own home with his family and friends. This combination of events suggests to Peter that God had declared Cornelius and his household clean, and that he thus was free also to eat unclean foods there. According to this reading, the leap from the vision of unclean animals to Peter's interpretation of them as gentiles is not as Olympian as many exegetes have thought. Indeed, it is God's insistence that Peter go to the home of Cornelius that provides the meaning of the vision.[38]

The portent at Aulis and its later imitations show that such allegorical leaps were routine. Ancient readers understood the animals in *Iliad* 2 as humans: the serpent was the Greek army and the mother sparrow was Troy. Most ancient imitations of the portent likewise symbolize humans through their depiction of animals. For example, the eagles in *Odyssey* 2 are Odysseus and the suitors; the two eagles in Aeschylus are Agamemnon and Menelaus and the rabbit is Troy; the serpent in Silius Italicus is Hannibal.[39] Luke and his readers would have been quite prepared to understand animal visions as allegories of human beings.

After receiving Oneiros's message, Agamemnon convened the council of elders to tell them about his dream. "He commanded the clear-voiced heralds to call the long-haired Achaeans to the assembly, and they gathered quickly. . . . After he had convened [συγκαλέσας] them, he designed a shrewd plan: 'Listen, my friends [φίλοι].' "[40] Luke similarly used a nominative aorist participle of συγκαλέω (συγκαλεσάμενος, "having summoned") and included in the group Cornelius's friends (φίλοι). Peter found "many people gathered"; in the epic the officers "gathered quickly."[41]

Verses 25–26 have no clear parallel in *Iliad* 2, but they too may have a Homeric backdrop: "It so happened that when Peter entered, Cornelius greeted him, fell at this feet, and lay prostrate. But Peter raised him up and said, 'Arise; I too am a mortal [ἄνθρωπος].'" The word translated here as "lay prostrate" is προσεκύνη-σεν, which may imply worship, whence the derivative *proskynesis*. Twice elsewhere in Acts people respond to the apostles as though they were gods (14:11–15 and 28:5–6), but in both cases the people were pagans, not worshipers of the Jewish God like Cornelius. Two interpretations of Cornelius's gesture are possible. On the one hand, one might conclude that "as an erstwhile pagan he continues to stand in danger of obscuring the boundary between God and creature."[42] Other interpreters, however, take Luke's depiction of Cornelius as a God-fearer more seriously and think that his proskynesis was merely a gesture of obeisance before a man of God or perhaps an angel.[43] According to this view, Peter merely demurred that such a demonstration of subordination was due God alone.

No matter which interpretation one prefers, this scene would have shocked Luke's readers: a Roman centurion in his own home prostrate before a Jewish fisherman! Here, again, the contrast with Agamemnon is intriguing. Homer used several epithets to show the king's lofty status, including ἄναξ ἀνδρῶν, "ruler of men," ποιμὴν λαῶν, "shepherd of the people," and δῖος, from the same Indo-European root that spawned Zeus, *deus,* and *divus.* This use of δῖος for heroes like Agamemnon does not imply their divinity any more that the related epithet διογενής, "born of Zeus," but it does exalt the mortal to heroic status. Homer used the epithet of Agamemnon once in *Iliad* 2 ('Αγαμέμνονι δίῳ).[44] More relevant to Luke's Cornelius is Agamemnon's arrogance, which repeatedly got him into trouble. He called himself "the best of the Achaeans" and would not tolerate insubordination.[45] His arrogant taking of Briseis resulted in Achilles' withdrawal from the war. Unlike Agamemnon, Cornelius is a model of humility. Though he could have wielded his power over Peter, he prostrated himself before him and treated him with deference, as in the polite expression "you have been kind enough to come."[46] The centurion's manners impressed John Chrysostom, among others.[47]

4.2. *Cornelius's speech to Peter (30–33).* In response to Peter's inquiry into the cause of the centurion's summons, Cornelius narrated an abbreviated version of his vision, a parallel to Agamemnon's recounting of his dream to the council of elders. The columns that follow are similar to those presented earlier, though here I have deleted the identification of motifs.[48]

Iliad 2.56–60 and 63–67	*Acts* 10:30b–32
Listen, friends, Oneiros, a divine dream,	Four days ago, at this very hour, at the ninth,
came to me during the ambrosial night.	I was praying in my house,
In shape, stature, and size	
he most resembled noble Nestor.	when suddenly a man *stood* [ἔστη] *before*
He *stood* [στῆ] *above my head*	*me* in dazzling clothes
and spoke to me, "Are you sleeping,	*and said,* "*Cornelius,*
son of Atreus . . . ?	
I am an angel to you from *Zeus,*	
who, though he is far away, cares for you	your prayers and *your alms* [ἐλεημοσύναι]
greatly *and takes pity* [ἐλεαίρει] on you.	have been remembered before *God.*
He ordered that you *arm the long-haired*	*Send* to Joppa and *summon Simon,* called
Achaeans at once, for now you can take	Peter. He is residing in the home of Simon,
the wide-laned city of the Trojans."	a tanner, near the sea."

4.3. *Peter's speech to the assembly (10:34–43).* The opening sentence of Peter's speech in Caesarea is his clearest articulation of the meaning of his vision: "Truly I perceive that God does not practice favoritism, but in every nation one who fears God and acts justly is acceptable to him."[49] What follows in 36–38 is a tangle of garbled grammar and oblique biblical allusions that need not detain us here insofar as they are not directly relevant to a comparison with the epic. But it may be worth noting that verse 39 begins with a phrase similar to Odysseus's introduction to the portent at Aulis. Luke's Peter says: "And we are witnesses [καὶ ἡμεῖς μάρτυρες] of everything that he [Jesus] did." Homer's Odysseus says, "We all know this well in our minds, and you are all witnesses [ἐστὲ δὲ πάντες μάρτυροι]."[50] In verses 40–43 Peter articulates Luke's interpretation of the Christian kerygma.

4.4. *The Coming of the Spirit (44–48).* This passage, too, has no apparent parallel in the epic: the Spirit fell on all who listened to Peter; Jews present in the house witnessed the event; and Peter baptized the gentiles. Parallels with the epic resume in the scene that follows.

Scene 5: The Report of Peter to the Church in Jerusalem (11:1–18)

Agamemnon's retelling of his dream to his war council led to an assembly of the entire army, at which, among other things, Odysseus reminded them of the portent of the serpent and sparrows. This second assembly differed significantly from the first, and a few of these differences apply also to Acts 10–11. For instance, the second assembly was much larger: Homer likens the gathering of troops to bees swarming into a meadow, "so from the ships and huts by the low beach many tribes marched out in companies to the assembly."[51] In the council no one opposed Agamemnon, but in the assembly the rogue Thersites spoke for others in denouncing the king's insistence on attacking Troy. The council focused on the validity of Agamemnon's dream; the assembly listened instead to Odysseus's recounting of the portent at Aulis. Finally, after the council, the officers dispersed in dignified obedience, but the assembled troops dispersed in frenzied excitement. When Odysseus stopped speaking, "the Argives shouted out, and round about the ships echoed terribly at the cries of the Achaeans, as they praised the speech of god-like Odysseus."[52] Similarly, after Agamemnon's final pep talk to the army, one reads that "the Argives shouted aloud as when a wave smashes a high cliff."[53] As we shall see, each of these differences from the council obtains also to the meeting at Jerusalem, for here, too, one finds a large assembly, stiff opposition, consideration of a symbolic vision, and an acclamation.

"The apostles and brethren who were in Judea heard that gentiles, too, received the word of God. So when Peter went up to Jerusalem, circumcised Jews disputed with him, saying, 'You went into the house of uncircumcised men and ate with them.' "[54] Peter's response is a rehearsal of events at Joppa and Caesarea, especially his vision of unclean beasts. Similarly, Odysseus's response to Thersites and other would-be deserters consisted primarily of a reminder of the portent at Aulis. I see no virtue in reproducing the parallels between the two visions. It will suffice to note that both in the epic and in Acts an earlier vision is narrated as a reply to opponents before a large audience. The visions narrated by Odysseus and Peter took place under open skies and involved reptiles, birds, and eating. Both visions coordinate with the content of a visitation by an angel earlier in the narrative through temporal correspondence. The portent at Aulis predicted victory in the tenth year, a correlate to the "now" of Agamemnon's dream. The vision at Joppa found its meaning in contemporaneity with the arrival of Cornelius's emissaries: "And behold suddenly three men stood before the house where I was."[55] Peter then briefly narrated what happened in Caesarea after he arrived, including an abbreviated version of Cornelius's vision and the gentiles' receiving the gift of the Spirit. Compare the response of those who heard Peter's speech with that of those who heard Odysseus's.

Iliad 2.333–35	Acts 11:18
So he spoke,	*When they heard these things,*
and the Argives shouted out, and round	they were quiet
about the ships echoed terribly at the cries	and *glorified God* [θεόν], saying:
of the Achaeans, as *they praised* the speech	"So *God* [θεός] has given to the gentiles
of *god-like* [θείοιο] Odysseus.	repentance that leads to life."
[Odysseus's speech would lead many of	
them to their deaths.]	

This chapter compared the twin visions in Acts 10–11 with the dream and portent in *Iliad* 2 to assess the density and sequence of the parallels (criteria three and four). The dream to Cornelius follows the order of motifs in the lying dream to Agamemnon and its imitators. Furthermore, Odysseus interprets the dream as a confirmation of the portent at Aulis; Peter interprets the vision to Cornelius as the key to his vision at Joppa. Just as Agamemnon repeated his dream to his council of elders, Cornelius repeated his experience with the angel to those assembled at Caesarea. Just as Odysseus recalled the portent at Aulis to the army, Peter recounted his vision to the brethren at Jerusalem. The density and sequence of parallel motifs is impressive — even more impressive than most of the imitations of *Iliad* 2 presented in Chapter 3 — but mimesis is not the only possible explanation. Chapter 5 will recapitulate the four criteria applied thus far and extend the analysis to the last two: the presence of distinctive traits (criterion five), and the ability of the similarities to explain why the author would have gone to the trouble to recast his model (criterion six).

5

Local Legend or Homeric Imitation?

The Introduction presented six criteria for detecting mimesis: accessibility, analogy, density, order, distinctive traits, and interpretability. The first criterion is the availability of the proposed model. Luke and his educated readers clearly could have known Agamemnon's lying dream and the portent at Aulis. The *Iliad* was the most famous book in Greek antiquity, and surviving school exercises witness to it as the most common mimetic target for ancient education, as I attempted to show toward the end of Chapter 2.

The second criterion is analogy, evidence that other authors used the same proposed model for their creations. Imitations of the lying dream appear in the *Odyssey*, Lucan, Vergil, and Statius; imitations of the serpent-sparrows portent appear in the *Odyssey*, Aeschylus, Vergil, Philostratus, and Nonnus; and imitations of both the dream and the portent appear in Herodotus and Silius Italicus (Chapter 3). This list is by no means complete.

Criterion three concerns the density of the parallels, and criterion four their order. A case for imitation strengthens with an accumulation of parallels, especially if they appear in the same sequence. Three of the five scenes that comprise Acts 10:1–11:18 have parallels in the same order in *Iliad* 2, and a fourth has a potential parallel. Cornelius's vision (Acts 10:1–18) parallels Agamemnon's dream (*Iliad* 2.16–47); the meeting at Caesarea (Acts 10:23b–48) resembles the council of elders (*Iliad* 2.48–83); and the assembly at Jerusalem (Acts 11:1–18) echoes the assembly of the army (*Iliad* 2.84–335). Peter's vision parallels the portent at Aulis, but because the portent took place nine years earlier, it appears in the epic only as a flashback told by Odysseus. It should be noted, however, that the flashback resembles Peter's account of his vision to those in Jerusalem. Only the third scene, the arrival of the emissaries in Joppa (Acts 10:17–23a) has no parallel in the epic. Luke created this section to emphasize the temporal coincidence of the two visions.

The columns that follow summarize the findings of Chapter 4 and surely demonstrate that the similarities between *Iliad* 2 and Acts 10–11 are dense and sequential.

Scene 1: *The Vision of Cornelius*

Iliad 2 begins with Zeus's instructions to Oneiros (motif *1. sending the messenger*). There is no equivalent to this episode in Acts, as is the case also in the imitations of the lying dream in Herodotus and Lucan.

Iliad 2.1–52	Acts 10:1–8
THE SETTING	
• The Greek army was bivouacked at Troy, near their ships.	• Cornelius was stationed at Caesarea Maritima, a famous harbor.
• Agamemnon was the commander of the Greek army, known both for his piety as well as his arrogance.	• Cornelius was a centurion of the Italian cohort, pious and righteous.
• Agamemnon slept at night.	• ≠ Cornelius, however, was diligently at prayer at 3 P.M.
2. DELIVERING THE MESSAGE	
2.1. The Appearance of the Messenger	
Oneiros, an "angel of Zeus," appeared to Agamemnon as he slept.	An "angel of God" appeared to Cornelius as he prayed.
2.2. Rebuke	
Oneiros rebuked Agamemnon for sleeping.	≠ There is no rebuke in Acts; Cornelius was fully awake and at prayer.
2.3. Expression of Divine Favor	
"Zeus . . . cares for you greatly and takes pity on you."	"Your prayers and your alms have ascended to remembrance before God."

2.4. Command to the Mortal

"Arm the . . . Achaeans" against Troy.

"Send men to Joppa and summon a certain Simon."

2.5. Assurance of Victory

Oneiros assures Agamemnon that Troy "now" will fall.

There is no assurance of victory in the narrator's version of the vision, but see Peter's account of it in 11:14.

2.6. Departure of the Messenger

"When he had spoken, he went away."

"When the angel who spoke to him went away . . ."

3. RESPONDING TO THE MESSAGE

Agamemnon convened his council and told them the dream.

Cornelius summoned two servants and a soldier and told them his vision.

Scene 2: The Vision of Peter

Because the portent took place nine years earlier, it is not told by the narrator. What follows is a reconstruction based on Odysseus's account looking back to it.

[*Iliad* 2.301–35]

Acts 10:9–16

THE SETTING

• The Greek army was about to sail from the harbor at Aulis.
• They were offering hecatombs, after which there would have been a meal.
• "A great sign appeared."

• Peter was residing at Joppa at the home of Simon the Tanner, "near the sea."
• He was praying on the roof, hungry, while others prepared his meal.
• "An ecstasy overtook him."

THE SIGN

• A serpent slithered up a tree and devoured eight sparrows before devouring the mother.

• A container resembling a sail descended in which were unclean beasts, including reptiles and birds. A voice from heaven told Peter to kill and devour them.

• The serpent descended and turned into stone.

• The container ascended into heaven and disappeared.

BAFFLEMENT

"[They] just stood there amazed at what had happened."

"Peter was at a loss what the vision he saw might mean."

INTERPRETATION OF THE SIGN

Calchas interpreted the sparrows each as one year: the Greeks would take Troy in the tenth year of the war, which Odysseus, nine years later, understood to correlate with the "now" of Agamemnon's dream.

Later Peter would take the contemporaneity of his vision with that of Cornelius to mean that the unclean animals represented gentiles. He ought not consider unclean what God had declared clean.

Scene 3: The Summoning of Peter from Joppa

Acts 10:17–23a: Luke created this scene to link to two visions together. While Peter was contemplating the vision, the emissaries arrived. The Spirit told Peter he had sent the men, and the men told Peter that an angel had directed Cornelius to send them. Because of the correlation of the messages and the correspondence in the timing of the arrival of the emissaries, the apostle left with them for Caesarea.

Scene 4: The Meeting of Peter and Cornelius

Iliad 2.48–83

Acts 10:23b–48

THE GATHERING

• Agamemnon convened the council of elders. "After he had summoned [συγκαλέσας] them, he designed a shrewd plan: 'Listen, my friends [φίλοι].'"
• Homer called Agamemnon god-like (δῖος) and depicted him as arrogantly misusing his authority.

• "Cornelius was waiting for them, having convened [συγκαλεσάμενος] his relatives and intimate friends [φίλους]."

• ≠ Cornelius fell at Peter's feet in worship, and Peter objected: "I too am a mortal."

CORNELIUS'S SPEECH

The centurion told Peter his vision, which parallels Agamemnon's telling the council his dream. Here again the two works share motifs.

2.1. *The Appearance of the Messenger*

"Oneiros, a divine dream, came to me
in the ambrosial night. In shape, stature,
and size he most resembled noble Nestor.
He stood [στῆ] above my head
and spoke to me."

"Four days ago, at this very hour,
at the ninth, I was praying in my house
when suddenly a man stood [ἔστη]
before me in dazzling clothes
and said . . ."

2.3. *Expression of Divine Favor*

"I am an angel to you from Zeus, who . . .
cares for you greatly and takes pity
on you."

"Your prayers and your alms have
ascended to remembrance before God."

2.4. *Command to the Mortal*

"He ordered that you arm the . . .
Achaeans" against Troy.

"Send men to Joppa and summon
Simon."

PETER'S SPEECH

Acts 10:34–43 is heavy with biblical allusions employed to articulate Luke's understanding of the Christian kerygma; thus there is no equivalent to this section in the epic.

THE COMING OF THE SPIRIT

Acts 10:44–48 also has no correlate in the *Iliad*.

Scene 5: *The Report of Peter to Jerusalem*

Iliad 2.84–335

• Agamemnon convened the entire army.

• Thersites spoke for those opposed to the king's plan to attack Troy.
• Odysseus countered the opposition by reminding them of the portent nine years earlier.
• "The ships . . . were assembling at Aulis. . . . [W]e were sacrificing perfect hecatombs to the immortals. . . . There a great sign appeared."

Acts 11:1–18

• Peter addressed an assembly of believers at Jerusalem.

• "Those of the circumcision" opposed Peter's association with "the uncircumcised."
• Peter countered the opposition by telling them of his vision.

• "I was in the city of Joppa praying, and in ecstasy I saw a vision: a container descending like a huge sail let down from heaven by four corners."

• A serpent slithered from under an altar, climbed a tree to the highest branches, and devoured nine sparrows.

• The serpent descended and turned into stone.
• Calchas interpreted the serpent to be Greeks, the sparrows to be Trojans; each of the sparrows also represented one year.
• Odysseus took the nine years to confirm the "now" of Agamemnon's dream.
• "So he spoke,
and the Argives shouted out, and round about the ships echoed terribly at the cries of the Achaeans, as they praised the speech of god-like [θείοιο] Odysseus."

• Inside the container were beasts, including reptiles and birds. "And I also heard a voice saying to me, 'Arise, Peter, sacrifice and eat.'"
• "Everything was drawn back into the sky."

• Immediately, Cornelius's emissaries arrived, prompting Peter to interpret the unclean animals as gentiles.
• The temporal correlation of the two visions confirmed each other.
• "When they heard these things, they were quiet
and glorified God [θεός], saying,
'So God [θεόν] has given to the gentiles repentance that leads to life.'"

Form critics might grant that these parallels are dense and often sequential but insist that direct literary imitation is not the best explanation. One might argue, for example, that dreams and visions were so common in ancient religious experience, both among pagans and Jews, that their appearance in early Christian texts is hardly surprising. Furthermore, the narration of a dream or a vision might naturally follow a standard pattern such as one finds in Acts: the setting, the appearance of a heavenly messenger, a statement of divine approval, instructions, and the messenger's departure. Symbolic portents, too, often are formulaic: appearance of a sign (often involving a serpent, bird, or both), bafflement of the witnesses, authoritative interpretation by a holy man or an *angelus interpres*, and appropriate response. Dreams and portents sometimes were combined so that the private and subjective dream finds confirmation in the public and objective portent interpreted by someone else.

These observations present the interpreter with several gnarly problems. How can one decide whether Luke imitated the *Iliad* or merely adapted a popular literary convention? Even if Luke had in mind a single literary model, is it not possible that it was one of Homer's well-known imitators? Did he expect readers to detect his transvaluation of the epic or the tradition of dreams and portents to military leaders that the epic spawned?

The last two criteria are designed to answer such questions: distinctive traits (criterion 5) and interpretability (criterion 6). The presence of unusual traits can separate the proposed imitation from tales of the same genre as a collectivity and join it to the model as a hermeneutical partner. For example, distinctive traits bind each of the pagan imitations discussed in Chapter 3 to *Iliad* 2, even though no two authors linked them in precisely the same manner. Ancient authors frequently used unusual features as flags alerting their readers to the influence of their models. Four peculiarities link Acts 10–11 with *Iliad* 2 so distinctively that the two are best viewed as imitation and model: references to the sea, temporal correspondence of the visions, repetition, and the importance of the visions for the narrative as a whole.

Commentators seldom give weight to the importance of the sea in Acts 10–11. Caesarea Maritima was noted for its magnificent harbor, and Joppa's harbor was famous in the Jewish scriptures. For example, it was the point of departure for Jonah's flight from his mission to gentiles. The angel makes a point of locating the home of Simon the tanner "by the sea."[1] Only in Acts 10–11 does Luke place Peter in a location near a harbor or the sea.

The visions in *Iliad* 2 also take place beside the sea. Zeus told Oneiros to go to Agamemnon who was sleeping "by the swift ships," and this is where he found him.[2] Failing Agamemnon's test, the troops bolted for their ships to escape, and it was by the sea that Athena and Odysseus called them back to the assembly.[3] The portent of the serpent and the sparrows took place at Aulis, the famous harbor that launched the ships for Troy. In response to Odysseus's recounting of the portent, "the Argives shouted out," and "the ships echoed terribly."[4] None of the imitations of the lying dream treated in Chapter 3 makes a point of a location near the sea, and of the imitations of the portent only Vergil's does so. Seaside visions are distinctive to the *Iliad* and Acts.

The misperceived temporal correspondence between the portent at Aulis and the dream of Agamemnon shaped the Greeks' interpretation of both. The "now" of the dream represented the completion of the nine years in the portent. Similarly, Herodotus and Silius Italicus imitated both the dream and the portent so that the two interpreted each other, but neither author made them coordinate temporally.[5] In Acts, however, it is the temporal correspondence between the visions that is crucial; indeed, the arrival of Cornelius's emissaries precisely when Peter was contemplating the meaning of his vision prompted him to interpret the unclean beasts as gentiles.

Ancient literature is rife with dreams and visions, and one can find several examples of two such visions confirming each other, but examples of combined visions followed by repeated narrations are rare. Homer first reports the content of the lying dream in the instructions Zeus gave to Oneiros; he repeats the content nearly verbatim in Oneiros's appearance to Agamemnon, except for adding five lines at the beginning and two at the end; and the king narrates it once again, nearly as he had heard it, to his council of elders. This triple telling both establishes the significance of the dream for the next several books and fixes it in the reader's memory. The poet expected the reader to have the dream in mind as late as Book 9, when Agamemnon, having lost many men, recognizes that Zeus deceived him.[6]

Herodotus may have imitated this repetitive aspect of *Iliad* 2 in the multiple dreams that came to Xerxes and Artabanus and in Xerxes' recognition, after several setbacks, that his dreams may have been deceptions.[7] Apart from Herodotus, the imitations never renarrate the dream; never elsewhere does the military leader repeat it to others — never elsewhere but in Acts.

Cornelius's vision likewise is narrated three times and alluded to twice more. Even though Luke uses repetition elsewhere in Acts — most notoriously in the triple telling of the conversion of Saul — the repetitions in Acts 10–11 are striking and noteworthy. The first version appears in the third-person voice of the narrator after which one reads that the centurion "told everything" to his three messengers. The second allusion is Peter's first notification of the vision, after which one finds the second full version on the lips of Cornelius himself to Peter. The third and final version is Peter's truncated tale for the assembly at Jerusalem. Neither in *Iliad* 2 nor in Acts 10–11 is the repetition of the vision necessary for the success of the story; in each case a simple reference to the dream or vision would have sufficed. Scholars both of the epic and of the Acts have debated the function of the repetition, but none apparently has seen the similarities in the two books.[8]

Furthermore, both *Iliad* 2 and Acts 10–11 have multiple assemblies for making corporate decisions on the basis of the apparitions. In the epic, Agamemnon first convenes his counselors, and then assembles the entire army, which Odysseus must reassemble after many of the troops bolt for home.[9] In the first of these assemblies Agamemnon narrates his dream, in the second Odysseus narrates the portent at Aulis. Similarly, in Acts there are two assemblies. The first occurs at the home of Cornelius where Peter "found many people gathered." In this setting Peter briefly alludes to his vision, but Cornelius narrates his vision in detail.[10] The second, apparently larger assembly takes place back in Jerusalem where it is Peter's vision that gets center stage and in fact is narrated first; Cornelius's vision gets second billing and only one sentence.[11] Surely these distinctively similar scenes suggest mimesis.

The last distinctive trait binding Acts to *Iliad* 2 is the importance of each set of visions for their host narratives. In commenting on the various functions of dreams in ancient literature, *Iliad* 2 above all, one scholar has emphasized the triple significance of the dream: the nobility of the dreamer, the gravity of the message, and the importance of the situation.[12] Zeus sends the dream to Agamemnon, the preeminent commander of the Greek army, considered by some "the best of the Achaeans." Nestor claimed that had the dream come to anyone else, "we might say it was a lie."[13] Oneiros's command to Agamemnon was momentous: it would involve the entire army (except Achilles and his Myrmidons) in a ferocious battle. The situation, too, was significant; the Trojan War was one of the defining events in Greek cultural consciousness. The reader of the epic is reminded of Zeus's deceit again in Book 9, when the king finally understands he has been duped.[14] This assessment also applies to imitations of Zeus's lying dream. The messenger usually comes to a king or a commander of a powerful army, ordering him to attack a foe in a situation of national crisis. Characteristically the dreamer obeys the dream at once and by so doing fundamentally redirects the flow of events.

This triple significance also applies to the story of Cornelius. The angel appears to a Roman military official with a momentous command: to summon the apostle to hear a message that will "save" him and his household. Indeed, his conversion will make possible the social inclusion of all gentiles seeking to join Jewish followers of Jesus. Cornelius wastes no time in obeying the angel's command and by so doing sets in motion events that will become the turning point in the gentile mission. Peter's defense of the mission at the Jerusalem council looks back on the event as clear proof of God's acceptance of gentiles.[15]

What does the reader gain through a comparison of the two works? Answering this question is the task of the sixth criterion, interpretability, which often includes emulation, the improvement of the model, whether aesthetically, philosophically, or morally. I propose that a comparison of Acts with its parallels in *Iliad* 2 reveals a threefold emulation: the virtues of Cornelius exceed those of Agamemnon; the vision to Cornelius was truthful, unlike the dream to Agamemnon; and the result of the two visions was the removal of hostility between East and West, not deadly warfare.

First, the character of Cornelius. Even though the centurion resembles Agamemnon in being a pious military leader, the Greek commander was morally flawed. He had sacrificed Iphigenia, his daughter, on an altar to Artemis; he had taken Briseis from Achilles; and he would take Cassandra home as a concubine, infuriating his wife. When Oneiros came to him at his hut, he rebuked him for sleeping despite his enormous responsibilities in the war.[16] In Acts, however, Cornelius was not asleep; he prayed constantly to God and received his vision in broad daylight. For that reason there is no rebuke (motif 2.2) but only an expression of divine favor (motif 2.3): "Your prayers and your alms have ascended to remembrance before God." Agamemnon was famous for his arrogance, claiming to be "the best of the Achaeans," even though on the field of battle he was no equal to Achilles. Cornelius, on the other hand, had shown compassion on Jews and humbly worshiped the apostle as though he were divine.

Second, the nature of the dream. The dream to Agamemnon was a deadly lie, and the same holds true for most of its imitators. The dreams to Xerxes (Herodotus), Turnus (Vergil), Pompey (Lucan), Etiocles (Statius), and Hannibal (Silius) all were divine deceptions that led to their deaths or the deaths of many other soldiers. Ancient moralists struggled to exculpate Zeus from his destructive lie, while Christian apologists relished Homer's recognition of Zeus's duplicity and cruelty. Though on the face of it, the dream and the portent at Aulis both predicted victory over Troy, the reader recognizes the mendacity of the dream and thus the irony of the next six books. In Acts, on the other hand, Cornelius's vision is entirely true and correlates precisely with the vision of Peter. God had told Cornelius to send for Peter and warned Peter not to consider gentiles unclean.

Third, the result of the dream. Oneiros instructed Agamemnon to fight against the Trojans; the dream to Xerxes told him to march westward against Greece; the dream to Pompey told him to attack Caesar; the dream to Turnus told him to resist the Trojan settlers; the dream to Etiocles told him to fight against Polynices; the dream to Hannibal told him to attack Rome.[17] In each case, the commander would lose the war, many men, and sometimes his own life. Cornelius's vision, on the other hand, commanded him not to fight but to summon the apostle to his home so that he and his household might "be saved." Instead of enflaming the hostilities between Europeans and barbarians, as in the other imitations of the lying dream, Luke's emulation overcomes differences between Jews and gentiles, or at least makes possible the inclusion of gentiles in a Jewish context.[18] "Truly I am coming to understand that God does not practice favoritism, but in every nation one who fears God and acts justly is acceptable to him."[19]

PART Two

Paul's Farewell at Miletus and Iliad 6

6

Hector's Farewell to Andromache

Few passages in Acts have attracted as much scholarly attention as Paul's farewell address to the Ephesian elders at Miletus (20:18–35). More than in any other speech in Acts, it is so saturated with echoes of Paul's epistles that many interpreters think, perhaps rightly, that Luke had access to several of them.[1] But the epistles alone cannot explain the form, function, and genre of the speech. Nearly all commentators of Paul's farewell address suppose that Luke modeled it after Jewish testaments.[2] According to the detailed treatment by Hans-Joachim Michel, Luke's account follows the testamentary form in Paul's summoning listeners (vs. 17), presenting himself as an example (18–21, 31, and 33–35), asserting his ethical integrity (26), announcing his death (22–25), exhorting his listeners to moral conduct (28, 31, and 35), prophesying future woes (29–30), transmitting his authority to his followers (28), blessing them (32), and praying (36). The narrative conclusion adheres to the pattern with weeping as a gesture of final farewell (37).[3]

Despite this near consensus concerning the genre of the speech, a few scholars have warned against linking it to the form too woodenly.[4] For example, three motifs that Michel found to be typical of Jewish testaments are absent in Acts: instructions for burial, promises and oaths, and the narration of the death itself. Second, at least two of the motifs Michel identified as characteristic of the genre—the collecting of listeners and emotional responses—are found in discourses of various genres. Third, although several of the testamentary motifs seem to fit Acts, some of them are forced, as Michel himself notes. For example, the presentation of the speaker as an example and the defense of his integrity are rare in Jewish testaments, and nowhere are they as prominent as in Acts 20. The final objection, and potentially the most damaging, is the delivery of the speech several years before Paul's death and in a document that avoids narrating his death entirely. Virtually all other examples of the testament in Jewish literature occur just before the speaker's demise. The pseudo-Pauline letter known as 2 Timothy provides a telling point of comparison insofar as it clearly contains features of the Jewish testament, but unlike Acts 20, this Pauline farewell takes place just before his death (see 4:6–8), conforming to the traditional pattern. Despite the recognition of these problems, scholars continue to suppose that Luke composed the speech after the tradition of Jewish testaments, even though the closest parallel to the passage appears in *Iliad* 6, Hector's farewell to Andromache.[5]

In the midst of a ferocious battle between Greeks and Trojans, Hector's brother Helenus told him to return to Troy and tell Hecuba, their mother, to "gather the older women to the temple of Athena" to pray for victory.[6] The hero encouraged his warriors to fight bravely in his absence so that he could go to Troy and "tell the elders who speak counsel and our wives to pray to the gods."[7] After entering the palace of Priam, he told his mother to "gather together the older women" at the temple of Athena to pray that the goddess "may have mercy on the city and the wives of the Trojans and the infant children."[8] He then went to the home of Paris and Helen to cajole his brother back to the battle. Helen asked Hector to linger, but he was eager to leave. "I will go home to see my own family, my beloved wife and infant son. For I do not know if ever again I shall return to them or if the gods will subdue me at the hands of the Achaeans."[9] This statement is the first of several potential parallels with Paul's speech in Acts, and we will refer to it as shared motif 1: the hero states that he does not know what dangers he must face.

When Hector arrived home, his family was not there; Andromache had gone to the walls to observe the war. In frustration, he rushed toward the gate to rejoin his troops. As he was about to leave the city, Andromache ran to him, bringing their son Scamandrius, whom the Trojans had nicknamed Astyanax, Lord of the City, "for Hector alone was saving Ilium."[10] His final farewell thus took place not at their home but near the gate.

Andromache begged him not to return to the battlefield, for he was her "father, queenly mother, and brother," as well as her husband. "Come now, take pity and stay here on the wall, lest you make your son an orphan and your wife a widow." Hector's response consists of three parts: (1) his recognition that he will die and that Andromache will be enslaved; (2) his prayer for Astyanax; and (3) his final instructions to his wife. Paul's speech in Acts also divides into three parts that largely correspond with the three parts of Hector's response, though the motifs appear in a somewhat different order. Here is the first section of Hector's response, together with an identification of motifs that it shares with Acts.

Part 1: Hector's Recognition that He Will Die

Motif 2: the hero boasts that he never shirked his duty. "Woman, all these things concern me, too, but I would be terribly ashamed before the Trojans and the Trojan women with trailing robes, if, like a coward, I were to shrink from the battle. My heart commands me not to, for I have learned always to be valiant and to fight on the front line with the Trojans, winning great renown both for my father and for myself."

Motif 3: the hero warns of disaster. "For this I know well in my mind and heart: a day will come when sacred Ilium will be destroyed—Priam and the spear-savvy people of Priam."

Motif 4: the hero expresses fears concerning the captivity of his loved ones.

> It is not so much the subsequent pain of the Trojans that concerns me . . . as yours, when some bronze-armored Achaean leads you away, weeping, and robs you of your day of freedom. . . . Someday someone seeing you shedding tears may say, "This is the wife of Hector, the best soldier of all the horse-taming Trojans when they fought for Ilium." Someday someone will say this, and it will be a fresh wound for you to be deprived of such a man to stave off the day of slavery. May a heap of earth cover my corpse before I learn of your crying and your dragging off to captivity.[11]

Part 2: Hector's Prayer for Astyanax

Hector's second response is a prayer for his son, Astyanax.

> So saying, glorious Hector reached for his boy, but the lad immediately shrank back into the breast of his fair-belted nurse, crying, upset by the sight of his dear father, terrified when he saw the bronze and the horsehair crest, watching it wave terribly atop the helmet. His dear father and queenly mother then laughed out loud, and immediately glorious Hector took the helmet from his head and laid it, gleaming, on the ground. Then he kissed his dear son, rocked him in his arms, and spoke a prayer to Zeus and the other gods.

Motif 5: the hero invokes his gods. "Zeus and you other gods . . ."

Motif 6: the hero prays that his successors may be like him. "Grant that this lad, my son, may be as I am—distinguished among the Trojans, as great in strength—and may he rule Ilium with might."

Motif 7: the hero cites a comparative quotation. "May someone say of him as he returns from battle, 'He is much better than his father.' After killing a foe, may he haul off the bloody spoils, and may his mother's heart rejoice."[12]

Part 3: Hector's Final Instructions

The third section consists of Hector's final instructions to Andromache, including his famous lines about the inexorability of fate.

Motif 8: the hero states his willingness to face his destiny with courage. "So saying, he placed the child in the arms of his dear wife, and she received him to her fragrant bosom, laughing as she wept. Looking at her, her husband took pity, stroked her with his hand, and addressed her by name: 'My bemused lady, do not let your heart excessively grieve for me; no man will hurl me to Hades beyond my lot. I say that no man, whether cowardly or courageous, ever has escaped fate after he has been born.' "

Motif 9: the hero commands his audience to attend to their tasks. "But go home, and look after your own tasks, the loom and the distaff, and command your maidservants to pursue their work. War will concern all the men who live in Ilium, especially me."

Conclusion

The poet concludes the scene with their tearful separation.

Having so said, glorious Hector took up his horsetailed helmet, and his beloved wife went home, frequently turning back, swelling with tears. Quickly then she came to the comfortable home of man-slaying Hector and found there her many maidservants; among them all she incited wailing. So they wailed for Hector in his own house while he was still alive, for they said that he would never again return from battle, escaped from the fury and hands of the Achaeans.[13]

There can be little doubt that Luke and his readers had been exposed to Homer's tale. One commentator has called Hector's farewell to Andromache the "most famous of all Homeric scenes."[14] Ancient sources leave little doubt about its popularity. Luke's contemporary, L. Mestrius Plutarchus, wrote how the wife of Marcus Iunius Brutus was forced to return to Rome alone. Just before her voyage, Porcia saw a painting of "Andromache bidding farewell to Hector. She was taken from his arms while her eyes were fixed on her husband. When Porcia saw this, the image of her own sorrow presented by it caused her to burst into tears, and she would visit it many times a day and weep before it."[15] One of Brutus's friends knew the *Iliad* so well that he could recite two lines from Book 6 to characterize her weeping; Brutus responded by quoting another.[16] The final meeting between Hector and Andromache depicted in this painting was a subject for several ancient Greek and Roman artists, especially vase painters.[17] Typically, an armed Hector stands ready to return to battle opposite his disconsolate wife, with or without their son Astyanax. Plutarch expected his readers to recall the Homeric scene and empathize with Porcia as an avatar of Andromache.

Not surprisingly, Hector's farewell to Andromache became a favorite target for imitations in the *Odyssey*, Herodotus's *History*, Sophocles' *Ajax*, Aristophanes' *Lysistrata*, Plato's *Phaedo*, Xenophon's *Cyropaedia*, Apollonius's *Argonautica*, Chariton's *Chaereas and Callirhoe*, Xenophon of Ephesus's *Ephesiaca*, Heliodorus's *Aethiopica*, Vergil's *Aeneid*, Seneca's *Troades*, Ovid's *Heroides*, and Silius Italicus's *Punica*.[18] Apsines (third century c.e.) encouraged future rhetors to keep *Iliad* 6 in mind as an example of how to move readers to pity, especially Hector's prediction of Andromache's captivity and her prediction that Astyanax would be orphaned.[19]

I will argue that Paul's farewell discourse to the Ephesian elders at Miletus in Acts 20:17–38 is yet another such imitation. The next chapter will compare Acts 20 with *Iliad* 6. Chapter 8 will argue that a mimetic interpretation has more to commend it than the prevailing view that Luke composed Paul's farewell as a final testament modeled after Jewish prototypes.

7

Paul's Farewell to the Ephesian Elders

The reader of Acts learned already in 19:21 that Paul, in Ephesus, "resolved in the Spirit to go through Macedonia and Achaea, and then to go on to Jerusalem [πορεύεσθαι εἰς Ἱεροσόλυμα]. He said, 'After I have gone there, I must also see Rome.'" As many commentators have noted, this passage echoes Jesus' resolve in Luke 9:51: "He set his face to go to Jerusalem [τοῦ πορεύεσθαι εἰς Ἱερουσαλήμ]." Jesus was crucified in Jerusalem; similarly, nothing but trouble awaits Paul there. It also would be his fate (δεῖ) to see Rome, where he would die.[1]

Acts 20 and 21 contain three farewell scenes, the first of which is the farewell to the Ephesian elders. In each instance Paul demonstrates his resolve to continue to Jerusalem. In the first, he tells the elders that he is not afraid to face his Jewish opponents; he does not know precisely what will happen to him, except that "chains and afflictions await" him. In the second farewell "the Spirit" warned the believers at Tyre of Paul's perils, and they begged him "not to continue on to Jerusalem."[2] Paul was determined to go on. The faithful, including "women and children," went with him outside the city to the shore, where he bade them farewell and embarked. "But they returned home." As in the Hector-Andromache scene, here one finds warnings of danger, heroic resolve to face them, and farewells to women and children. The hero left to meet his fate, while the others returned home in sorrow.[3]

According to the last of the three episodes, Acts 21:7–14, Paul and companions arrived in Caesarea where a prophet named Agabus

> took Paul's belt, bound his own feet and hands, and said: "The Holy Spirit says this: in just such a manner will the Jews in Jerusalem bind up the man who owns this belt and deliver him unto the hands of the gentiles." When we heard these things, we and the local residents begged him not to go up to Jerusalem. Then Paul said, "Why are you weeping and breaking your hearts? I am willing not only to be bound but even to die in Jerusalem for the name of the Lord Jesus." Since he was not persuaded, we left him alone and said, "May the will of the Lord be done."

Paul's address resembles Hector's farewell to Andromache, especially his famous statement about fate.

Iliad 6.485–89	*Acts 21:13–14*[4]
He spoke to her and said,	*Then Paul said,*
"My bemused lady, *do not let your*	*"Why are you weeping*
heart excessively grieve for me.	*and breaking your hearts?*
No man will hurl me to Hades beyond	I am willing not only to be bound
my lot. I say that after birth no man,	*but even to die in Jerusalem."*
whether cowardly or courageous,	. . . We left him alone and said,
ever has escaped fate."	"The will of the Lord be done."

Neither Hector nor Paul knows what will befall him, but each faces danger with courageous resignation: Hector to fate; Paul to "the will of the Lord."

The combination of these three scenes prepares the reader to expect the worst for the apostle and to admire his adamantine resolve to bear witness in Jerusalem and Rome. Luke's placement of these episodes years before the apostle's death brilliantly sets the scene for the last eight chapters of Acts. The reader and the hero both know that he will die at the hands of his opponents, yet he willingly does his duty. Luke's model for the placement of these farewells early in the narrative could not have been Jewish testaments, which characteristically place the speech just before the hero dies.

Like Hector's farewell, Paul's consists of three parts: (1) Paul's courage in the past and present (verses 18–27), (2) the challenges facing the elders in the future (28–31), and (3) Paul's prayer for them (32–35). Each section has its parallels with the speeches of Hector in *Iliad* 6, though in a different order. Hector gave two speeches to Andromache separated by a prayer for Astyanax. In Acts, however, the prayer comes last. Luke also shifted motifs from Hector's two speeches within the first two sections. Chapter 8 will discuss sequencing in more detail; this chapter concentrates on the density of the parallels.

1. Paul's Courage (Acts 20:18–27)

Luke begins Paul's speech to the Ephesian elders with a sixty-eight-word sentence reminding the elders of his courageous proclamation despite the plots on his life.

> You yourselves know how I was with you the entire time from the first day that I arrived in Asia — serving the Lord with all lowliness, tears, and testings that came to me through the plots of the Jews — that I did not hold back anything beneficial, to preach to you and to teach you in public and from house to house, by testifying both to Jews and to Greeks about repentance toward God and faith toward our Lord Jesus.[5]

Earlier in Acts Luke had said nothing about persecutions from Jews in Ephesus, but by the time the reader gets to the Ephesus section the pattern of Jewish opposition has been set. Paul was engaged in a battle of sorts. At Damascus "the Jews plotted to kill him, but their plot became known."[6] At Jerusalem Jews "were attempting to kill him."[7] At Pisidian Antioch "the Jews incited the devout women of high standing and the leading men of the city, stirred up persecution against Paul and Barnabas, and drove them out of their region."[8] At Lystra "the unbelieving Jews stirred up the Gentiles and poisoned their minds against the brothers" such that they attempted "to mistreat and stone them."[9] At Thessalonica "the Jews became jealous and . . . formed a mob and set the city in an uproar."[10] At Beroea, "when the Jews of Thessalonica learned that the word of God had been proclaimed by Paul . . . , they came . . . to stir up and incite the crowds."[11] At Corinth "the Jews made a united attack on Paul and brought him before the tribunal."[12] At Achaea "a plot was made against him by the Jews."[13] When one reads in Acts 20:19 that Paul endured persecutions also in Asia "through the plots of the Jews," it comes as no surprise. The theme of Paul's courageous preaching despite violent opposition recurs throughout his speech to the Ephesian elders.

The beginning of the speech resembles the opening lines of Hector's first speech to Andromache. Here we find shared motif 2: the hero boasts that he never shirked his duty.

Iliad 6.440–46	Acts 20:18–21
Then great *Hector* of the flashing helmet	*He said to them*
said to her [τὴν . . . προσέειπεν],	[εἶπεν αὐτοῖς],
"Woman, all these things concern me, too,	
but I would be terribly ashamed before	
the Trojans and the Trojan women with	"You yourselves know . . . how I was with you
trailing robes, if, like a coward,	. . . that
I were to shrink from the battle.	*I did not hold back anything beneficial:*

My heart commands me not to, for I have
learned always *to be valiant and to fight*
on the front line with the Trojans,
winning great renown *both* for my father
and for myself."

to *preach* to you *and to teach* you
in public and from house to house,
testifying both to Jews *and* to Greeks
about repentance toward God
and faith toward our Lord Jesus."[14]

The structure of these statements by Hector and Paul are strikingly similar. In both cases the hero witnesses to his courage by stating, in the first person singular, that he never shirked his duty (ἀλυσκάζω/ὑπεστειλάμην). Hector's danger came from Greeks; Paul's from Jews. In both cases the hero then expands on his courage, using two infinitives linked by "and" (ἔμμεναι . . . καὶ . . . μάχεσθαι/ἀναγγεῖλαι . . . καὶ διδάξαι) with the public location of action expressed by an adverb (πρώτοισι/δημοσίᾳ), followed by a nominative singular circumstantial participle in the present tense (ἀρνύμενος/διαμαρτυρόμενος) with an accusative object (μέγα κλέος/μετανοίαν καὶ πίστιν).[15]

In a similar passage in 1 Thessalonians, Paul himself spoke of his "boldness" using the verb παρρησιάζομαι; elsewhere he uses the cognate noun παρρησία.[16] Deutero-Pauline authors frequently used these words for Paul's preaching, and Luke himself used them of Paul elsewhere in Acts.[17] Here in Acts 20, however, Paul twice uses an expression found nowhere else in the New Testament: "I did not hold back anything [οὐδὲν ὑπεστειλάμην] that was profitable"; "I did not shrink from [οὐ . . . ὑπεστειλάμην] proclaiming." The verb ὑποστέλλω sometimes was used of furling a sail when the winds became dangerously strong, as in Pindar's image of a brave sailor: "never did an oncoming wind cause him to furl [ὑπέστειλ'] the sails."[18] Demosthenes claimed that unlike his opponent who groveled before Philip of Macedon, he courageously defended the Athenian captives: "I withheld nothing [οὐδὲν ὑπεστειλάμην]" to save them.[19] Philo used the same expression in connection with boldness: "I will speak with boldness [μετὰ παρρησίας], holding back nothing [οὐδὲν ὑποστειλαμένη]."[20] Two Hellenistic inscriptions commemorating the courage of politicians state that they "held back nothing" despite danger (κίνδυνος) and suffering (κακοπαθία).[21]

Why does Luke here, and nowhere else, speak of Paul's boldness by using the negative alternative to παρρησιάζομαι?[22] *Iliad* 6 may have influenced Luke's choice. Homer told Andromache he would never "shrink from the battle." The verb ἀλυσκάζω appears almost exclusively in epic poetry. Its cousin ἀλύσκω appears in prose more or less contemporary with Luke, but it, too, was rare. It never appears, for example, in the Septuagint. Luke seems to have preferred the more common ὑποστέλλω as an appropriate substitute for Homer's verb ἀλυσκάζω. Both in the epic and in the Acts, the hero describes his heroism as not shrinking from his duty.[23]

Paul continues to defend his heroism in Acts 20:22–27.

> And now, captive to the Spirit, I am on my way to Jerusalem, not knowing what will happen to me there, except that the Holy Spirit testifies to me in every city, saying that chains and afflictions await me. But I do not count my life of any value to myself, so that I may complete my race and the ministry that I received from the Lord Jesus, to testify to the gospel of the grace of God. And now I know that none of you will ever again see my face—you among whom I have gone about proclaiming the kingdom. For this reason I testify to you this day that I am pure from the blood of all, for I did not shrink from proclaiming the entire will of God.[24]

Some commentators have noted an apparent contradiction between Acts 20:22 where Paul states that he does not know what will befall him in Jerusalem, and vs. 25, where he states that he knows the elders will never see him again.[25] This is no contradiction at all. Paul knows that he will die, but he does not know how or when. The combination of certainty of his death and uncertainty about how it will happen makes Paul's resolution to continue to Jerusalem all the more heroic.

Hector, too, knew he soon would die but not how or when. His statement to Helen in *Iliad* 6 resembles Paul's uncertainty in Acts (shared motif 1: the hero states that he does not know what dangers he must face).

Iliad 6.361–62 and 367–68	Acts 20:22–23
For my heart is already impatient to assist the Trojans. . . .	And now, captive to the Spirit, I am on my way to Jerusalem,
I do not know [οὐ . . . οἶδ'] if ever again I shall return to them	*not knowing* [μὴ εἰδώς] *what* will happen to me there, except that the Holy Spirit
or *if the gods will subdue me at the the hands of the Achaeans.*	testifies to me in every city saying that *chains and afflictions await me.*

In each column the hero states his determination to face the dangers before him and confesses his ignorance of the future with a negated form of οἶδα. Hector suspects that the gods may subdue him; Paul expects imprisonment.

Despite his awareness of the dangers, Paul insists on continuing his journey (shared motif 8: the hero states his willingness to face his destiny with courage): "I do not count my life of any value to myself, so that I may complete my race and the ministry that I received from the Lord Jesus." Such insistence on doing one's duty despite the cost defines courage in the *Iliad,* and no hero in the epic more exemplifies valor than Hector.[26] He learned always to fight courageously at the front, confident that "no man will hurl me to Hades beyond my lot. I say that no man . . . ever has escaped fate."[27]

Willingness to face one's fate also characterizes imitations of Hector's fare-well. For example, according to Apollonius's *Argonautica*, Jason tried to comfort his mother in a speech transparently modeled after Hector's to Andromache. "Mother, do not excessively take thought of bitter sorrows. . . . For unknown are the woes that the gods mete out to mortals." One must simply bear with courage "things determined by fate [μοῖραν]."[28] The attentive reader will detect here Apollonius's imitation of *Iliad* 6.486–88: "My bemused lady, do not let your heart excessively grieve for me. . . . No man, whether cowardly or courage-ous, ever has escaped fate [μοῖραν]."[29] The motif also appears in Silius Italicus's *Punica*, where Hannibal lectures Imilce on destiny: "Have done with foreboding and with tears, my faithful wife. In war, as in peace, the end of each man's life is fixed, and the first day leads but to the last."[30] Here again is an imitation of Hector's statement about fate. Hector thought it impossible to avoid his fate. Paul was not bound by fate but "bound by the Spirit" and obedient to "the will of the Lord."[31]

Even though Hector and Paul did not know precisely what the future held for them, they did know that they soon would die. The left-hand column contains Hector's "famous line" of recognition that he would not prevail; he and Troy will fall.[32] The right-hand column contains Paul's recognition that he would never again see Ephesus (shared motif 3: the hero warns of disaster).

Iliad 6.447–49	Acts 20:25
For *this I know* well [εὖ γὰρ ἐγὼ τόδε οἶδα] in my mind and heart: a day will come when *sacred Ilium* will be destroyed — Priam and the spear-savvy people of Priam.	And now *I know that* [καὶ νῦν ἰδοὺ ἐγὼ οἶδα ὅτι] none of you will ever see my face again— you among whom I have gone about proclaiming *the kingdom.*

Homer and Luke both have their heroes say "I know" and use precisely the same words to do so: ἐγὼ οἶδα. In both cases they know that their violent deaths are inevitable and perhaps imminent.

Knowing that he will never again see the elders, Paul declares his innocence (again, shared motif 2: the hero boasts that he never shirked his duty): "I testify to you this day that I am pure from the blood of all, for I did not shrink [οὐ . . . ὑπεστειλάμην] from proclaiming the entire will of God."[33] Luke had used this same expression in verse 20: "I did not hold back anything [οὐδὲν ὑπεστειλάμην] beneficial," apparently inspired by Hector's claim that he would never "shrink from battle." By courageously doing his duty, Paul was innocent of Ephesian blood. He was their savior. Similarly, as defender of Troy, Hector was in no way responsible for the death of anyone in the city, for it was he more than anyone who protected the weak, especially the women and children. "Hector alone was saving Ilium."[34]

2. Challenges Facing the Elders (Acts 20:28–31)

Acts 20:28 represents a major transition in the speech insofar as Paul turns attention from himself to the elders in 28–31. The shift in focus is quite abrupt and unaided by explicit linkage to what has preceded.[35] This verse may echo Hector's final command to Andromache, which also is an abrupt shift in focus. Just before the text in the left-hand column Hector has given his famous statement concerning the inevitability of fate. Just before the text in the right-hand column Paul has stated he "did not shrink from proclaiming the entire will of God." Then, quite without warning, each speaker switches from reasserting his courage to a command to his audience (shared motif 9: the hero commands his audience to attend to their tasks).

Iliad 6.490–93	Acts 20:28
Look after your own tasks,	*Attend to yourselves*
the loom and the distaff,	
and command your maidservants	*and over all the flock,* in which
to pursue their work.	the Holy Spirit has placed you
War will concern all the men	as overseers to shepherd the church of God
who live in Ilium, especially me.	that he rescued with his own blood.[36]

In each column the hero gives a command in the imperative mood. The command first applies to his immediate auditor(s) and uses a reflexive ("look after your own tasks"; "attend yourselves"); the command then extends to underlings ("command your maidservants to pursue their work"; "attend to . . . all the flock, in which the Holy Spirit has placed you as overseers"). Hector followed his command by restating his willingness to defend the city: "War will concern all the men who live in Ilium, especially me." Similarly, Paul reminded the elders of Jesus' sacrifice on behalf of the flock. Just as Hector shed his blood trying to rescue Troy, Jesus shed his blood to rescue the church.

If Luke did imitate this command, he was in good company. According to *Odyssey* 1, Telemachus, son of Odysseus and Penelope, commanded his mother to return to her room, using lines virtually identical to Hector's command that Andromache return home. In the following excerpt, the only differences are the words underlined. "Go home and look after your own tasks, the loom and the distaff, and command your maidservants to pursue their work. *Speech* will concern all the men, especially me. *Mine is the power in the house.*"[37] Here it is speech not war that concerns the men. Penelope's subsequent return to her chamber resembles Andromache's return, complete with weeping and attending servants.[38] Commenting on these lines, one interpreter has written: "Recalling as they do one of the most memorable scenes of the *Iliad,* Hector's farewell to

Andromache, they have for us the effect of a quotation, and their callousness in this context is enhanced by the contrast with their earlier occurrence" in the *Iliad*.³⁹

According to Aristophanes, male citizens had bungled the governance of Athens by prolonging the Peleponnesian War, so the women decided to take matters into their own hands. In the following dialog between Lysistrata and a magistrate, the heroine begins her harangue by complaining that the men kept quoting the *Iliad* to keep their wives at home.

> *Lysistrata.* We would ask, "Husband, how come you're handling this so stupidly?" And right away he'd glare at me and tell me to get back to my sewing if I didn't want major damage to my head: "War will concern the men [πόλεμος δ' ἄνδρεσσι μελήσει]."
>
> *Magistrate.* He was right on the mark, by Zeus.
>
> *Lysistrata.* How could he be right, you sorry fool, when we were forbidden to offer advice even when your policy was wrong?⁴⁰ But then—when we began to hear you in the streets openly crying, "There isn't a man left in the land," and someone else saying, "No, by Zeus, not a one"⁴¹—after that we women decided to lose no more time and to band together to save Greece. . . . So, if you're ready to take your turn at listening, we have some good advice, and if you shut up, as *we* used to, we can put you back on the right track.
>
> *Magistrate. You* put *us* — outrageous! I won't stand for it! . . .
>
> *Lysistrata.* Now hitch up your clothes and start sewing; chew some beans while you work. War will concern the women [πόλεμος δὲ γυναιξὶ μελήσει]!⁴²

Aristophanes surely expected his audience to take pleasure in Lysistrata's statement as a parody of Hector's command that Andromache return to "the loom and the distaff," for "war will concern all the men [πόλεμος δ' ἄνδρεσσι μελήσει]." This passage "is modelled on the famous conversation between Hektor and Andromache in the sixth book of Homer's *Iliad*."⁴³

According to the great Byzantine Homeric commentator Eustathius, the very same conversation served Herodotus as a model for his tale about a woman named Pheretime who asked for an army from Evelthon of Salamis to pursue the interests of her family against her foes. Instead of sending her an army he sent "a golden spindle and distaff."⁴⁴ Herodotus apparently expected both Pheretime and his readers to see here an insult inspired by the *Iliad*.

According to Vergil, Turnus, Aeneas's foe, told one of the Furies (female powers of retribution) to turn her attention to tasks more appropriate for women, looking after the "images and temples of the gods," and not to interfere in matters pertaining to war: "Men will attend to war and peace, as men should."⁴⁵ The Fury was not amused: she drove him mad.

These imitations are useful not only for understanding the popularity of the scene but also for clarifying Luke's transformation of it. Hector's command to Andromache was dismissive; he insisted that she excuse herself from warfare and content herself with household tasks. Aristophanes, Herodotus, and Vergil saw his instructions as demeaning of Andromache and potentially of women in general.

Paul's command to the elders was not demeaning but empowering. After his departure, they would have to carry on the fight without him. He ordered them to exercise the authority given them by God to shepherd the flock. Just as Paul never shrank from proclaiming his message despite Jewish opposition, they must seize their authority to withstand the coming onslaught of false teachers, as the verses that follow make clear. "I know that after my departure savage wolves will come in among you, not sparing the flock. And from your own ranks men will arise speaking perverse things to draw the disciples after them. Therefore, be alert, remembering that for three years night and day I did not cease to warn everyone with tears."[46] Similarly, Hector warned Andromache of future devastation: "For this I know well in mind and heart: a day will come when sacred Ilium will be destroyed — Priam and the spear-savvy people of Priam."[47] Earlier, when discussing Paul's awareness that the elders would never again see him, I compared the beginning of this passage with Hector's famous lines that he knew Troy would fall after his death. This Homeric passage is even more relevant to Acts 20:29 (again, shared motif 3: the hero warns of disaster).

Iliad 6.447–49	Acts 20:29
For *this I know* well [εὖ γὰρ ἐγὼ τόδε οἶδα] in my mind and heart: *a day will come* when *sacred Ilium will be destroyed* — Priam and the spear-savvy people of Priam.	*I know that* [ἐγὼ οἶδα ὅτι] *after my departure* *savage wolves will come* in among you, *not sparing the flock.*

In both columns the hero confidently predicts future devastation using nearly identical expressions [εὖ γὰρ ἐγὼ τόδε οἶδα/ἐγὼ οἶδα ὅτι). Soon after Hector's death, Greek warriors swarmed into the city and slew the residents without mercy. Paul's warning expresses similar fears for the church.

Paul calls his opponents "wolves," a metaphor used of religious rivals elsewhere in early Christian literature with potential roots in Judaism.[48] To my knowledge, no one has recognized that Homer's wolf similes provide an even richer conceptual complex. Two of these similes, both in *Iliad* 16, are particularly relevant. The first is the description of Achilles' Myrmidons who would play a decisive role in the sack of Troy. "[T]hey rushed out like ravening wolves [λύκοι] in whose hearts is fury unspeakable — wolves that have slain in the hills a great horned stag, and rend him, and the jaws of all are red with gore; and in a pack they go to lap with their slender tongues the surface of the black water from a dusky spring, belching forth blood and gore, the heart in their breasts unflinching, and their bellies gorged full."[49] In the second simile, Homer compares Greek troops to wolves attacking lambs unprotected by shepherds; the similarities to Acts 20 are transparent. "[A]s ravening wolves [λύκοι] fall on lambs or kids, choosing them out of the flocks, when through the folly of the shepherd [ποιμένος] they are scattered among the mountains, and the wolves seeing this immediately snatch the young whose hearts are cowardly, so the Danaans fell on the Trojans."[50] Post-Homeric narratives of the fall of Troy use wolf similes of their own.[51]

As we have seen, Acts 20:29 expresses fears concerning those from outside the community who "will come in among" the believers to do harm. The next verse, however, speaks of insiders, those "from your own ranks," who "will arise . . . to draw the disciples after them." Those from the outside will destroy; those from the inside will lead away captive. This fear, too, corresponds to Hector's.

> It is not so much the subsequent pain of the Trojans that concerns me . . . as yours, when some bronze-armored Achaean leads you, weeping, away and robs you of your day of freedom. . . . Someday someone seeing you shedding tears may say, "This is the wife of Hector, the best soldier of all the horse-taming Trojans, when they fought for Ilium." Someday someone will say this, and it will be a fresh wound for you to be deprived of such a man to stave off the day of slavery. May a heap of earth cover my corpse before I learn of your crying and your dragging off to captivity.[52]

Sophocles targeted this passage for imitation in *Ajax*. Tecmessa appealed to Ajax not to kill himself and thereby render her a slave once again. The following parallels suggest that she wanted Ajax to show her the same pity that Hector expressed for Andromache. "*Then one of my masters will address me bitterly with taunting words: 'Behold the concubine of Ajax, who was the mightiest of the army! What servitude she has instead of such bliss!' Such things someone will say.*"[53] Like Andromache, Tecmessa had lost her father and mother in the Trojan War; Ajax was her only means of support, but he shows her none of Hector's compassion.[54] "Tecmessa's farewell to Ajax in Sophocles' *Ajax* has been recognized since antiquity . . . as an adaptation of the scene between Hector and Andromache."[55]

Paul was concerned that some Ephesian believers might be taken off to captivity: "[F]rom your own ranks men will arise speaking perverse things to draw the disciples after them. Therefore, be alert, remembering that for three years, night and day, I did not cease to warn everyone with tears." Paul's constant efforts for three years staved off destructive wolves from without and schismatics from within. At his death, responsibility for the flock would fall to the elders, who must be on guard (γρηγορεῖτε) lest disciples be drawn away, like Andromache, whom Neoptolemus hauled off to Epirus. This command, like the one in vs. 28, echoes Hector's command to Andromache (again, shared motif 9: the hero commands his audience to attend to their tasks).

Iliad 6.490–93	Acts 20:31
Look after your own tasks, . . .	Therefore, *be alert,*
	remembering that for three years night and
War will concern all the men	day I did not cease
who live in Ilium, especially me.	to warn everyone with tears.

To be sure, the verbal similarities between these columns are not impressive, but in both the hero gives a command to his audience and boasts of his eagerness to perform his duty.

3. *Paul's Prayer for the Elders (Acts 20:32–36)*

Paul continues his speech as follows: "And now I entrust you to God and to the Logos of his grace, who has the power to build you up and grant you the inheritance with all who have been made holy."[56] The verb παρατίθεμαι, "I entrust," implies a prayer, as in Acts 14:23: "by praying . . . they entrusted [παρέθεντο] them to the Lord."[57] Entrusting the elders to God apparently was the purpose of Paul's prayer after his speech: "He knelt with all of them and prayed."[58]

The relationship of the intervening verses (33–35) to these bracketing references to prayer is by no means obvious, and many interpreters have argued that they introduce a pronounced change of topic: a defense of Paul's integrity similar to verses 18–21.[59] But it seems best to take these verses as a continuation of vs. 32.[60] The reader probably should assume that the content of Paul's prayer after his speech conformed to the content of his instructions to them. I have rewritten Acts 20:32–36 as a prayer to demonstrate the point. To indicate my alterations of the text, I have italicized them. Words rearranged appear between square brackets.

> [He knelt with them all and prayed.] "I entrust *these elders to you,* O God, and to the Logos of *your* grace, who has the power to build *them* up and grant *them* the inheritance with all who have been made holy. I desired of no one silver or gold or clothing, *and they them*selves know that these hands ministered to my necessities and to those who were with me. In all ways I showed *them,* that it is necessary to work like this to support the weak and to remember the words *that you,* O Lord Jesus, said, 'It is more blessed to give than to receive.'" And when he had said these things . . . there was much weeping among them all. They fell on Paul's neck and kissed him.[61]

When Acts 20:32–36 is taken as a unit in this manner, it establishes a chain of tradition from Jesus, who said, "It is more blessed to give than to receive," to Paul who worked with his own hands to assist others, and then to the elders who similarly must "work to support the weak."[62] The focus here is Paul's example: "In all ways I showed you . . ." He prays that they may follow his lead, empowered by "God and the Logos of his grace."

I have transliterated and capitalized "Logos" to highlight the personification of God's Word. A personified, divine Logos was common in ancient Judaism and Christianity, and Luke here uses it as a title for Christ.[63] Paul prays that the Logos/Christ will "build up [οἰκοδομῆσαι]" the elders and "grant them the inheritance," implying that the elders are, in some sense, sons. Paul here plays a role similar to that of fathers in testaments who hand on their property and power to offspring.[64] Paul can give them no "silver or gold or clothing"; their inheritance is eternal life "with all who have been made holy."[65]

Between Hector's two speeches to Andromache he reached for his son, but the baby recoiled in fear of the crest of horsehair waving atop of his father's helmet. Hector and Andromache then shared a laugh. He put down his helmet,

> kissed his dear son, rocked him in his arms, and spoke a prayer to Zeus and the other Gods. "Zeus and you other gods, grant that this lad, my son, may be as I am — distinguished among the Trojans, as great in strength — and may he rule Ilium with might. May someone say of him as he returns from battle, 'He is much better than his father.' After killing a foe, may he haul off the bloody spoils, and may his mother's heart rejoice."[66]

Hector returned the boy to his mother, "and she took him to her fragrant breast, laughing as she wept." The reader knows that Hector's prayer will not be realized; indeed, Astyanax would not live to see his next birthday. Seneca's Andromache warns him as much: "God has rejected prayers. You will not wield a scepter in power over Ilium in your royal hall. . . . You will not slay Greeks in retreat."[67]

Hector's simple prayer, six poetic lines, served as a model for prayers in Sophocles, Chariton, Vergil, and Silius Italicus, all of whom cast light on Luke's interests in *Iliad* 6. For clarity I have divided Hector's prayer into three parts, each of which finds a parallel in Acts 20 and these other ancient imitations: (1) the setting and invocation; (2) the wish that Astyanax be as great as or greater than his father, (3) the hypothetical quotation of someone who compares him to his father.

SETTING AND INVOCATION

Vergil's account of Aeneas's prayer for Ascanius, his son, clearly imitates Hector's for Astyanax.[68] Hector, fully armed, reached for his infant son, who cried when he saw his father's helmet. The hero removed his helmet, kissed his son, rocked him in his arms, and offered his prayer. Similarly, Aeneas, "eager for battle, . . . enclosed his legs in gold, left and right. He scorns delay and waves a spear. . . . He embraced Ascanius in his arms, lightly kissed his cheek through the helmet, and said . . ."[69] Both heroes are eager to return to battle; both kiss and embrace their sons, one wearing a helmet and one with one in hand; and both utter a prayer for a glorious military future for their boys. Later I will compare the content of the two prayers, but for now it is sufficient to note the similarities of setting.

Chariton's novel imitated the Andromache scene several times. In one passage the plutocrat Dionysius read a letter from his wife, Callirhoe, explaining why she had left him. He then turned to the boy he supposed was his son by her and mourned their future separation. "Looking at *his little boy, he rocked him in his arms* [πήλας ταῖς χερσίν; cf. *Iliad* 6.474: πῆλέ τε χερσίν]: 'You too will leave me some day, my son, and go to your mother.' "[70] "Chariton here adapts a phrase from a famous scene in the *Iliad* (6.474) where Hector plays with his son, Astyanax, for the last time before going, as he knows, to meet his death at the hands of Achilles."[71]

The reference to Paul's prayer following the speech has its own similarities to *Iliad* 6.

Iliad 6.466 and 474–75	Acts 20:36–37
When he had thus said [ὣς εἰπών],	And *when he had said these things*
glorious Hector reached out for the boy. . . .	[ταῦτα εἰπών], he knelt with them all
And then he *kissed his dear son*,	*and prayed* [προσηύξατο]. There was
rocked him in his arms, and spoke	much weeping among them all; they *fell on*
in prayer [ἐπευξάμενος] to Zeus.	Paul's *neck* and *kissed him*.
[After the prayer, Andromache wept.]	

In both columns the protagonist had finished a speech (ὣς εἰπών/ταῦτα εἰπών) and prayed (ἐπευξάμενος/προσηύξατο; both are compounds of ευχ-). Hector hugged and kissed his son before the prayer; the elders hugged and kissed Paul after the prayer. After both prayers, those present wept. As extensive as these parallels may appear, they are not particularly compelling insofar as one ought not be surprised that the motifs of farewell prayers, hugging, and kissing form a natural cluster and appear in texts without any literary interconnection. It helps only modestly that the prayers of Aeneas and Dionysius, clearly rewritings of *Iliad* 6, contain the same motifs.

Fortunately, the parallels between the prayers do not end here. Both begin by invoking their gods (shared motif 5: the hero invokes his gods).

Iliad 6.475–76	Acts 20:32
[Hector] spoke in prayer *to Zeus*	I entrust you
and the other gods [θεοῖσιν]:	*to God* [θεῷ] *and to the Logos* of his grace.
"*Zeus and you other gods* [θεοί], . . ."	

It may be mere coincidence that both prayers address not only the highest gods (Zeus/God) but lesser gods as well (other gods/the Logos). The content that follows, however, surely comes from mimesis.

HECTOR'S WISH THAT ASTYANAX MIGHT BE LIKE HIM

Hector's prayer for Astyanax was this: "Grant that this lad, my son, may be as I am," and that someone would even say of him, "He is much better than his father" in warfare. Such comparisons of the son and the father are common in literary imitations of the scene.

As we have seen, Sophocles imitated Hector's farewell to Andromache in the farewell of Ajax to Tecmessa; he also imitated Hector's prayer for Astyanax in Ajax's blessing on his son Eurysaces. Tecmessa had kept the boy away from his demented father lest he be afraid of the sight and in danger, but Ajax called for him and said: "May you be happier than your father, but like him otherwise."[72] Ajax hoped Eurysaces would be like him in battle, as Hector had prayed that Astyanax would.[73] But he also prayed that his son would be happier than he. One certainly would hope so: Ajax was a tragic figure, and not long after uttering this prayer he took his life.

According to Vergil, Aeneas prayed that Ascanius would grow into a man like himself and his uncle Hector. Vergil clearly imitated Hector's prayer in *Iliad* 6.

> *He embraced Ascanius in his arms,* lightly *kissed his cheek* through the helmet, *and said, "My son,* learn *courage* and true *labor from me. . . .*[74] When your youth gives way to maturity, see to it that you remember [my accomplishments], and may *your father* Aeneas and your uncle Hector inspire your soul when you call to mind the example of your kinsmen." *Having offered these words, he went through the gates in might,* waving a huge spear in his hand, *and with him,* like a tight column, *rushed Antheus and Mnestheus.*[75]

If Vergil's readers detected the Homeric backdrop to this prayer, they may well have remembered that Zeus did not grant Hector's request: Greek soldiers hurled Astyanax to the earth from the walls of Troy. Aeneas's wishes for Ascanius, on the other hand, would find fulfillment. He would rule in Italy in the tradition of his father and uncle Hector. Hector's prayer for Astyanax here is answered indirectly. His son would not rule; his nephew would.

Hannibal's prayer for his son, according to Silius Italicus, drew extensive comparisons between himself and his son. "May you, I pray, be more glorious than your father and make a name for yourself by works of war that will surpass your grandsire's. . . . I recognize my father's countenance and the defiant eyes beneath a frowning brow; I note the depth of your infant cries and the beginnings of a fierceness like my own."[76] Here as in *Iliad* 6 one finds a favorable comparison between the lad and his father and an expression of hope that he will slay his foes. Silius probably had no historical source for this passage. In fact, the poet himself seems to have created the name Imilce — to sound Punic — and the very existence of Hannibal's son.[77]

In Acts 20 the comparison between Paul and the elders may be less explicit, but it is present nonetheless.

Iliad 6.476–78	Acts 20:32
[Hector] spoke in prayer *to Zeus and the other gods* [θεῶσιν]: "*Zeus and you other gods* [θεοί], grant [δότε] that *this, my son, may be as I am* — distinguished among the Trojans, as *great in strength*."	And now I entrust you *to God* [θε ῷ] *and to the Logos* of his grace, who *has the power to build you up* and grant [δοῦναι] *you* the inheritance with all who have been made holy.

Paul had lived by Jesus' beatitude in working to satisfy the needs of others, and his efforts were an example (ὑπέδειξα) for the elders to "support the weak." Paul is saying, after a fashion, "I pray that they be as I am, as great in strength for the needy" (shared motif 6: the hero prays that his successors will be like him).

COMPARATIVE QUOTATION

Hector ended his prayer with a hypothetical quotation in which someone in the future would say that Astyanax was greater than his father. "May someone say of him as he returns from battle, 'He is much better than his father.' After killing a foe, may he haul off the bloody spoils, and may his mother's heart rejoice."[78] Earlier we saw how Chariton imitated the prayer in *Iliad* 6 when narrating Dionysius's speech to the boy he thought he had sired by Callirhoe. In the same novel, Callirhoe, his mother, offers a prayer for him that echoes Hector's and contains another hypothetical quotation. But first Callirhoe prays that he may be comparable to his venerable ancestors.

> [H]olding up *her infant in her arms, she said* [to Aphrodite], "*Lady,* I know your grace for this child . . . *Grant that my son may be* happier than his parents and the *equal of his grandfather. May he, too, sail on a battle trireme, and may someone say when he fights at sea, 'The grandson is greater than Hermocrates.'* His grandfather, too will be happy to have a successor in valor, *and we, his parents, shall feel delight,* even though we are dead."[79]

Here the section of the prayer most relevant to Acts is the embedded discourse; the hypothetical quotation concerning the comparative greatness of the offspring to the sire. "*And may someone say when he fights at sea, 'The grandson is greater than Hermocrates.'* "

Surely it is not accidental that Luke ends Paul's sermon with an embedded direct discourse that makes a comparison of its own, but whose content sharply contrasts with the *Iliad* (shared motif 7: the hero cites a comparative quotation).

Iliad 6.479–80	Acts 20:35
May *someone say* of him	[R]emember the words of the Lord Jesus,
as he returns from battle,	that *he himself said,*
"*He is much better than his father.*"	"*It is more blessed to give than to receive.*"

The two comparative quotations are closer in English than in Greek; even so, in both works one finds in the context of a prayer for one's descendents a quotation consisting of a single comparative statement. Hector prays that someone will say that Astyanax is an even greater warrior than his father; Luke prays that the elders will remember Jesus' words that giving is even greater than receiving.[80]

The structure of these quotations may be similar, but the content can hardly be more antithetical. Hector hopes that Astyanax will be judged greater in war than his father: "After killing a foe, may he haul off the bloody spoils, and may his mother's heart rejoice." Ajax's prayer for Eurysaces included the hope that he would "show in the presence of enemies what kind of son of what kind of father you are."[81] Callirhoe prayed that her son would be a victorious admiral. Hannibal's prayer for his son included the following lines: "Rome, sick with fear, already reckons up your years — years that shall make mothers weep. If my prophetic soul does not deceive my feeling, vast suffering for the world is growing up in you."[82] Paul's prayer for the elders, however, has nothing to do with military accomplishments. Instead, the apostle prays that they, like he, would seek no one's "silver or gold or clothing" and would support the weak by working with their own hands.

Paul's Departure (Acts 20:37–38)

After Hector's speeches to Andromache and his prayer for Astyanax, they part.

> Having so said, glorious Hector took up his horsetailed helmet, and his beloved wife went home, frequently turning back, swelling with tears. Quickly then she came to the comfortable home of man-slaying Hector and found there her many maidservants; among them all she incited wailing. So they wailed for Hector in his own house while he was still alive, for they said that he would never again return from battle, escaped from the fury and hands of the Achaeans.[83]

Several of the imitations of the Hector-Andromache scene conclude with similar separations. For example, Telemachus's command to Penelope in *Odyssey* 1, which repeated nearly verbatim Hector's command that Andromache go home, is followed by Penelope's departure: "then she, in amazement, went home [οἴκόνδε βεβήκει; the same construction appears in *Iliad* 6.495]. . . . Having ascended to her upper room with her maidservants [ἀμφιπόλοισι; cf. ἀμφιπόλους in *Iliad* 6.498], she then wept for Odysseus, her dear husband [φίλον πόσιν/ cf. ἄλοχος . . . φίλη, "dear wife" in *Iliad* 6.495]."[84]

The Persian general Abradatas bid farewell to his wife Panthea in a passage of Xenophon modeled after the Hector-Andromache scene. Like Hector, Abradatas prayed to Zeus and then told his wife to return home. "Then the eunuchs and maid-servants took her and conducted her to her carriage, where they bid her recline, and hid her completely from view with the hood of the carriage," apparently so she could weep in privacy.[85] In Chariton's novel, the heroine Callirhoe, separated from her husband Chaereas, imitated Andromache's weeping for Hector. "So Callirhoe spent that night in lamentation mourning for Chaereas while he was still alive."[86]

Vergil may have used *Iliad* 6 as a model for Dido's farewell to Aeneas: "So saying, she breaks off her speech midway, flees daylight in turmoil, turns herself from his eyes, and runs away, leaving him waiting in fear and ready to say much more. Her maidservants catch her, carry her swooning to her marble chamber, and lay her prone on her bed."[87] There she lamented with her sister, nurse, and maidservants, until she finally killed herself at the end of Book 4.[88] As in the Hector-Andromache scene, here one finds a constellation of related motifs: a farewell speech, deliberations of suicide, sympathetic maidservants, and weeping in the bedroom.

The separation of Hannibal and Imilce in Silius Italicus's *Punica* again echoes Homer: "While they conversed together thus and mingled their tears, the steersman, feeling that he could trust the sea, hailed the unwilling wife from his high seat on the stern. Torn from her husband's arms she is carried away. Her eager eyes still cling to him and watch the shore, until the sea made sight impossible and the land fell back, as the swift ship sped on its watery way." Hannibal went back "to drown his love in the business of war."[89] Especially suggestive of *Iliad* 6 is the relationship of Imilce's persistent gaze for her husband to Andromache's "frequently turning back, swelling with tears."

The most famous final farewell in ancient literature is that of Socrates in Plato's *Phaedo*, and it, too, seems to imitate the Homeric scene. Some of the parallels pertain to elements of Hector's farewell prior to his separation from Andromache, but it is the separation itself that seems most appropriate for understanding Acts 20. Required by Athens to drain the hemlock, Socrates bade adieu to family and friends. Phaedo, Plato's narrator, says that "a very strange feeling came over me, an unaccustomed mixture of pleasure and pain together, when I thought that

Socrates was presently to die, and all of us who were there were in much the same condition, sometimes laughing and sometimes weeping [ὅτε μὲν γελῶντες, ἐνίοτε δὲ δακρύοντες]."[90] Plato surely would not have been surprised if his readers saw here the famous paradox of Andromache "laughing as she wept [δακρυόεν γελάσασα]."[91]

The first sight that greeted Socrates' friends when they arrived at the prison was Xanthippe "holding his little son [ἔχουσάν τε τὸ παιδίον αὐτοῦ]," a detail reminiscent of Andromache's maidservant, "holding the child to the breast [παῖδ᾽ ἐπὶ κόλπῳ ἔχουσ᾽]."[92] Just as Andromache's first words to Hector predicted doom, "soon the Achaeans will rush against you and kill you," Xanthippe's first — and only — words to Socrates were: "This is the last time your friends will speak with you."[93] Plato's reader might expect Socrates to show his wife tenderness and pray for their son; instead, he immediately ordered them to leave. Plato reserved Socrates' final farewell not for his family but for his philosophical circle. Xanthippe's removal from the prison once again calls to mind *Iliad* 6. " 'Crito, let somebody take her home.' And some of Crito's people took her away wailing and beating her breast."[94] In his speeches to his friends Socrates lectured on death, the nature of the soul, immortality, and courage, the courage of the philosopher when facing his own demise.[95] Hector's speech to Andromache, of course, emphasized his courage and willingness to die.

Crito asked Socrates, "Do you wish to leave any directions with us about your children?" Once again Socrates ignores his family in favor of this friends: "If you take care of yourselves you will serve me and mine and yourselves."[96] His friends were his true family: "We felt that he was like a father to us and that when bereft of him we should pass the rest of our lives as orphans."[97] Socrates' biological family reappears nearer his death. When his three sons and "the women of the family had come, he talked with them in Crito's presence and gave them such directions as he wished; then he told the women and children to go away." He then prayed to the gods for a happy departure and drained the cup. Those present wept profusely, like Andromache and her maidservants. Andromache had "swelled with tears [δάκρυ]." So did Socrates' friends.

> Most of us had been able to restrain our tears [τὸ δακρύειν] fairly well, but when we watched him drinking and saw that he had drunk the poison, we could do so no longer, but in spite of myself my tears [τὰ δάκρυα] rolled down in floods, so that I wrapped by face in my cloak and wept for myself; for it was not for him that I wept, but for my own misfortune in being deprived of such a friend. Crito had got up and gone away even before I did, because he could not restrain his tears [τὰ δάκρυα]. But Apollodorus, who had never stopped weeping [δακρύων], then wailed aloud in his grief and made us all break down, except Socrates

himself. But he said, "What conduct is this, you strange men! I sent the women away chiefly for this very reason, that they might not behave in this absurd way; for I have heard that it is best to die in silence. Keep quiet and be brave." Then we were ashamed and controlled our tears [τοῦ δακρύειν].[98]

Like Hector, Socrates courageously went to face his fate; he did not want his friends to weep like Andromache and her servants.

Similarly, after Paul's prayer in Acts 20, "There was much weeping among them all; they fell on Paul's neck and kissed him, grieving especially because of what he had said, that they would never again see his face. Then they brought him to the ship."[99] This passage finds no closer parallel in ancient literature than *Iliad* 6.

Iliad 6.498–501	Acts 20:37–38
[Andromache went home and] found there her many maidservants; *among them all* [πάσῃσιν] she induced *wailing*. So *they wailed* for Hector in his own house while he was still alive; *for they said that he would never again* [οὐ . . . ἔτ'] *return from battle* [Hector went back to the battle.]	There was much *weeping among them all* [πάντων]. They fell on Paul's neck and kissed him, *grieving* especially *because of what he had said, that they would never* again [οὐκέτι] see *his face.* And they sent him off in the ship.

In both columns those who heard the hero's final farewell wept at what was said: "he would never again return from battle"; "they would never again see his face." Homer's οὐ . . . ἔτ' "never again," matches Luke's οὐκέτι. Homer's infinitive ἵξεσθαι correlates with Luke's θεωρεῖν. Hector will never escape "from the fury and hands of the Achaeans"; Paul will never escape the Jews who will hand him over to "the hands of the gentiles."[100]

8

Jewish Testament or Homeric Imitation?

This chapter concludes the discussion of Acts 20 and seeks to answer one simple question: Why should one abandon the rich tradition of Jewish testamentary literature in favor of a single Greek literary model to explain the composition of Paul's farewell at Miletus? The answer lies in the application of the six criteria. Criteria one and two surely apply: Hector's farewell to Andromache not only was accessible to Luke and his readers, it was a popular target for analogous imitations. Aristophanes, Sophocles, Plato, Herodotus, Xenophon, Apollonius Rhodius, Chariton, Vergil, and Silius Italicus not only imitated the scene, some of them apparently expected their readers to catch their allusions to it.

Criteria three and four assess the density of the parallels and their relative sequence. Chapter 7 identified nine motifs shared by Homer and Luke that I numbered according to the order their appearance in the epic. Paul's speech begins with shared motif 2, and so does Hector's speech to Andromache. The first motif appeared in his speech to Helen a few lines earlier (the hero states that he does not know what dangers he will face). The following columns contain Paul's entire speech on the right, with the Homeric parallels on the left. The number and description of the relevant motif introduce each section. (Most of these columns appear in the Appendix in Greek.)

Motif 2: The Hero Boasts that He Never Shirked His Duty

Iliad 6.440–46
Then *he said to her*, . . .
"But I would be terribly ashamed before
the Trojans and the Trojan women with
trailing robes,

if, like a coward,
I were to shrink from the battle.
My heart commands me not to, for I have
learned always *to be valiant and to fight
on the front line* with the Trojans,
winning great renown *both* for my father
and for myself."

Acts 20:18–21
He said to them,
"You yourselves know how I was with you
the entire time from the first day that I
arrived in Asia — serving the Lord with all
lowliness, tears, and testings that came to
me through the plots of the Jews — that
I did not hold back anything beneficial:

to *preach* to you *and to teach* you
in public and from house to house,
testifying both to Jews *and* to Greeks
about repentance toward God
and faith toward our Lord Jesus."

Motif 1: The Hero States that He Does Not Know What Dangers He Will Face

Iliad 6.361–62 and 367–68
For my heart is already impatient to
assist the Trojans. . . .
I do not know if ever
again I shall return to them
or *if the gods will subdue me at
the hands of the Achaeans.*

Acts 20:22–23
And now, captive to the Spirit,
I am on my way to Jerusalem,
not knowing what will happen
to me there, except that the Holy Spirit
testifies to me in every city saying that
chains and afflictions await me.

Motif 8: The Hero States His Willingness to Face His Destiny with Courage

Iliad 6.486–89
[D]o not let your heart excessively
grieve for me. No man will hurl me
to Hades beyond *my lot.* I say that
after birth no man, whether cowardly or
courageous, ever has escaped fate.

Acts 20:24
But I do not count my life of any value
to myself so that I may complete *my race
and the ministry that I received* from the
Lord Jesus, to testify to the gospel
of the grace of God.

Motif 3: *The Hero Warns of Disaster*

Iliad 6.447–49	Acts 20:25
For *this I know* well in my mind and heart:	And now *I know that*
a day will come when *sacred Ilium*	none of you will ever see my face again —
will be destroyed — Priam and the	you among whom I have gone about
spear-savvy people of Priam.	proclaiming *the kingdom*.

Motif 2: *The Hero Boasts that He Never Shirked His Duty*

Iliad 6.441–43	Acts 20:26–27
I would be terribly ashamed before	For this reason I testify to you this day that
the Trojans and the Trojan women with	
trailing robes, if, like a coward,	I am pure from the blood of all,
I were to shrink from the battle.	for *I did not shrink from* proclaiming
	the entire will of God.

Motif 9: *The Hero Commands His Audience*

Iliad 6.490–93	Acts 20:28
Attend to your own tasks,	*Attend to yourselves*
the loom and the distaff,	
and command your maidservants	*and all the flock*, in which
to pursue their work.	the Holy Spirit has placed you
War will concern all the men	as overseers to shepherd the church of God
who live in Ilium, especially me.	that he rescued with his own blood.

Motif 3: *The Hero Warns of Disaster*

Iliad 6.447–49	Acts 20:29–30
For *this I know* well in my mind and heart:	*I know that*
a day will come	*after my departure*
when *sacred Ilium will be destroyed* —	*savage wolves will come* in among you,
Priam and the spear-savvy people of Priam.	*not sparing the flock.*
[Homer used wolf similes of the soldiers	
who would sack Troy without mercy.	And from your own ranks men will arise
Hector feared the enslavement and	speaking perverse things to draw the
deportation of his wife to Greece.]	disciples after them.

Motif 9: The Hero Commands His Audience

Iliad 6.490 and 492–93
Attend to your own tasks, . . .

War will concern all the men
who live in Ilium, especially me.

Acts 20:31
Therefore, *be alert,*
remembering that for three years night
and day I did not cease to warn
everyone with tears.

Motif 5: The Hero Invokes His Gods

Iliad 6.475–78
[Hector] spoke in prayer *to Zeus*
and the other gods:
"*Zeus and you other gods, grant that this,*
my son, may be as I am — distinguished
among the Trojans, as *great in strength.*"

Acts 20:32
And now I entrust you
to God and to the Logos of his grace, who
has *the power to build you up* and *grant you*
the inheritance with all who have been
made holy.

Motif 6: The Hero Prays that His Successors Will Be Like Him

Iliad 6.476–78

[G]rant that this lad, my son, *may be*
as I am — distinguished among the Trojans,
as great in strength.

Acts 20:33–35a
I desired of no one silver or gold
or clothing. You yourselves know that
these hands ministered to my necessities
and to those who were with me.
In all ways I showed you that it is necessary
to work like this to *support the weak.*

Motif 7: The Hero Cites a Comparative Quotation

Iliad 6.479–80
May *someone say* of him
as he returns from battle,
"*He is much better than his father.*"

Acts 20:35b
[It is necessary] to remember the words of
the Lord Jesus that *he himself said,*
"*It is more blessed to give than to receive.*"

Clearly these parallels satisfy the criterion of density, but the order of shared
motifs varies from that of the *Iliad*: 2, 1, 8, 3, 2 (again), 9, 3 (again), 9 (again), 5,
6, and 7. This significant deviation in order at first sight would seem to militate
against literary dependence, but a closer look allows one to appreciate Luke's
rearrangement.

As we have seen, Paul's speech is organized into three units: Paul's heroism (verses 18–27, containing motifs 2, 1, 8, 3, and 2), the challenges facing the elders (28–31, containing motifs 9, 3, and 9), and Paul's prayer for the elders (32–35, containing motifs 5, 6, and 7). Homer inserted the prayer for Astyanax between Hector's two speeches to Andromache, while Luke put the prayer for the elders at the end of the speech. This moving of the prayer explains why motifs 5, 6, and 7 appear at the end and not toward the middle, as in the epic.

The logic of the first section (18–27) is this: Paul claims that he did not shrink from fear (motif 2), even though he was unsure of the future except that he would suffer wherever he went (motif 1). In order to fulfill the ministry Christ had given him, he did not consider his life as precious (motif 8). He did know that the elders would never see him again (motif 3), but Paul could leave them with a clear conscience insofar as he never shirked his duty (motif 2). The repetition of the second motif (not shirking) provides an elegant inclusion around a chiasm.

A. Paul never shirked his duty (motif 2)
   B. He *did not know* what the future would hold (motif 1)
      C. He did not consider his life precious so he could perform his duty (motif 8)
   B¹. He *did know* that the elders would not see him again (motif 3)
A¹. He never shirked his duty (motif 2)

A and A¹ speak of Paul's courageous preaching; B and B¹ state what Paul did and did not know, though both passages presage suffering; C stands at the center of the chiasm and forms its climax: Paul was willing to die to complete his mission.

The second section of the speech (28–31) consists of commands. Whereas Hector gave instructions to Andromache at the very end of their encounter (motif 9), Luke uses the motif to introduce the commands to the elders. Earlier Luke had used motif 3 (warnings) of Paul's own death, in verses 29–30 he uses it again to warn of dangers to the church. Verse 31 completes another chiasm by reiterating commands (motif 9).

A. Paul commands the elders to be on guard (motif 9)
   B. He knows that wolves will come and threaten the church (motif 3)
A¹. He commands the elders to be on guard, as he had been (motif 9)

In this chiasm B stands in the center position: a warning of dangers.

The third and last section is a prayer consisting of three motifs that appear in the same order as in the epic (motifs 5, 6, and 7). The prayer section appears here, after motifs 8 and 9, to complete the speech. It then segues into the prayer prior to the sendoff. Once again Luke has adapted the motifs to produce a chiasm.

A. Paul commends the elders to "God and the Logos of his grace" (motif 5)

   B. He prays that the elders may be like him in caring for the needy (motif 6)

A^1. He reminds the elders of the "words [λόγοι] of the Lord Jesus" (motif 7)

This chiasm focuses on B: the prayer that the elders follow Paul's example in caring for the weak.

   The three major divisions of the speech form a chiasm of their own.

A. Paul never shirked his duty to the elders, despite the danger of doing so (18–27)

   B. He commands the elders to be watchful because of coming disasters (28–31)

A^1. He prays that the elders may be like him, doing their duty to others (32–35)

The organization of motifs from the *Iliad* would suggest the following macrostructure.

A. Paul never shirked his duty to the elders, despite the danger of doing so (18–27)

   AA. He never shirked his duty (motif 2)

     AB. He *did not know* what the future would hold (motif 1)

       AC. He did not consider his life precious (motif 8)

     AB^1. He *did know* that the elders would not see him again (motif 3)

   AA^1. He never shirked his duty (motif 2)

B. Paul commands the elders to be watchful because of coming disasters (28–31)

   BA. He commands the elders to be on guard (motif 9)

     BB. He knows that wolves will come and threaten the church (motif 3)

   BA^1. He commands the elders to be on guard, as he had been (motif 9)

A^1. Paul prays that the elders may be like him, doing their duty to others (32–35)

   A^{1}A. He invokes "God and the Logos of his grace" (motif 5)

     A^{1}B. He prays that the elders may be like him (motif 6)

   A^{1}A^1. He reminds the elders of the "words [λόγοι] of the Lord" (motif 7)

In this larger chiasm, Paul's warning of future dangers stands at the very center (BB). If this treatment of the speech is correct, it would explain why the order of motifs in Acts 20 differs from their order in the epic.

Defenders of the speech as a Jewish testament are likely to argue that the parallels I have drawn to the epic likewise appear in the testament, such as the hero's defense of his integrity, warnings of future disasters, readiness to die, instructions to descendants, and prayer. This is correct, but I would contend that if one were to mine the entire body of Jewish testaments for parallels to Acts 20, one could not compile parallels closer to those in the Hector-Andromache scene. Defenders of the testamentary hypothesis also might object that my chiastic structure for the speech is simply a clever ploy to disguise the deviation in the sequence of shared motifs. The detection of chiasms in ancient literature is notoriously subjective, and other structural assessments of the speech in Acts are possible.

To decide the matter it would be helpful to find evidence of shared features seldom found in exemplars of the genre as a whole, features that link the two texts together into a unique hermeneutical tension. The significance of the fifth criterion, distinctive traits, is its capacity to cement two texts together. Furthermore, the presence of unusual traits can distinguish a mere echo from an allusion. Does Acts 20 display traits distinctive to it and *Iliad* 6 and not to final testaments as a whole?

Both Hector and Paul speak of not shirking their duty, declare both what they know and what they do not know about the future, and both direct their prayers to more than one deity: "Zeus and you other gods"; "God and the Logos." But it is their literary contexts that make the speeches most alike, a topic I have put off until now.

Jewish testaments characteristically take place just before the death of the patriarch, usually in his own home, at his deathbed. Those who view Paul's farewell as a final testament based on Jewish models must explain why Paul does not die immediately afterward. In fact, Luke never narrates Paul's death; after this speech, the apostle continues his ministry for another eight chapters and at the end of the book continues preaching in Rome for two years. Had Luke wanted Paul's farewell to be a final testament, he could have placed it at the end of Acts while Paul awaited his execution. The location of the speech here, near the beginning of his final journey to Jerusalem, makes it less a final testament than a hero's departure for battle. Furthermore, Paul's speech at Miletus establishes his courageous willingness to do God's will, even though he knew that dangers awaited him in Jerusalem from his primary foes, the Jews.[1]

Similarly, readers ancient and modern have wondered why Homer placed Hector's farewell so early in the epic, in Book 6, even though he would not die until Book 22, several days later. The hero returns to Troy again in Book 7, where the poet could have placed the scene.[2] In fact, he could have made Hector say his good-byes at the beginning of Book 22, just before he faced Achilles. Noting the premature location of the farewell and observing that Hector never accomplished what he set out to do — to consult the elders in Troy — some interpreters have supposed that the scene once existed as an independent poem that later was grafted into Book 6.[3]

Other scholars, however, "find it inspired that Homer chose to place this scene early on in the poem, where it establishes Hector's importance and, more materially, gives readers an idea of what Hector is fighting for, all in vain, and casts an ominous shadow over his subsequent appearances, grimly presaging Troy's doom and the human waste the war will entail."[4] Even though Hector knows that his efforts ultimately will fail, he does not know precisely how or when. In any case, he states that nothing can be gained by hiding in the city, for "no man, whether cowardly or courageous, ever has escaped fate."[5] From this early moment in the epic and for the next sixteen books the reader is aware of Hector's courage and anticipates his tragic but noble death.

Some of Homer's imitators similarly used farewell scenes early in their narratives to highlight the courage of their heroes in the face of danger. According to Apollonius Rhodius, as the Argonauts were about to sail to Colchis to fetch the golden fleece from the sleepless dragon, the women of Iolchus came to the ship, weeping. Alcimede, Jason's mother, thought it better to have died before seeing her only son sail off to his doom. Now she would be left behind alone, like a slave. "Thus with mourning she wept, and her maidservants standing by also lamented."[6] Jason comforted her by saying that no one can escape fate, a statement almost certainly modeled after Hector's statement about fate to Andromache. Jason would return safely at the end of the epic, but he did not know before embarking what the gods and fate held for him. The placement of the farewell scene early in the epic sets the stage for the drama that would follow.

According to Vergil, Aeneas told Dido that when he was about to leave Troy to fight the attacking Greeks, his wife Creusa met him at the threshold "holding up little Iulus to his father" and begging him to take them with him.[7] The scene clearly imitates *Iliad 6*. Aeneas did take them with him, but before Creusa could escape, Cybele transported her to the heavens. Later, Creusa's ghost would bid Aeneas farewell. She told him that he must not grieve, for her death was the will of the gods, and that she "will not suffer the fate of Andromache," who was taken off as a slave.[8] Aeneas one day would rule a kingdom on the banks of the Tiber.[9] "The Trojan princess instructs her husband to look after their son, and in this she evokes for the last time the gentleness of *Iliad 6*."[10] Vergil, like Homer, uses the farewell as Aeneas fled Troy to cast a shadow over the subsequent narrative — the last ten of its twelve books.

Silius Italicus used *Iliad 6* as his model for the farewell of Hannibal to his wife, Imilce, including a restatement of the inalterability of fate.[11] A soldier, said Hannibal, cannot let cowardice deter him from warfare insofar as no one knows his lot. From this point to the end of Latin's longest poem — ten thousand lines later! — the reader appreciates Hannibal's courage. These Homeric imitations may explain why Luke placed Paul's farewell so early in a narrative that never mentions his death. It is not the final testament of a dying man; it is a courageous declaration of a hero who is intent on performing his duty despite dangers.

The placement of the speech so early in Acts is not the only peculiarity with the setting. Luke states that Paul and company sailed along the western shore of Asia — Mitylene, Chios, Samos — bypassing Ephesus in favor of Miletus; "for Paul had decided to sail past Ephesus, so that he might not have to spend time in Asia. He was eager to be in Jerusalem, if possible, on the day of Pentecost. From Miletus he sent to Ephesus and summoned the elders of the church. "[12] As many commentators have noted, Luke's explanation for bypassing Ephesus is unconvincing. If Paul were in a hurry, he surely would have been wiser to have stopped at Ephesus than to have sailed to Miletus, sent a messenger back to Ephesus to call for the elders, and then waited for them to arrive.[13]

Luke's model for this hurried and awkward choreography again could have been *Iliad 6*, where Homer repeatedly emphasizes Hector's eagerness to return to the battlefield. Helen asked him to linger, but he responded, "Helen, do not make me sit. . . . Already my heart is hastening me to defend the Trojans."[14] Instead, he asked her to hasten Paris's reentry into the battle.[15] Hector then went "quickly" to his home, but he did not find Andromache there; she had gone to the ramparts to watch the battle, hoping to get a glimpse of her husband. He decided to waste no more time and "hurried back" toward the gates "at which he was about to exit for the plain."[16] It was there that Andromache met him for their final goodbye.[17] In Acts 20 Paul's eagerness (ἔσπευδεν) to face his opponents at Jerusalem similarly caused his final farewell to the elders to take place not at Ephesus but at Miletus.

Here is how I would compare the two settings:

Iliad 6	Acts 20
• Hector was a target of violence.	• Paul was a target of violence.
• Hector returned to Troy to have the elders pray to the gods.	• Paul had left the Troad and summoned the elders for instruction and prayer.
• Hector was eager to return to the battle despite the danger.	• Paul was eager to return to Jerusalem despite the danger.
• Hector's farewell to Andromache took place not at their home but at the gate.	• Paul's farewell to the Ephesian elders took place not at their home but at Miletus.
• Hector would not die until days later.	• Paul would not die until years later.

The unusual setting of the speech in Acts 20 thus teases the reader to view it as a variation of the Hector-Andromache scene.

One might say the same of the response of the elders after the speech. Lest the reader earlier had missed the similarities between Paul and Hector, the conclusion makes it certain.

Iliad 6.466, 474–75, and 498–502	Acts 20:36–38
When he had thus said [ὣς εἰπών],	And *when he had said these things* [ταῦτα
glorious Hector reached out for the boy.	εἰπών], he knelt with them all
… And then he *kissed his dear son,*	*and prayed* [προσηύξατο].
rocked him in his arms, and spoke	
in prayer [ἐπευξάμενος] to Zeus. …	
[Andromache went home and] found	
there her many maidservants; *among*	There was much
them all she induced *wailing.*	*weeping among them all.*
So *they wailed* for Hector in his own house	They *fell on* Paul's *neck* and *kissed him,*
while he was still alive;	*grieving* especially
for they said that he would never again	*because of what he had said, that they would*
[οὐ … ἔτ'] *return from battle*	*never* again [οὐκέτι] see *his face.*
[Hector went back to the battle.]	And they sent him off in the ship.

My sixth and final criterion is interpretability: how does the proposed intertextual reading contribute to understanding the text? Put otherwise, what does one gain hermeneutically by comparing the two? In what way might the imitation transvalue the model?

The most obvious difference between the two scenes pertains to their depictions of heroism. Hector boasted that he never shrank from battle, he had won renown for himself and his father through valor, and he prayed that his son would be a greater warrior than he: "May someone say of him as he returns from battle, 'He is much better than his father.' After killing a foe, may he haul off the bloody spoils, and may his mother's heart rejoice." Paul, on the other hand, did not fight but provided "what was beneficial"; he "desired of no one silver or gold or clothing"; and he used his strength not to slay his opponents but to care for the weak. Unlike Hector who wanted his son to distinguish himself in battle, Paul wanted the elders to live by the maxim, "It is more blessed to give than to receive." Hector felt bound by his fate; Paul was bound to the Holy Spirit, willing to do the will of God. Hector dismissively commanded Andromache to return home and leave the war to the men. Paul commanded the elders to take charge of their flock, to keep alert against the savage wolves that would attack it. Finally, Zeus rejected Hector's prayer for Astyanax, who soon would die in the sack of Troy. The reader of Acts, however, may assume that God and the Logos would strengthen the elders and grant them their inheritance, just as Paul had prayed they would. It thus would appear that Luke did not merely imitate the Hector-Andromache scene, he emulated it to make it serve a new interpretation of heroism.

The Selection of Matthias and Iliad 7

9

The Selection of Ajax to Face Hector

After Hector bade farewell to Andromache, he rushed back to the field and challenged the Greeks to send him their best man for a battle of champions, man-to-man. The Greek army sat in stunned silence; no one dared meet the challenge until Menelaus, whose wife had caused the war, thought it his duty to face Hector himself. As he put on his armor, his brother Agamemnon told him to sit down with the others; he was no match for the Trojan.

Then "Nestor rose up among the Argives and spoke."[1] He complained that their cowardice was disgraceful. If he still had the strength of his youth, he would rise up and fight Hector himself. Long ago Lycurgus ambushed the warrior-king Areïthous in a narrow defile and "stabbed him with a spear in the middle, and he was forced backward to the earth."[2] The victor later gave the armor of the fallen king to the giant Ereuthalion, and in this armor he challenged the Pylians to send their best man against him. None of the army dared face him, until Nestor himself, the youngest in the ranks, rose to the challenge and slew him. "Athena gave me the glory. He was the tallest and mightiest man I ever slew, for he lay there enormous, sprawled here and there."[3] Nestor ended his speech like this. " 'Even though you men are the best of all the Achaeans, you are unwilling to go against Hector.' Thus the old man rebuked them, and nine men all stood up."[4] The poet then named them: Agamemnon, Diomedes, the two Ajaxes, Idomeneus, Meriones, Eurypylus, Thoas, and Odysseus.

All these wanted to fight noble Hector. Then the horseman, Nestor of Gerenia, addressed them, "One after the other now cast your lots [to determine] who wins by lot, for that one will help the well-greaved Achaeans, and will help his own heart as well, provided he escapes the destruction of battle and the terrible combat."

So he spoke, and each man marked his lot and cast it into the helmet of Atreides Agamemnon, and the people prayed and lifted their hands to the gods, looking up to the broad heaven. One would speak like this: "Father Zeus, [I pray that] Ajax may win the lot, or the son of Tydeus, or the king of gold-rich Mycene himself." So they spoke, and the horseman, Nestor of Gerenia, shook them, and out from the helmet popped the lot that they had wanted: that of Ajax.

When Ajax recognized his lot, he rejoiced and asked the army to pray to Zeus for victory, and pray they did.[5] The fight between Ajax and Hector ended in a draw; each survived to fight again.

Insofar as this passage appears in the *Iliad* it clearly was accessible to Luke and his readers (criterion one).[6] But this episode fails criterion two, analogy. Even though *Iliad* 7 appears in several elementary school exercises and in one advanced exercise, it was not as popular as the other books imitated in Acts. More significantly, I have not found a single imitation of this scene in ancient literature other than a possible parallel in Acts 1, the casting of lots to replace Judas and to complete the number of the Twelve.

Despite the absence of analogous imitations, we shall see that the parallels between Acts 1 and *Iliad* 7 are sufficiently extensive and distinctive to establish a literary connection. The six criteria for detecting mimesis do not constitute a checklist of requisite conditions. They are best used *ensemble* to create a coherent case for — or against — imitation.

The Selection of Matthias to Replace Judas

Luke wrote that after the Ascension the church at Jerusalem cast lots to determine whether Joseph Barsabbas Justus or Matthias would replace Judas among the Twelve. Throughout Acts 1:15–26 one can hear echoes of the casting of lots to determine who would fight Hector.[1] According to Acts 1:13–14, the believers who gathered after the ascension consisted of the eleven apostles together with "the women, Mary the mother of Jesus, and his brothers," but in verse 15 the group inexplicably expands to one hundred and twenty.[2] By inflating the number, Luke set the stage for a situation somewhat more like that in *Iliad 7*, where Nestor spoke to the entire army.

Peter's speech begins like Nestor's.

Iliad 7.123	Acts 1:15
Nestor rose up [ἀνίστατο] *among the Argives and spoke* [μετέειπεν].	*Peter rose up* [ἀναστάς] *in the midst of the brethren and spoke* [εἶπεν].

There is nothing particularly unusual about these parallels insofar as Luke frequently uses the verb ἀνίστημι to introduce speeches.[3] But the speeches that follow in both books contain stories of violent deaths. Nestor told the troops of Lycurgus's murder of Areïthous and his own victory over Ereuthalion; the content of Peter's speech had to do with the death of Judas.

Men brothers, the text had to be fulfilled that the Holy Spirit predicted through the mouth of David about Judas, who became a guide for those who arrested Jesus, for he was numbered among us and received the lot of this service. This one then purchased a field from the reward of his injustice and, falling face down, burst in the middle, and all his guts poured out. And it became known to all the inhabitants of Jerusalem, so that that field was called in their language Hakeldamach, that is "Field of Blood." For it was written in the Book of Psalms, "May his fold be desolate, and may no inhabitant be in it, and let another take his responsibility."[4]

The speech displays characteristic Lucan vocabulary and style.[5] The biblical quotation is a combination of two texts from the Psalms (69:26 and 109:8) that more closely resembles the Septuagint than the Hebrew versions. If Luke found these biblical allusions combined in a source, it probably was written in Greek.[6] Furthermore, it is unlikely that the historical Peter — or a Semitic source — would have said that the "field was called in their language Hakeldamach," as though Aramaic were a foreign tongue needing translation.[7]

On the other hand, Luke clearly inherited traditional information concerning the death of Judas. Unlike the other examples discussed in this book, for which there exists no significant external evidence of pre-Lucan tradition, Acts 1:15–20 finds partial confirmation in descriptions of Judas's death in Matthew and a fragment of a second-century bishop in Phrygia named Papias.[8] Matthew and Luke agree that Judas came to a violent end as a fulfillment of scripture; that the money Judas received for betraying Jesus purchased a plot of land; and that the plot thus came to be known as the "Field of Blood." At least this much of Luke's story must have been traditional.

According to Matthew, Judas repented of betraying Jesus, returned the money to the high priests, and hanged himself. The priests then used the money to purchase "the potter's field" as a tomb for foreigners, known to the locals as the Field of Blood. By so doing, the authorities fulfilled the predictions of Zech 11:12–13 and Jer 18:1–3 and 32:6–15. Luke, too, knew of this plot of land, but in Acts it is Judas himself who bought it, and it was his own blood, not Jesus', that rendered it a Field of Blood. Like Matthew, Luke thought that the purchase of the field fulfilled prophecy — not the predictions of Jeremiah and Zechariah but of David.

Here is Papias's version: Judas

became so bloated that he was unable to pass through an opening large enough for a chariot easily to pass. Not even the massiveness of his head could get through! They say that his eyelids were so swollen that he was entirely unable to see the light, and even physicians with magnifying glasses could not see his eyes, so deeply had they sunk beyond sight. His penis appeared to be more repulsive and larger than any such disgraceful member, and pus and maggots poured from his entire body. . . . They say that after many tortures and punishments, he died in his own field, which even now remains deserted and uninhabited due to its stench. Still today no one can pass by that place without pinching the nostrils, such was the efflux that seeped from his flesh to the ground.[9]

This gruesome description agrees more with Acts 1 than with Matthew 27. Papias and Luke agree that Judas did not commit suicide but that God struck him down, and that the efflux from his body befouled his property. One point of contact between Papias and Acts is particularly intriguing. Papias's description emphasizes the expansion of his body: he was bloated, his head was as large as a chariot, his eyes swelled shut, and his penis enlarged. My translation "became bloated" renders the verb πρησθείς, which probably relates somehow to Luke's notoriously awkward πρηνὴς γενόμενος ("falling face down"). The word πρηνής, "face down," is a hapax legomenon (a word used only once in the New Testament), and it appears only four times in the Septuagint. According to Wis 4:19, one day God will throw the wicked "speechless to the ground [πρηνεῖς]."[10] The textual tradition of this verse suggests the word was problematic to ancient readers. "[T]he corrector of Codex Vaticanus added a note in the margin ἐπὶ πρόσωπον ['on his face'], showing that although he knew what it meant he thought that it might trouble the readers of the ms. which he was preparing."[11]

Readers of Acts 1 might have had the same trouble. The Armenian and Old Georgian versions—presumably derived from the Old Syriac—read as though the Greek text behind them read πρησθείς or perhaps πεπρησμένος: *Being swollen up,* he burst in the middle and all his guts poured out." Some scholars have conjectured that πρησθείς is, in fact, the original reading in Acts 1:18, as in Papias.[12]

Most scholars, however, conclude that Luke wrote πρηνὴς γενόμενος and that its awkwardness soon led to misunderstandings. In fact, the text of Acts known to Papias already may have read πρησθείς. Additional evidence for this reading may come from the *Acts of Thomas,* which speaks of the apostle slaying a dragon "that swelled up, burst open, and died, and poison and gall poured forth from him [ὁ δὲ δράκων φυσηθεὶς ἐλάκησεν καὶ ἀπέθανεν, καὶ ἐξεχύθη αὐτοῦ ὁ ἰὸς καὶ ἡ χολή]."[13] The passage almost certainly imitates Acts 1:18, and the use of φυσηθείς, "swelled up," makes best sense if the text it imitated read πρησθείς. The *Acts of Thomas* was composed in Syria, and apparently it was the Old Syriac version of the Acts of the Apostles that informed the Armenian and Old Georgian accounts of Judas's death, perhaps based on a similar Greek text. Unfortunately, it is impossible to know if the scribal variant in Acts 1 influenced Papias or if knowledge of Papias's account prompted a scribe to produce the variant.

If Luke indeed wrote the word πρηνής, why? Although it was rare in Luke's day, it was common in Homer's to describe the deaths of cowards. When epic heroes fought bravely, they received their wounds facing their enemies and thus fell backwards (ὕπτιος). But cowards who turned from battle were struck from behind and fell πρηνής, "face down." The weapon, usually a spear, struck the coward in the back and drove him forward, face down to the earth, πρηνής. The spear, entering the back, forced his bowels through the stomach to the earth. For example, as the Trojan Scamandrius fled, Menelaus sent a spear through his chest and he "fell forward [ἤριπε. . . πρηνής]."[14] Menelaus again sent a spear through the back of a warrior, Dolops, "and he slumped forward [πρηνὴς ἐλιάσθη]."[15] Menoetius's spear slew Areilycus as he turned to flee, "and he fell on his face on the ground [πρηνὴς ἐπὶ γαίῃ κάππεσ']."[16]

Luke's depiction of Judas's death also states that he "burst in the middle [ἐλάκησεν μέσος]." This form of the verb can be the aorist of two verbs, neither of which appears elsewhere in the New Testament or in the Septuagint. The verb λακάω means "to burst"; it is quite rare. More common is the verb λάσκω, meaning "to sound out," or "to crack," which the *Iliad* uses for the cracking of bones in warfare. Menelaus struck Peisander in the head with a spear. "The bones cracked [λάκε], and his bloody eyeballs fell at his feet in the dust. Doubling over, he fell."[17]

Luke ends the depiction of Judas's death by saying that "all his guts poured out [ἐξεχύθη πάντα τὰ σπλάγχνα αὐτοῦ]." This revolting expression, too, finds parallels in Homer, who described the death of Polydorus like this: "Swift-footed noble Achilles struck him square on the back with a cast of his spear as he darted past . . . ; clean through went the spear point beside the navel, and he fell to his knees with a groan and a cloud of darkness enfolded him, and as he slumped he clasped his intestines to him with his hands."[18] Two passages in the epic use an identical formula for disgorging that approaches Acts 1:18: ἐκ δ' ἄρα πᾶσα χύντο χαμαὶ χολάδες ("and out on the ground gushed all his bowels"; ἐκ . . . χύντο is tmesis for ἐκχέω).[19] Readers familiar with Homer would have taken Judas's falling forward to suggest cowardice. His bursting in the middle with his insides spilling to the earth suggest that he was struck with an invisible shaft from behind, like the cowards of epic. But readers less familiar with Homer would have found the expression strange. In his speech in *Iliad* 7, Nestor does not use the word πρηνής, but he does use its antonym to describe the fall of noble Areïthous: Lycurgus "stabbed him with a spear in the middle [μέσον], and he was forced backward [ὕπτιος] to the earth."[20] Eustathius's note on this text shows the importance of the use of ὕπτιος here: "The expression 'he was forced backward' makes it clear that the club-bearer [Areïthous] was not fleeing when he fell but was fighting him face-to-face. If he were fleeing, he would have fallen face down [πρηνής]."[21]

Peter's speech continues by developing the theme of the lottery that he had adumbrated earlier. When speaking of Judas's inclusion among the Twelve, Luke used the unusual expression "he received the lot [ἔλαχεν τὸν κλῆρον] of this service." Luke understood Ps 109 to require someone else to take Judas's place, someone "who has traveled with us the whole time that the Lord Jesus came and went among us, beginning from the baptism of John until the day he was taken from us."[22] One of those eligible and willing would be chosen by lot.

The responses to the speeches of Nestor and Peter again are similar.

Iliad 7.161	Acts 1:23
And nine men all stood [ἀνέσταν].	*And they presented* [ἔστησαν] *two men.*

What follows in both works are the names of those who volunteered. These lists of names do not resemble each other — in Acts only two men stood — but the list in the epic does resemble the list of the eleven disciples earlier in Acts 1. Compare the following, especially the end of the list.

Iliad 7.161–69	Acts 1:13–14
And nine men all stood.	They ascended to the upper room
The first by far to stand was Agamemnon,	where they stayed — Peter, and John, and
lord of men, then arose mighty Diomedes	James, and Andrew, Philip and Thomas,
of Tydeus, and after them the two Ajaxes,	Bartholomew and Matthew, James son of
clothed in impetuous valor, and after them	Alphaeus and Simon the Zealot and
Idomeneus and Idomeneus's comrade	Judas son of James —
Meriones, equal to man-slaying Enyalius,	
and after them Eurypylos, glorious son of	
Euaemon, and up jumped Thoas of	
Andaemon and noble Odysseus —	
all these [πάντες ἄρ᾽ οἵ γ᾽] wanted to	*all these* [οὗτοι πάντες] were continuing
fight with noble Hector.	together in prayer.

Lists of apostles appear three other times in the New Testament, but in no other case does a summary statement conclude it as here in Acts 1:14.[23]

To decide between Barsabbas Justus and Matthias, the disciples cast lots, the same procedure used in *Iliad* 7. Nestor told the contenders, "One after the other now cast your lots [to determine] who wins [κλήρῳ . . . ὅς κε λάχησιν]." In fact, the two accounts are arrestingly similar.

Iliad 7.175–83	Acts 1:24–26a
And *each man marked his lot* [κλῆρον]	[Peter's statement in 1:17 anticipates
and cast it into the helmet of Atreides	the casting of lots: Judas won his ministry
Agamemnon.	with the Twelve in a lottery of sorts
	(ἔλαχεν τὸν κλῆρον).]

And the people prayed and lifted their
hands to the gods, looking up to broad
heaven, one would *speak* [εἴπεσκεν] like
this: "*Father Zeus,*
[I pray that] Ajax may *win the lot*
[λαχεῖν], or the son of Tydeus,
or the king of gold-rich Mycene himself."

So they spoke, and the horseman, *Nestor*
of Gerenia, *shook them,* and out from the
helmet popped *the lot* [κλῆρος] that
they had wanted: that of Ajax.

And they prayed

and *said* [εἶπαν]:
"*Lord,* knower of hearts,
indicate which of these two men
you select *to take* [λαβεῖν]
the place of this service and apostleship
that Judas forsook to go to his own place."
And *they gave them lots* [κλήρους],

and *the lot* [κλῆρος] fell
for Matthias.

In both columns the volunteers who stand mark lots, and in both columns the large group of those present pray for a favorable selection. Each prayer begins with a direct address ("Father Zeus"/"Lord, knower of hearts"). The army in the *Iliad* asks Zeus to select Ajax; the crowd in Acts asks God or, more likely, Christ to select the more worthy of the two. In both columns the volunteers cast lots to determine the winner.

These parallels are remarkable, but apparently have never before been investigated for evidence of imitation. Scholars have sought for the origin of the election of Matthias not in the *Iliad* but in pre-Lucan tradition. The next chapter will survey the proposals advanced for the genesis of the story and will apply our criteria for mimesis.

Jerusalem Legend or Homeric Imitation?

As we have seen, Luke surely knew a tradition about the death of Judas insofar as he shares intriguing details with Matthew's version; some of Papias's account likewise may be independent of Acts. For the casting of lots to replace Judas, however, no independent evidence exists. Furthermore, "The structure, vocabulary, style, motifs, and line of thought in verses 21ff point to Lucan formation so strongly that any underlying tradition in these verses is unrecognizable."[1] But typically Lucan traits have not deterred form critics from positing a tradition behind this material as well. The proposals run the gamut from oral tradition to a written source and from an Aramaic environment to a Greek.[2] The case for a pre-Lucan tradition usually consists of a combination of the following arguments: (1) the names Joseph Barsabbas Justus and Matthias are traditional; (2) the casting of lots was common among Palestinian Jews; and (3) the selection of Matthias is inconsistent with Luke's understanding of apostleship elsewhere.

1. It is indeed unlikely that Luke created ex nihilo the names Joseph Barsabbas Justus and Matthias; the names are not significant of themselves, and neither appears later in Acts.[3] Luke's interest in the men resides solely in their eligibility to complete the number of twelve apostles. But the appearance of traditional names is no guarantee that the narrative in which they appear also is traditional.

2. The claim that the casting of lots was a Palestinian Jewish practice appears so frequently in modern commentaries that it has become an axiom.[4] Perhaps the

most exhaustive treatment of casting lots in antiquity is that of Victor Ehrenberg, published in 1927 in the prestigious *Real-Encyclopädie der classischen Altertumswissenschaft,* known as Pauly-Wissowa in honor of its editors.[5] Without evidence or argumentation, Ehrenberg stated that "no influence is discernible" on ancient Christianity "from the lottery of the profane pagan world."[6] Christians inherited the practice from Jewish culture.

As we shall see, this assessment is too facile. Casting lots was indeed common in ancient Israel, but it became increasingly unpopular after the Exile, and by the first century, some Jewish intellectuals ridiculed it as a method for selecting leaders. Quite apart from the literary parallels in *Iliad* 7, the most analogous lotteries in Luke's day were pagan.

Throughout ancient Mediterranean cultures, people cast lots to remove human interference in decision-making. Everyone in the lottery placed a distinctive token such as a pebble, a potsherd, or a bean into an open-topped container, like Agamemnon's helmet in *Iliad* 7. A neutral party then shook the container and the lot "went out" or "was cast" from the container and "fell" to the earth. The lot thus "falls" for the person identified with the token. The lottery is not a drawing in which someone blindly takes the winning token. In the casting of lots, no one touches the token itself until it pops out. For this reason, the casting of lots ensured fairness. In some cases, however, the lot functioned as divination, offering the deity the opportunity to act. "The lot is cast into the lap, but the decision is the Lord's alone."[7] Pagan sailors cast lots to expose Jonah's guilt.[8] A lottery thus might follow a prayer for a favorable outcome, as in Acts 1 and *Iliad* 7.[9]

One finds evidence of casting lots for the distribution of property in ancient Israel.[10] According to the Book of Joshua, by casting lots the twelve tribes of Israel parceled out the conquered lands of Palestine.[11] The author of 1 Samuel tells of the selection of Saul as Israel's first king. Candidates for the lottery included all adult males, whom the first casting of lots narrowed to the tribe of Benjamin. From the families of Benjamin the second lot chose the family of the Matrites. The last lot chose Saul, who reluctantly accepted the job.[12] Lots never again selected an Israelite king, and lotteries for the distribution of property likewise became increasingly rare.[13]

One arena of Jewish life in first-century Palestine, however, used lots often. Priestly families in Judea used a lottery for assigning the times of service and responsibilities of the priestly families at the Temple. 1 Chronicles 24–26 describes the practice, and Luke himself refers to it. "Once when he [Zechariah] was serving as priest before God and his section was on duty, he was chosen by lot, according to the custom of the priesthood, to enter the sanctuary of the Lord and offer incense."[14] Some scholars have argued that this sacerdotal lottery informed the election of Matthias in Acts, but the usage is not as parallel as some have suggested.[15] Sacerdotal lotteries did not select priests — who had obtained their status by heredity — but merely distributed temporary duties among them. In Acts, however, the lottery was used to fill the position of leadership and the outcome was permanent.

Josephus records an incident during the Jewish War in which Zealots seized the Temple and insisted that the high priesthood originally was not hereditary but had been determined by lot. They cast lots among the members of an obscure priestly family, and the lot fell to a buffoon named Phanni, who became a laughingstock and an outrage.[16] Even though their use of the lottery in this instance produced a debacle, its motivation was antihierarchical and democratic, at least among priestly families. The revolutionaries justified it with a claim that the lotteries were ancient, perhaps informed by the selection of Israel's first king by lot.

Several scholars have proposed that a Jewish sectarian document among the Dead Sea Scrolls known as the *Rule of the Community* (1QS) provides the key to the selection of Matthias. The *Rule* delineates conditions for membership and leadership at Qumran, and it mentions the lot as one stage in the process of selection. But in each case "the lot" apparently refers not to a ritual of divination but metaphorically to a vote by the leadership, a vote understood to be in accord with the divine will. This text retains the language of the lottery but apparently not the practice.[17]

William A. Beardslee argued that Luke received a tradition that similarly spoke metaphorically of casting lots to describe a vote of the early church to include Matthias among the Twelve. It was Luke who transformed the vote into a literal lottery as it was done among pagans.[18]

> In the Book of Acts, there is little doubt that the choice of Matthias is presented by Luke as a choice by actual casting of lots. Many commentaries observe that in Jewish circles such a method of choice was to be expected, because lot casting was so frequent. The rather fragmentary evidence suggests, on the contrary, that the choice of a responsible official by lot would have been entirely normal in Hellenistic pagan circles, but is unexpected in Judaism. . . . Pseudepigraphic and later rabbinic writings both show that the lot as a medium of numinous presence was remembered from ancient times, but do not suggest that in the present the lot was expected to function for such mediation.[19]

Surely Beardslee was correct. In Greco-Roman antiquity people frequently cast lots to distribute property among equally worthy claimants. The potential beneficiaries might be children, victorious soldiers, or citizens.[20] According to Greek mythology, Zeus, Poseidon, and Hades cast lots to divide the universe; Zeus won the sky, Poseidon the sea, and Hades the netherworld.[21] So common was the practice among Greeks that the word for inheritance was κληρονομία, the word for heir was κληρονόμος, and the verb for inheriting was κληρονομέω, all referring to the law (νόμος) of the lottery (κλῆρος). These words became theologically significant in the New Testament, especially for Paul. The word κλῆρος later was used of religious offices, whence our word "cleric."

Lots proved useful for purposes other than inheritance as well, such as deciding who would win the post position in races, who would go first in contests, and who would marry Helen.[22] According to Socrates, souls preparing for reincarnation cast lots for the order in which they would select their new lives back on earth.[23]

The most famous and controversial uses of lots in antiquity involved classical Athens, where a lottery selected magistrates. Every male citizen was eligible to rule, regardless of pedigree or ability. The practice may first have been religious, but it became a hallmark of Athenian democracy.[24] Socrates reportedly ridiculed the practice: Who would feel safe at sea if the pilot were chosen by lot?[25] The Jewish philosopher Philo raised the same objections and contrasted the irrational Athenian practice with Mosaic instructions on the selection of rulers in Deut 17:15 — he cleverly passed over the selection of Saul by lot in silence.[26] Clearly Philo considered lotteries for filling political office more characteristic of pagan culture than Jewish.

If one were looking for analogies to the selection of Matthias one might look to the selection of pagan priests. According to Demosthenes, Athenian nobility nominated candidates for the priesthood of Heracles, and a lottery decided which of them would serve.[27] Syracuse had a law that the citizenry would nominate three men as priests of Jupiter; the lot chose one of them.[28] Even though these practices clearly resemble Acts 1, they shed less light than the selection of Ajax in the *Iliad*.

3. The third argument advanced to defend a tradition behind Acts 1:21–26 claims that these verses conflict with Luke's understanding of apostleship elsewhere in Acts. Clearly, the significance of the Twelve was firmly rooted in the tradition.[29] Furthermore, Luke later shows no interest in Matthias. The completion of the ranks of the Twelve would have been most important in a Palestinian context and in the mission to Jews.[30] The completion of the Twelve also excludes Paul as an apostle, something Luke would not have done on his own, so the argument goes; later he refers to Paul and Barnabas as apostles.[31]

Other scholars have argued, however, that Acts 1:21–26 is central for understanding Luke's apostles and is consistent with his views throughout Acts. In the first place, the selection of Matthias does not exclude others from being apostles. Peter did not propose the lottery to limit the circle of apostles to Twelve but to provide a twelfth "witness of the resurrection." Furthermore, Acts repeatedly emphasizes the evangelism of Jews, by both Peter and Paul.[32]

Luke had sufficient motivation for creating the selection of Matthias insofar as he left a glaring problem unresolved at the end of his Gospel. In Luke 22 the devil enters Judas "who was of the number of the twelve." Jesus eats the Last Supper with his disciples, after which he promises that in his kingdom they will "sit on thrones to judge the twelve tribes of Israel."[33] The reader knows that one of the Twelve will be unworthy of his eschatological duties, and apparently for this reason Luke does not number the thrones, even though the text surely implies that there would be one apostle per tribe.[34] This promise of thrones to the disciples came to Luke from Q, and in this case Matthew probably preserves Q more faithfully: "When the Son of Man sits upon the throne of his glory, you too will sit on twelve thrones, judging the twelve tribes of Israel."[35] Q never mentioned the betrayal of Jesus by Judas, so there is no conflict in Q with Jesus' promise. Matthew seems not to have recognized the problem when he incorporated this saying into his rewriting of Mark, where Judas's betrayal is prominent.[36] But Luke ends his Gospel with Jesus' promise that the disciples would judge the twelve tribes even though one of the twelve was an unrepentant traitor. Luke 24 mentions "the eleven and all the rest," and "the eleven and others with them," thus reminding the reader of Judas's vacancy.[37] By the time the reader completes the Gospel, she may well wonder how Jesus' promise would be fulfilled: Would there be a twelfth judge?

Luke's solution was to complete the ranks of the Twelve with someone who had accompanied the eleven from the beginning, someone whom God (or the risen Jesus) would select through the lot. This person then would become an authoritative witness to the resurrection and accordingly a worthy judge of Israel.[38] Support for this view comes from the death of James, the brother of John, after which there is no effort to find a replacement.[39] The problem presented to Luke by the death of Judas was not his vacating the office but his disqualification as a judge over a tribe of Israel in the kingdom of God.

What Luke needed was a procedure by which the early church could allow God to select someone worthy to replace Judas, and the lottery in *Iliad* 7 was ideal for this purpose. Here nine worthy heroes offer to fight Hector, the army prays that Zeus will select the right man, and the lot indeed selects the one they most want. For the creation of a replacement for Judas Luke needed no historical memory, oral tradition, or source. All he needed was an appropriate literary model; he found it in Homer.

To test the case, one might apply the criteria for mimesis that inform the rest of our study of Acts. Clearly Luke could have had access to this tale insofar as it appears at an important stage in the *Iliad,* the most famous book in Greek antiquity (criterion 1, accessibility). But the parallels fail the criterion of analogy; I have found no imitation of the casting of lots in *Iliad* 7.[40] On the other hand, the third and fourth criteria (density and order) apply to Acts 1 and *Iliad* 7 spectacularly. (Most of the parallels appear in Greek in the Appendix.)

Iliad 7	Acts 1
• The Greek army convened, and no one was both fit and willing to fight Hector.	• One hundred and twenty people — all men [ἄνδρες ἀδελφοί]? — were gathered.
• "Nestor rose up [ἀνίστατο] among the Argives and spoke [μετέειπεν]."	• "Peter rose up [ἀναστάς] in the midst of the brethren and spoke [εἶπεν]."
• Nestor told them how Areïthous had been speared in the middle (μέσον) and fallen back. Lycurgus gave the armor of the slain king to the giant Ereuthalion, whom Nestor then slew.	• Peter told them how Judas had died — falling forward bursting in the middle (μέσος), and spilling his insides.
• Aroused by this speech, "nine men stood [ἀνέσταν]." Homer named all nine, and ended his list with the words,	• Aroused by this speech, "they presented [ἔστησαν] two men." Luke named the two men, and earlier had listed the names of the eleven. He ended that list with the words, "all these [οὗτοι πάντες] were continuing together in prayer."
"all these [πάντες ἄρ' οἵ γ'] wanted to fight with noble Hector."	
• To decide which of the nine would face Hector, Nestor ordered: "One after the other now cast your lots [κλήρῳ] [to see] who wins [λάχῃσιν], for that one will help the well-greaved Achaeans."	• Peter apparently proposed the casting of lots. Note that Judas's own selection as an apostle anticipates the casting of lots: "he was numbered among us and received the lot [ἔλαχεν τὸν κλῆρον] of this service."
• "And each man marked his lot [κλῆρον] and cast it into the helmet of Atreides Agamemnon."	• "And they gave them lots [κλήρους]."
• "And the people prayed and lifted their hands to the gods, looking up to broad heaven, one would speak [εἴπεσκεν] like this: 'Father Zeus, [I pray that] Ajax may win the lot [λαχεῖν], or the son of Tydeus, or the king of gold-rich Mycene himself.'	• "And they prayed and said [εἶπαν]: 'Lord, knower of hearts, indicate which of these two men you select to take [λαβεῖν] the place of this service and apostleship that Judas forsook to go to his own place.' And they gave them lots [κλήρους],
So they spoke, and the horseman, Nestor of Gerenia, shook them, and out from the helmet popped the lot [κλῆρος] that they had wanted: that of Ajax."	and the lot [κλῆρος] fell for Matthias."

Surely these parallels satisfy the criteria of density and order.

Criterion five, distinctive traits, is essential for linking two texts mimetically. No tale in antiquity more closely resembles Acts 1 than *Iliad* 7. Each begins with a crisis (the challenge of Hector or the death of Judas) that prompts a senior statesman (Nestor or Peter) to address the crowd. The contents of the speeches remind the men present of a violent death or deaths (Areïthous and Ereuthalion or Judas) and ends with a proposal that evokes some in the audience to demonstrate their willingness and fitness for the task. The lottery itself in each case consists of the collection of tokens, a prayer by all assembled, and the successful outcome. Furthermore, both works use similar vocabulary for the standing of the speaker (ἀνίστημι in both cases), the presentation of the volunteers (ἀνίστημι or ἵστημι), the lots (κλῆρος in both cases), and the selection (λαγχάνω in both cases).

Several elements in the description of the death of Judas likewise point to the epic, such as the use of the Homeric adjective πρηνής and the verb λάσκω, both of which appear nowhere else in the New Testament. The spilling of Judas's bowels resembles the deaths of many Homeric warriors, especially the death of Patroclus. Luke's combination of Homeric images creates a picture of Judas dying like a fleeing coward struck from behind by a spear and bursting to the ground face first.

The sixth and final criterion is interpretability: What does the reader gain by recognizing Acts 1:15–26 as an imitation of *Iliad* 7.123–83? The purpose of the lottery in the epic was to select a warrior to slay Hector. During the lottery the army prayed that Zeus would select Ajax, their incomparable champion (apart from Achilles who had refused to fight). But in Acts 1 the lottery does not select someone to kill but to serve others as a witness to life through Jesus' resurrection. The qualifications to participate in the lottery were not might and courage but faithfulness in having accompanied the eleven others during Jesus' entire ministry. When the crowd prayed, they did not prefer one candidate to the other but asked that God or Christ choose between them. The next scene in the epic is hand-to-hand between champions, one from the East and one from the West. The next scene in Acts is the reception of the Spirit manifest in the speaking of tongues that allowed the message to be understood by all nations, East and West.

PART Four

Peter's Escape from Prison and Iliad 24

12

Priam's Escape from Achilles and Its Imitators

Ancient literature is peppered with stories of gods, heroes, or "divine men" escaping dangerous situations by means of magically opening doors. In fact, in the Acts of the Apostles one finds three prison escapes: two by Peter (5:17–42 and 12:3–17) and one by Paul (16:16–40). Some scholars have interpreted the empty tomb stories in the gospels as adaptations of the tale-type, and the apocryphal Acts of the Apostles employ the genre repeatedly.[1] Over a dozen other examples appear in ancient texts. According to Acts 12, while Peter slept in prison an angel woke him and facilitated his escape by opening the prison doors and apparently shedding sleep on the guards.

> When Herod was about to bring Peter forth — that very night — he was sleeping between two soldiers bound with two chains, while guards were keeping their watch outside the door. Suddenly an angel of the Lord stood by him, and a light shone in the cell. He struck Peter's side and roused him, saying, "Get up quickly!" His chains fell from his hands, and the angel said to him, "Tie up your belt and put on your sandals." And so he did. The angel said to him, "Throw on your cloak and follow me." Peter went out following him and did not know that what was happening because of the angel was real; he thought he was seeing a vision. They passed through the first guard station, and the second, and came to the iron gate leading to the city that opened for them on its own. Having left, they proceeded along one street, and suddenly the angel left him.[2]

In 1929 Otto Weinreich published an extensive treatment of ancient escape stories that has dominated the discussion ever since.[3] He paid special attention to the motif of the opening door as evidence of an epiphany and found the motif in a wide variety of ancient sources, including Homer, Vergil, Ovid, Philostratus, Apuleius, and especially in Dionysian writings by Euripides and Nonnus. Weinreich concluded that the escape miracles in Acts 12 and 16 came to Luke as independent traditions whose closest analogs may be found among pagan beliefs in miracles and magic, but Luke redacted the stories under the influence of Euripides' *Bacchae,* where the god manifests his power by breaking his shackles and producing an earthquake that opens the prison doors.[4]

Fifty years later, Reinhard Kratz reinvestigated the matter and concluded that Luke did not compose Acts 12 with an eye on the *Bacchae* but with an ear attuned to such epiphanic tales in popular religion.[5] Both studies are indispensable for understanding this fascinating and popular form of religious propaganda, but both lamentably ignored *Iliad* 24, where Hermes shed sleep on guards and opened doors to allow Priam, in a daring rescue of Hector's corpse, to enter and leave the Greek camp unharmed.[6]

This oversight of Priam's escape apparently issues from two causes. First, Homer spent more ink on the king's miraculous entry into the camp of Achilles than on his escape, even though the escape, too, required the guards to be sleeping and the doors open. Second, researchers have focused on the motif of opening doors; had they studied the motif of sleeping guards, they would have shifted their attention from Dionysus to Hermes and from the *Bacchae* to the *Iliad.* The literary tradition concerning Dionysus says nothing concerning the god putting guards to sleep; in fact, the purpose of prison breaks is to demonstrate the god's power to witnesses. The point is not to escape notice but to attract it. Sleep, on the other hand, is the domain of Hermes.[7]

The definitive depiction of Hermes the soporific helper is his appearance at the end of the *Iliad,* one of the most privileged narratives of Greek antiquity. Indeed, "Priam's visit to Akhilleus was the most popular scene to be represented in Greek and Roman art of all the episodes in the *Iliad.*"[8] The scene is especially common in Greek vases, though it appears as well on copper and silver cups, and, as one might expect given the necrotic topic, on sarcophagi. No educated Greek reader would have been ignorant of this final, dramatic book of the most famous work of Greek antiquity.

Furthermore, *Iliad* 24 was a favorite mine for literary imitations. Scholars long have recognized the influence of the last book of the *Iliad* on the first book of the *Odyssey.*[9] Aeschylus wrote a play entitled the *Ransoming of Hector,* as did the tyrant and aspiring playwright Dionysius I. Ennius wrote his *Ransoming of Hec-*

tor on the basis of Latin translations of *Iliad* 24.[10] None of these plays survives, nor does Sophocles' *Priam*, which probably dealt with the same subject. Imitations of the rescue of Hector's corpse surface at several points in the *Aeneid*.[11] Statius repeatedly imitated the final book of the *Iliad* in the final book of the *Thebaid*.[12] According to Quintilian, students of rhetoric were required to compose speeches as though they were Priam asking Achilles for Hector's body.[13]

When the curtain opens on *Iliad* 24, Achilles is desecrating Hector's corpse, dragging it behind his chariot. Apollo preserved the body intact and entreated the other gods to show pity because of Hector's piety. Zeus agreed insofar as Hector "was the most beloved of mortals in Ilium to the gods."[14] Zeus sent Iris to Priam to tell him to ransom his son, making the dangerous journey himself and alone, taking only one servant to drive the wagon with the ransom.

Despite the objections of Hecuba, his wife, the king of Troy gathered an enormous ransom and drove across the plain with his servant Idaeus. Zeus took pity on them and spoke to Hermes: "Go and take Priam to the hollow ships so that no one sees or recognizes him."[15] Immediately, Hermes "tied under his feet his sandals — beautiful, immortal, golden — that carried him over the waters and over the boundless land swift as the blasts of the wind. And he took the wand he used to cast spells over the eyes of whomever he wished and also to awaken others who sleep. With this in hand, the mighty Argeiphontes flew and quickly arrived at the land of Troy and the Hellespont."[16] Hermes would use his wand to put Greek guards to sleep.

Several authors imitated this depiction of Hermes' descent. For example, the author of the *Odyssey* says that when Hermes left Olympus to rescue Odysseus from Calypso, he "took the wand he used to cast spells over the eyes of whomever he wished and also to awaken others who sleep."[17] The lines are identical to *Iliad* 24.343–44, but Hermes does not use the wand to put people to sleep in *Odyssey* 5, nor again in Book 24, even though "he held in his hands his beautiful, golden wand that he used to cast spells over the eyes of whomever he wished and also to awaken others who sleep."[18]

Hermes' wand (ῥάβδος in Homer, elsewhere κηρύκειον; Latin *caduceus*) became a frequent prop in ancient fiction and an identifying feature in art, including representations of Priam before Achilles.[19] Vergil probably had *Iliad* 24 in mind when he depicted Mercury (= Hermes) "taking the wand with which he calls pale souls from Orchus and sends others down to miserable Tartarus, gives and deprives sleep."[20] Ovid mentioned Mercury's soporific wand several times: the god used it so he could kill Argus and seduce Chione.[21] He also used it to open locked doors.[22]

Back to Homer: Priam and Idaeus were terrified when they saw Hermes approach disguised as a young soldier. To reassure them, the god took Priam's hand and spoke gently, telling him that even though he was one of Achilles' troops, he meant them no harm. The king then asked him to guide them to the bivouac of Achilles. He agreed, leaped into the chariot, took the reins, and led the way to the camp. The following passage contains motifs particularly relevant to Acts 12.

> When they arrived at the walls and the ditch protecting the ships, where the guards [φυλακτῆρες] were beginning to prepare their supper, the messenger Argeiphontes shed sleep over all of them, instantly opened the gates [πύλας], thrust aside the bolts, and brought Priam inside together with the glorious gifts on the wagon. . . . [At Achilles' hut] only one bar of pine secured the door [θύρην], but one that three Achaeans used to drive home, and three used to draw back the great bolt of the doors [θυράων] — three of the others, though Achilles would drive it home on his own. Then Hermes the Helper opened it for the old man and brought in the marvelous gifts for the swift-footed son of Peleus. He dismounted from behind the horses to the ground and said: "Old man, I who have come to you am an immortal god, Hermes; for my father sent me to escort you. But now I am going back. . . ." When he had said this, Hermes went off to high Olympus.[23]

Priam went to Achilles, knelt before him, and "kissed his terrible, murderous hands that had slain his many sons."[24] He offered the ransom, and Achilles agreed to the exchange: "I know in my mind — nor has it escaped my attention — that one of the gods brought you to the swift ships of the Achaeans. For no mortal would dare come into the camp — not even one in his prime. And no mortal could escape the notice of the guards [φυλάκους] or easily shove back the bar of our doors [θυράων]."[25] The two men then dined and went to bed; Priam intended to return to Troy with the corpse in the morning.

Here Priam does not escape danger; he safely enters it. The first imitation of this passage appears in *Odyssey* 7: Odysseus must enter the palace of King Alcinous of the Phaeacians without being seen, if he would win his request for a ship to return to Ithaca. Just as Hermes had come to Priam disguised as a young man to sneak him into Achilles' bivouac, Athena came to Odysseus disguised as a young woman for a similar purpose.[26] Priam and Odysseus both asked the strangers to guide them to the dangerous setting, and both gods agreed.[27] Just as Hermes "quickly [καρπαλίμως] took in his hands the whip and reins," Athena "quickly [καρπαλίμως] led the way."[28] Athena would not put the guards to sleep; instead, she shed a mist about Odysseus to render him invisible.[29] Priam and Odysseus both bypassed ships on their way. Athena told Odysseus to enter the palace and seek favor from Queen Arete. "Having so spoken, owl-eyed Athena left over the barren sea." In the *Iliad* Hermes had told Priam: " 'Go in and clasp the knees of Achilles. . . .' Having so spoken, Hermes left for high Olympus."[30] Both heroes entered the houses unseen, past guards and protective doors, and found a powerful leader finishing dinner.[31] In the *Odyssey* it is Athena, not Hermes, who facilitates the entry, but Hermes is not entirely absent. When Odysseus entered the palace, he found the Phaeacians engaged in their customary evening ritual: pouring libations to Hermes for a good night's sleep.[32] Odysseus then grasped the knees of Queen Arete as the mist dissipated; Priam had grasped the knees of Achilles and then was recognized. Achilles and his comrades were filled with wonder; the Phaeacians fell silent.[33] Priam and Odysseus both presented their requests, won approval, dined, and retired for the night. The following five lines are nearly identical in the two epics: in each tale the host commanded maid-servants "to place a bed under the portico, throw over it beautiful purple blankets, spread over them a bedspread, and place over these wooly cloaks to wear. They went from the hall holding torches in their hands. When they had quickly made the plush bed . . ."[34] Although one may explain the parallels by appealing to the conventions of epic performance, the distinctive verbal similarities between the two stories and the gratuitous reference to Hermes just as Odysseus crosses the palace threshold suggest literary borrowing.[35]

Lucian expected his readers to know of Hermes' soporific powers sufficiently to appreciate his parodies of it. For example, in one of his works a rooster claims that Hermes had empowered one of his feathers to open locked doors and keep people from being seen.[36] Another character says that he wants Hermes to give him a magic ring, "to put to sleep anyone I want and open every door when I approach, releasing bolts and removing bars."[37] Here almost certainly is a parody of *Iliad* 24.

Here is the conclusion of Homer's tale of Priam's journey. Priam and Idaeus slept in Achilles' home, expecting to return to Troy with the corpse in the morning.

> The others—both gods and men, chariot-fighters—slept throughout the night, subdued by soft sleep. But sleep did not overtake Hermes the Helper, who debated in his mind how to escort King Priam from the ships unnoticed by the powerful gatekeepers. He stood over his head and spoke to him, saying: "Old man, you have no concern for harm—the way you are still sleeping among your enemies—since Achilles has spared you. Now you have ransomed your dear son and have given much for him. But if Agamemnon, son of Atreus, learns of you, or if all the Achaeans learn of you, your sons whom you left behind might have to give three times such a ransom for your life."
>
> So he spoke, and the old man was terrified and awoke his herald. Hermes yoked the horses and mules for them, and he himself swiftly drove them through the camp. No one knew about them. But when they came to the ford of the fair-flowing river . . . , then Hermes went up to high Olympus.[38]

Priam was able to escape because Hermes kept the guards sleeping and the doors and gates open.

Priam's escape seems to have been the model for several literary escapes from danger. For example, according to the *Argonautica* Hera frightened Medea by reminding her of plots against Jason; the young woman decided to flee Colchis with the Argonauts. She rushed out of the house at night, barefoot and veiled, hoping the guards would not see her. Because of her magical powers, "the bolts of the doors [θυρέων] receded for her on their own," and "none of the guards [φυλακτήρων] knew it, as she rushed away unseen by them." The density of Homeric vocabulary implies mimesis of *Iliad* 24.[39]

Nonnus of Panopolis, a prolix and pretentious poet of late antiquity, told several versions of Dionysian prison breaks, but he also imitated *Iliad* 24. Nonnus wrote that Hermes descended from Olympus and "with his all-enchanting wand shed sweet sleep on the tireless eyes of the guards [φυλάκων] right down the line," to protect the worshipers of Dionysus. "The women made no noise as wingless Hermes led them secretly through the city. With his divine hand he opened the strong bolt of the high gates [πυλάων]."[40] The concentration of distinctive vocabulary shared with *Iliad* 24 and the presence of Hermes once again suggest imitation.[41]

Thus far we have seen evidence of imitations of Priam's breaking into Achilles' camp (the *Odyssey* and Lucian) and his breaking out again (Apollonius Rhodius and Nonnus). The Hellenistic Jewish author Artapanus (first century B.C.E.) has Moses breaking into danger and breaking out again, as in *Iliad* 24, but in the opposite order: Moses escaped the prison and then broke into Pharaoh's palace. Underlining identifies elements most resonant with the *Iliad*.

> Upon learning this, the king imprisoned him. When *night* came, *all the doors* [θύρας] *of the prison opened of their own accord,* and *some of the guards* [φυλάκων] died while others *were overcome with sleep* [ὕπνου]; also, their weapons broke into pieces. Moses *left the prison* and went to the palace. *Finding the doors* [θύρας] *open,* he *entered the palace* and aroused the king while *the guards* [φυλάκων] were *sleeping on duty. Startled at what happened,* the king ordered Moses to declare the name of the god who had sent him. He did this scoffingly. Moses bent over and spoke into the king's ear, but when the king heard it, he fell over speechless. But Moses picked him up and he came back to life again.[42]

No biblical evidence exists for a Mosaic prison break. The inspiration for the passage was not Exodus but it could have been Priam's exodus from Achilles in *Iliad* 24. It is in traditions about Hermes that one is mostly likely to find sleeping guards and opening doors.

Early Christian narratives, too, show the influence of Priam's rescue of Hector's corpse. In *The Homeric Epics and the Gospel of Mark* I argued that Mark patterned Joseph of Arimathea after Priam. Like Priam, Joseph "dared" to go at night to Pilate to request Jesus' body to provide it a fitting burial. Like Achilles, Pilate was amazed by the request and allowed Joseph to shroud the body and take it away. Two women saw where Joseph laid the body, and three women came to the tomb Easter morning to give it appropriate care, like Andromache, Hecuba, and Helen in the epic.[43] In Mark, however, there is no equivalent to Hermes, sleeping guards, or opening doors: not until Easter morning.

It is Matthew's version of the empty tomb story that most resembles stories of Hermes. According to Matthew, the Jewish authorities stationed guards at the tomb to keep the corpse from being stolen. Then, at dawn, "there was a great earthquake; for an angel of the Lord, descending from heaven, came and rolled back the stone and sat on it. His appearance was like lightning, and his clothing white as snow. For fear of him the guards shook and became like dead men."[44] When the guards reported what had happened, the authorities bribed them to say, "His disciples came by night and stole him away while we were asleep." Priam, of course, had gone to Achilles at night and taken away the corpse of his son while the guards slept. To keep the guards from getting into trouble for confessing to sleeping on duty, the authorities promised that if Pilate learned of it, "we will satisfy him and keep you out of trouble."[45] The author of Matthew probably did not have *Iliad* 24 in mind when writing this tale, but the similarities with traditions about Hermes, Zeus's ἄγγελος, are intriguing.[46]

Priam's entry to Achilles' bivouac is more likely to have informed a passage in the *Acts of Andrew and Matthias,* where Andrew enters a Myrmidonian prison to rescue the apostle Matthias from cannibals.

> Andrew rose up and went to the city *without anyone seeing him*. They went to the prison, and Andrew saw *seven guards* [φύλακας] *standing at the door* [θύραν] *of the prison guarding it*. He prayed silently, and *the seven guards* [φύλακες] *fell and died. When he came to the prison door* [θύραν], *Andrew marked it with the sign of the cross and it opened automatically. On entering the prison* with his disciples, he saw Matthias sitting, singing by himself. When he saw Andrew, Matthias rose, and *they greeted each other with a holy kiss*.[47]

Several details here suggest imitation of *Iliad* 24. In the first place, the city was named Myrmidonia, or the city of the Myrmidons, who were Achilles' troops according to Homer. Andrew's entrance "without anyone seeing him" resembles Priam's entrance to the Greek camp. Achilles told Priam he knew a god had helped him: "No mortal could escape the notice of the guards." Instead of putting guards to sleep, Andrew killed them and opened the door with the sign of the cross. Priam's first gesture inside the house was to kiss Achilles' hand; Andrew and Matthias immediately kissed each other.[48] Several prison breaks appear in other Christian apocryphal writings, usually as imitations of biblical accounts or of earlier apocryphal stories.[49]

If Peter's escape in Acts 12 imitated Priam's in *Iliad* 24, it surely would satisfy the first two criteria, accessibility and analogy. The next chapter treats in detail an extensive parody of Priam's rescue that will make the case for Luke's imitation even clearer insofar as the mimetic devices and strategies used there illumine those used in Acts.

Alexander's Escape from Darius

A particularly fascinating imitation of Priam's escape from the Achaean camp appears in the *Alexander Romance,* pseudonymously attributed to Callisthenes, historian to Alexander the Great, and composed in the late second or the third century C.E. Among other things it tells how Alexander, disguised as Hermes, daringly entered and escaped from Darius's palace. This episode merits special treatment insofar as it entices its readers to recognize it as a parody of the end of the *Iliad.*[1]

> That night Alexander slept and in a dream saw Ammon standing by him in the guise of Hermes — with his herald's staff [κηρύκιον], cloak, wand [ῥάβδον], and a Macedonian cap on his head — saying to him, "Alexander, my child, when it is time for help, I am with you. If you send a messenger [ἄγγελον] to Darius, he will betray you; you yourself become a messenger [ἄγγελος] and go in the costume you see me in." Alexander said to him, "It is dangerous for me, a king, to be my own messenger [ἄγγελον]." Ammon said to him, "But with a god as your helper, no harm can befall you."[2]

The reader should see here an imitation of Hermes' appearances to Priam in *Iliad* 24. In the first appearance, Hermes takes with him his soporific wand and disguises himself as a Myrmidon; in the second, he appears as himself to Priam as he sleeps. In the novel, Ammon disguises himself as Hermes, wand in hand, and appears to Alexander as he sleeps.

The content of the speech, however, resembles Iris's appearance earlier in the same book when she tells the king to go to Achilles alone: "Do not let death or any fear concern your thoughts, for such a guide will go with you, Argeiphontes [Hermes] who will lead you. . . . Achilles himself will not kill you and he will thwart others from doing so."[3] Ammon told Alexander, "with a god as your helper, no harm can befall you." The responses to the visions also are similar. "Having received this oracle, Alexander arose rejoicing and shared it with his satraps; but they advised him not to do it." After Priam received his instructions from Iris, he told Hecuba, who was appalled by the idea of his going alone to Achilles and tried to talk him out it.[4] Despite the discouraging responses of others, Priam and Alexander both decided to undertake their dangerous journeys.

"Taking with him a satrap by the name of Eumelus and gathering three horses, Alexander set out immediately and reached the river Stranga."[5] According to the epic, Priam ordered his sons to yoke two horses to his chariot and two mules to the wagon to be driven by Idaeus.[6] The men set out at night and stopped at the river Scamander to allow the animals to drink.[7] The river Stranga that separated the camps of Alexander and Darius in the novel is fictional and is said to freeze and thaw with dangerous speed. When frozen, "beasts and wagons pass over it"; when thawed, it sweeps away anything trying to cross it.[8] In this respect it is treacherous, like the Scamander, which Priam had to cross to get to and from the Greek camp and which earlier had fought with Achilles. "Alexander found the river solid and put on the costume he had seen Ammon wearing in his dream," that is, Ammon's disguise as Hermes. In the epic, Hermes first appeared to Priam as he and Idaeus stopped at the river Scamander. It was at the river Stranga that Alexander dressed himself as Hermes. Alexander, as his own ἄγγελος, "messenger," now is decked out like Hermes, the ἄγγελος of Zeus.

Alexander then "sat on his horse and crossed alone." In the *Iliad* Hermes, disguised as a Myrmidon, leaped into Priam's chariot at the banks of the Scamander and drove it to the Greek camp. Eumelus wanted to accompany Alexander to Darius's palace, but Alexander refused: "Stay here with the two colts. I have the help of him who gave me the oracle to take on this appearance and to go on alone."[9] Similarly in the epic, Priam left Idaeus outside Achilles' home "holding the horses and mules."[10]

"Alexander went on his way and approached the gates [πυλῶν] of Persis. The guards [φρούραρχοι] there, seeing him in such a getup, supposed he was a god. Detaining him, they asked him who he was. Alexander said to them, 'Present me before King Darius, and I will report who I am to him.'"[11] Homer's Hermes, disguised as a Myrmidon, had led Priam past the guards and gates; ironically, it was Alexander disguised as Hermes that accomplished the same feat, though without sleeping guards and magically opening gates.

When Alexander presented himself to Darius, everyone marveled at "his strange appearance," and "Darius nearly fell down before him, thinking him a god descended from Olympus. . . . Darius was sitting . . . and had scepters on either side and ranks of thousands of men around him. Darius asked him who he was, gawking at him wearing a costume he had never seen before. . . . Alexander replied, 'I am the messenger [ἄγγελος] of King Alexander.' "[12] By claiming that he, as Hermes, was the messenger of Alexander, he implied that King Alexander was like Zeus. This scene resembles the beginning of the meeting of Priam and Achilles. Achilles, too, was seated when Priam "found him," and "Achilles was amazed when he saw god-looking [θεοειδέα] Priam, and the others, too, were amazed."[13]

In his conversation with Darius, Alexander spoke with authority that surprised the king: "You respond daringly as though you were my comrade." Darius then invited Alexander to dine: " 'I shall go to my usual dinner, and you will dine with me. . . .' Having spoken thus, Darius took Alexander by the hand and went inside his palace. Alexander took it as a good sign that he was led by the hand of the tyrant."[14] In the *Iliad* Achilles was amazed at Priam's courage and invited him to dine.[15] Three times Achilles took Priam "by the hand": once to push him away, once to raise him up, and once to reassure him: "When he had thus spoken, he took the old man's right hand."[16]

At the dinner, the wine flowed freely, and every time Alexander drained a golden cup he put it in his pocket, claiming that he was accustomed to doing so at the banquets of King Alexander. By so doing, he impressed the Persians with the Macedonian's wealth and generosity. When he fled, Alexander would take the cups with him.[17] Among the treasures that Priam had given Achilles for ransoming the body of Hector was a golden drinking cup.[18]

Achilles had Priam sleep outside his home to avoid being recognized by any counselor who might come to him during the night. "If one of them should see you during the swift black night, he might immediately disclose it to Agamemnon."[19] Hermes appeared to Priam during the night warning him to leave lest he be discovered.[20] Alexander ran the same danger of being discovered at Darius's banquet, where a Persian emissary did indeed recognize him.

After Hermes' warning, Priam woke Idaeus, mounted his chariot, and escaped unseen. When they arrived at the Scamander, Hermes left them. Alexander, on the other hand, had no god to guide him or put the guards to sleep, so he had to fend for himself—still in his Hermes disguise. "Darius and the feasters were very drunk. So Alexander . . . jumped up . . . and left secretly. Mounting his colt to escape the danger and finding a Persian guard [φύλακα] at the gate [πυλῶνι], he killed him and left the city of Persis."[21] Alexander outran and outwitted the Persian pursuers and crossed the river Stranga just as it was melting. It swept his horse downstream, but he himself won the shore, mounted a spare from Eumelus, and rode back safely to the camp.

This tale surely satisfies the criteria for mimesis. The story in the epic was accessible and we have seen analogous imitations of the scene, especially in stories about Hermes' wand. The following columns show that the parallels are dense and often sequential (criteria three and four).

Iliad 24	*Alexander Romance*
• Iris appeared to Priam telling him to go to Achilles alone and not to fear death; Hermes would go with him.	• Ammon appeared to Alexander in the likeness of Hermes telling him to go to Darius and not to fear death, for a god would aid him.
• Hermes went to Priam with his wand, but took on the appearance of a Myrmidon.	• He must dress himself as Hermes, with a "herald's staff, cloak, wand, and a Macedonian cap."
• Priam told Hecuba of the vision, but she begged him not to go.	• Alexander told his comrades of the vision, "but they advised him not to do it."
• Priam decided to go.	• Alexander decided to go.
• Priam's sons yoked the horses and mules.	• Alexander gathered three horses.
• Priam took Idaeus to drive the wagon.	• Alexander took Eumelus to bring the horses.
• Hermes appeared to Priam at the river Scamander.	• At the river Stranga Alexander donned his Hermes disguise.
• Idaeus would stay outside the gate with the animals while Priam entered.	• Eumelus stayed at the river with the horses while Alexander entered.
• Priam was able to approach Achilles because Hermes had opened the gates and put the guards to sleep.	• Alexander was able to approach Darius because the guards were taken aback by his disguise as Hermes.
• Homer called Priam "god-looking."	• Darius viewed Alexander as a god.
• Achilles was amazed at his boldness.	• Darius was amazed at his boldness.
• Achilles invited Priam to dine.	• Darius invited Alexander to dine.
• Achilles took Priam's hand to comfort him.	• Darius took Alexander's hand, which gave him comfort.
• Priam feared someone other than Achilles would learn his identity.	• Someone at the dinner recognized Alexander's identity.
• Priam and Idaeus rode away past the gates and guards with Hermes' aid.	• Alexander rode away past the gates and guards dressed as Hermes.
• The guards were sleeping.	• The soldiers were drunk; Alexander slew the guard.
• Priam and Idaeus crossed the Scamander and returned to Troy.	• Alexander crossed the Stranga and returned to the camp with Eumelus.

To alert his readers to the parody, the author used several distinctive traits (criterion five), including the naming of Hermes, the mention of his magical wand, and the double fording of a river. Particularly telling are the depictions of Eumelus and the river Stranga. The name Eumelus is a literary flag pointing to the *Iliad* where a character of the same name is a charioteer "excelling in horsemanship." The horses he drove were the best in the Greek cavalry, and he was awarded first prize at the famous chariot race in *Iliad* 23.[22] Ancient hippiatricians used his name as a pseudonymous authority for their craft.[23]

No less significant is the depiction of the Stranga River as freezing and thawing unexpectedly. Here is Homer's description of the river Scamander in *Iliad* 22: "They [Achilles and Hector] came to the two fair-flowing springs, where the two sources of the eddying Scamander pour forth. One of them flows with warm water, and smoke issues from it as from a blazing fire. The other even in the summer flows as cold as hail or frigid snow or ice from water."[24] The name of the river, too, may be significant. It comes from the root στραγγ- whence the English word "strangle" and cognates in other European languages via the derivative Latin *strangulo*. The root can be used passively of something strangled or actively of something that strangles. The river Stranga is described as "one stade wide," or about two hundred yards; it hardly seems to have been strangled to a trickle. Surely is it wiser to take the name in an active sense, the "Strangler River." In the next episode it unleashes its dangers and drowns many Persians.[25] If one takes Stranga in this active sense, the river again resembles the mighty Scamander as depicted in *Iliad* 21, where it fought to drown Achilles.

The author of *Alexander Romance* surely expected some of his readers to see in the story of Alexander's ruse an emulation of Priam's rescue of Hector's corpse (criterion six). Whereas the King of Troy needed Hermes to get safely to and from Achilles' home, the King of Macedon himself, disguised as Hermes, went safely to and from Darius using only his courage, wits, and strength. Priam was passive; Alexander was his own Hermes. Priam made his perilous request to Achilles in the presence of two other soldiers, whereas Alexander made his request to Darius in the presence of thousands. Priam gave Achilles an enormous ransom, including a golden cup; Alexander brought nothing to Darius and escaped with the king's own golden cups.

The previous chapter proposed that Priam's rescue of Hector's corpse served as a model for Odysseus's entrance into the palace of Alcinous, for Medea's escape from Colchis in Apollonius Rhodius, for Moses' escape from prison in Artapanus, for Joseph's rescue of Jesus' body in Mark, for the empty tomb story in Matthew, for Andrew's entry into the Myrmidonian prison to rescue Matthias in the *Acts of Andrew,* for the Maenads' escape in Nonnus, and for references to Hermes in Vergil, Ovid, and Lucian. This chapter compared a passage in the

Alexander Romance with Homer's tale of Priam and Achilles and argued that the parody works only if the reader is aware of its retelling of its antecedent. Many of these examples flag their relationship to the epic by naming Hermes explicitly (the *Odyssey,* Vergil, Ovid, Lucian, Nonnus, and the *Alexander Romance*). Apollonius Rhodius and all imitations by Jews and Christians (Artapanus, Mark, perhaps Matthew, and the *Acts of Andrew*) not surprisingly are silent about Hermes. The same is true of Acts 12.

14

Peter's Escape from Herod

According to the Acts of the Apostles, "King Herod" locked Peter in a prison, where, in the middle of the night, an "angel of the Lord" told him to leave, opened the doors of the prison, and apparently shed sleep over the guards so that the apostle could leave undetected. Only in Acts is Julius Agrippa I called Herod. The prison escape is sandwiched between his execution of James, John's brother, and his death as divine punishment for hubris. Acts 12:1–23 thus forms a literary unit bracketed by two passages on Herod Agrippa, both of which Luke probably received from tradition.[1] The intervening verses concerning Peter, however, find no external attestation; even so, scholars routinely attribute them to a Judean legend because of alleged "local coloration."[2] As we shall see, it is more likely that Luke himself created the narrative, using *Iliad* 24 as his model.

The mise-en-scènes of the stories in the *Iliad* 24 and Acts 12 are remarkably similar. The rescue of Hector's corpse requires its transport from the Greek encampment to Troy. Homer described Achilles' fortifications as follows: his private dwelling had a double door (θύρη) bolted with a single beam, "but one that three Achaeans used to drive home, and three used to draw back."[3] "No mortal could . . . easily shove back the bar of our doors [θυράων]."[4] Two soldiers waited on him: Automedon and Alcimus. Posted outside the doors, protecting the walls around the encampment, were guards (φυλακτῆρες/φύλακες) at bolted gates (πύλαι).[5]

Here is the scene set by Luke: Paul was shackled between two soldiers in a cell protected by guards outside the door (φύλακές τε πρὸ τῆς θύρας). These guards comprise the "first guard" (πρώτην φυλακήν). A second group was stationed within an iron gate (τὴν πύλην τὴν σιδηρᾶν) leading into the city.[6] Herod had assigned a total of sixteen guards—four squads of four soldiers—corresponding to the four watches of the night according to Roman practice.[7] At any one time during the night, at least four soldiers should have been awake to do their job, presumably two at the first guard and two at the second. The failure of the guards to stay awake would cost them their lives.[8] The following columns delineate the similarities in the scenes.

Achilles' lodging	Peter's prison
• bolted doors (θύρη/θύραι) with two attending soldiers	• bolted doors (θύρη) with two attending soldiers
• guards (φυλακτῆρες/φύλακες) posted at the bolted gates (πύλαι) around the encampment	• guards (φύλακες) posted outside the doors of the cell and others inside the gate (πύλη) leading to the street

After Priam escaped from Achilles, he traveled at night back to the city where the Trojans kept their prayerful vigil for him.[9] Similarly, after Peter left the prison, he made his way at night to the house of Mary, where "fervent prayer for him took place," where "quite a number of people were gathered and at prayer."[10]

Luke's account of Peter's escape mirrors that of Priam so closely that one can view them in parallel columns.

Iliad 24.673–74, 678–82, and 689–91	Acts 12:6b–9a[11]
There at the vestibule of the house they *fell asleep,* the herald and *Priam.* . . .	*That very night* [νυκτί]
They slept throughout the night [παννύχιοι]. . . . But sleep did not overtake Hermes the Helper, who debated in his mind how to escort King Priam from the ships unnoticed by the powerful *gatekeepers* [πυλαωρούς].	*Peter was sleeping* between two soldiers bound with two chains
[Iris is called an "angel" in 24.169 and 173]. *He stood* [στῆ] over *his head*	*while guards* [φύλακες] were keeping their watch *outside the door.* Behold, *an angel of the Lord stood by him* [ἐπέστη], and a light shone in the cell. He struck Peter's side and *roused* him,
and *spoke to him, saying:* . . . [Hermes warned Priam against staying.]	*saying, "Get up* [ἀνάστα] *quickly!"*[12]

So he spoke, and the old man was terrified
and *awoke* [ἀνίστη] his herald. Hermes
yoked the horses and mules for them,

and he himself
swiftly *drove them through the camp.*

His chains fell from his hands,
and the angel *said* to him, "*Tie up your belt
and put on your sandals.*" And so he did.
And he *said* to him, "*Throw on your cloak
and follow me.*"
He *went out following him.*

The similarities between these texts are remarkable. In both the endangered protagonist and his enemies sleep (κοιμήσαντο . . . εὗδον/κοιμώμενος) during the night (παννύχιοι/νυκτί) while guards keep watch at the door (πυλαωρούς/φύλακες . . . πρὸ τῆς θύρας). A divine messenger comes to each, stands (στῆ/ἐπέστη) above him, and wakes him (cf. ἀνίστη/ἀνάστα). Hermes and the angel both attend to details for the journey (the yoking of the chariot and wagon/the dressing of Peter), and lead the way out of danger. Homer does not use the word ἄγγελος of Hermes when he visits Priam, but elsewhere Hermes—like Iris, his female counterpart—was known as Διὸς ἄγγελος, "angel of Zeus."[13] As we have seen, it was Hermes' role as a messenger/angel that Pseudo-Callisthenes exploited for parody in making Alexander, disguised as Hermes, his own messenger to Darius. Other imitations of Hermes' appearance to the sleeping Priam in *Iliad* 24 appear in ancient literature, most obviously in Vergil's *Aeneid*.[14]

Luke describes Peter's escape as follows: "They passed through the first guard station, and the second, and came to the iron gate leading to the city that opened for them on its own. Having left, they proceeded along one street, and suddenly the angel left him. When Peter came to himself, he said, 'Now I know for certain that the Lord sent his angel and rescued me from the hands of Herod and from all that the people of the Jews had expected.'"[15] Even though the text does not say so explicitly, the reader surely is to assume that the guards, like the soldiers at the side of Peter, were asleep.

The text in the following left column describes the activities of Hermes that allowed Priam into the Greek camp, activities necessary also to allow Priam's escape. The text in the right column is Peter's escape.

Iliad 24.443–47
When they arrived at the walls and the
ditch to protect the ships where *the guards*
[φυλακτῆρες] were beginning to prepare
their supper, the messenger Argeiphontes
shed sleep over all of them,
thrust aside the bolts,
opened the gates [πύλας],
and *brought* Priam inside.

Acts 12:10–11a

They passed through the first guard post
[φυλακήν], and *the second,*
[The reader must assume that the angel had
put the guards to sleep.]
and came to *the iron gate* [πύλην] leading to
the city that *opened* for them on its own.
Having left, *they proceeded . . .*

In both columns the divine messenger and the hero pass undetected by sleeping guards and bolted gates. The parallels do not end here.

Before Hermes put the guards to sleep and opened the gates, Priam had supposed his helper was who he had said he was: "I am one of the Myrmidons," Achilles' comrade.[16] After performing these wonders, however, Hermes revealed his identity: " 'I who have come to you am an immortal god, Hermes; for my father sent me to escort you. But now I am going back. . . .' When he had said this, Hermes went off to high Olympus." Of course, Hermes later returned to escort Priam out of the Greek camp, after which he again vanished: "Hermes went up to high Olympus." Similarly, before the angel opened the gates, Peter thought he was dreaming: "He went out following him and did not know that what was happening because of the angel was real; instead, he supposed he was seeing a vision." Peter did not "come to himself" until after his miraculous release from prison. Only then did he tell himself, "Now I know for certain that the Lord sent his angel."

Compare the following:

Iliad 24.692 and 696–97	Acts 12:10b–11b and 12a
But when *they came* to the ford of the fair-flowing river, . . .	Having left, *they proceeded* along one street,
then Hermes went up to high Olympus,[17] but *they drove* the horses *into the city,* with moaning and wailing.	*and suddenly the angel left him. . . .* When he understood this, *he went to the house.*

In both columns as soon as the hero had escaped from danger and reached a neutral location (a river or a street), the divine messenger left (ἀπέβη/ἀπέστη), returning to Olympus or heaven. The heroes in both cases proceeded to their loved ones ("into the city" or "to the house").

When confronted with such parallels a form critic is likely to propose that they issue from Luke's knowledge of the prison escape genre, not necessarily from literary imitation. From the evidence supplied thus far, this would be a possible explanation, especially in light of the popularity of the genre in ancient literature. Even though the parallels are extensive and in many cases sequential, they may point to a common genre and not to mimesis. In the next chapter, however, it will become clear that one can best explain the return of Peter to the believers praying at the home of Mary and John Mark as a strategic imitation of *Iliad* 24.

15

Hellenistic Legend or Homeric Imitation?

For determining whether parallels between two texts are generic or mimetic, the greatest desideratum is the existence of shared features that bind two texts together, traits not found in the genre as a collectivity (criterion five, distinctive traits). To his credit, Reinhard Kratz recognized that one major aspect of Peter's escape is entirely foreign to escape miracles generically: Peter's reception at the home of Mary, the mother of John Mark.[1] Like Weinreich before him, Kratz avoids discussing Acts 12:12–17, and commentators usually ascribe the genesis of the tale to Jerusalem traditions preserved by Luke independent of Peter's escape.[2] It is the peculiarity of this tale that points directly to the *Iliad*. The stone rejected by form critics has become the mimetic cornerstone. Here is the passage in question.

> When he [Peter] understood this [that the angel had caused his escape], he went to the house of Mary, the mother of John who is called Mark, where quite a number of people were gathered and at prayer. When he knocked at the door of the gate, a servant girl named Rhoda came to answer it. Even though she recognized Peter's voice, out of joy she did not open the gate but ran inside and announced that Peter was standing outside the gate. But they said to her, "You're crazy!" She insisted that it was so, but they kept saying, "It is his angel." Peter himself continued knocking. When they finally opened the gate, they saw him and were bewildered. He gestured to them to keep silent, told them how the Lord

had brought him out of the prison, and said, "Report these things to James and the brothers." He left and went off to another place.

This curious episode parallels Priam's return to Troy, his recognition by Cassandra, and his delay in entering the gates.

Several commentators have noted that Mary's house was no hovel. A courtyard and a wall with a locked gate (πύλη) attended by a servant protected it from the street.[3] The house itself held a large group who had gathered for prayer (ἱκανοὶ συνηθροισμένοι). Some scholars have taken this detailed and unusual description of the home as evidence of historical memory, "local color."[4] The description also could come from the Homeric imitation. A wall and gates (πύλαι) protected Troy, where the residents prayed for Priam's return.

Commentators seldom give Rhoda her due: she was clairvoyant. Peter knocked at the door and apparently announced himself, for on the basis of his voice alone "she recognized [ἐπιγνοῦσα]" it was he. Those inside the house did not consider her insightful but witless. This passage resembles Cassandra's recognition of Priam.

Iliad 24.697–700 and 703–6	Acts 12:13–14[5]
[Priam and Idaeus returned to Troy.]	When he knocked at the door of the gate,
None of the men or fair-belted women recognized [ἔγνω] them,	
but *Cassandra*, peer of golden Aphrodite, *having gone up on Pergamus,*	*a servant girl named Rhoda came to answer it.*
recognized [εἰσενόησεν] *her dear father....*	Even though *she recognized* [ἐπιγνοῦσα] *Peter's voice, out of joy* [χαρᾶς] she did not
She wailed and shouted throughout all the city: "Come and see Hector,	open the gate but *ran inside and announced that Peter was standing outside the gate.*
men and women of Troy, if you ever *rejoiced* [χαίρετ'] when he was alive and returned from battle, for he was a great *source of joy* [χάρμα] to the city and to all the people."	

In Homeric epic Cassandra is not clairvoyant, but later readers saw in this text evidence of her supernatural powers of perception.[6]

This may be the last time in Greek or Latin literature that anyone believed Cassandra, the unheeded seer. According to one ancient mythographer, "Because Apollo wanted to make love with her, he promised to teach her to prophesy. She learned the art, but did not make love. For this reason, Apollo deprived her prophecy of persuasion."[7] The Hellenistic poet Lycophron wrote an entire work exploiting her notoriously unpersuasive portents. For 1474 lines a slave reports incredulously her forecasts of the fall of Troy, the return of the Achaeans, and a multitude of other mythic events. According to Quintus Smyrnaeus, Cassandra divined that the Trojan horse would be the city's undoing and told the others, but they would not listen. She complained, "You do not believe me, no matter how much I say."[8] Indeed, they thought her mad.[9] Rhoda, Luke's version of Cassandra, likewise failed to persuade others.[10]

The Trojans greeted Priam outside the gates, where they thronged and wailed so that the king could not enter the city for some time. Only when he told them to take their mourning inside did they allow him to pass. Peter, too, was stuck outside the gate. "Meanwhile, Peter continued knocking; and when they opened the gate they saw him and were amazed. He motioned to them with his hand to be silent, and described for them how the Lord had brought him out of the prison."

The parallels between Acts 12 and *Iliad* 24 are so extensive and in some cases distinctive that one should consider literary contact not only plausible but likely. Material in square brackets appears in Priam's entry into the Greek camp, not in his escape.

Iliad 24	Acts 12:1–17
• Achilles had slain many Trojans, including Hector.	• "King Herod laid violent hands" on many believers and killed James.
• Priam set out at night, while the Trojans, in fear, prayed for his safe return (299–321).	• The king arrested Peter, while the believers in Jerusalem prayed for his release.
• Priam and others slept (κοιμήσαντο) in Achilles' residence surrounded by enemy troops (673–75).	• Peter slept (κοιμώμενος) in jail between two soldiers.
• "Powerful gatekeepers" guarded the door (681).	• "Guards [φύλακες] were keeping their watch [φυλάσσειν] outside the door."
• In the middle of the night Hermes, angel of Zeus, stood (στῆ) over Priam's head and warned him of danger (682–88). Priam awoke Idaeus.	• In the middle of the night "an angel of the Lord" stood by him (ἐπέστη) and told him, "Get up quickly." Peter awoke.
• Hermes yoked the horses and mules (689–90).	• The angel told Peter to get dressed.
• Hermes drove the chariot out of the camp unnoticed by the sleeping guards (691).	• The angel led Peter out of the prison unnoticed by the sleeping guards.
• [To get Priam safely *into* the Greek camp, Hermes had put the Greek guards (φυλακτῆρες/φύλακες) to sleep, and	• To get Peter safely *out of* the prison, the angel apparently put the guards to

thrust back the bolts of the gates and the bar to the door (453–69).]
• [After opening the gates Priam learned that his companion was a god. Having revealed his identity, "Hermes went off to high Olympus" (460–68; cf. 694).]
• Priam proceeded to Troy (696–97).
• Cassandra saw Priam approaching and went to tell the others (697–706).

• Cassandra was often considered mad.
• Priam waited outside the gate (707–17).
• Finally, the gates opened and the Trojans continued their wailing (718–22).

sleep and opened the prison gate.

• After Peter escaped from the prison, the angel left him. Only then did the apostle "know for certain that the Lord sent his angel."
• Peter proceeded to the home of Mary.
• Rhoda heard Peter knocking at the door, recognized his voice, and went to tell the others.

• Those inside the house thought Rhoda mad.
• Peter waited outside the gate.
• ≠ Finally, the gate opened and told them what wonderful things "the Lord" had done.

One final possible parallel between the two stories merits attention. Acts 12 stands at an important juncture insofar as it concludes the first half of the book, in which Peter is primary. The apostle appears again only once in Acts, at the Jerusalem council where he speaks in favor of the evangelizing of the gentiles by referring to the conversion of Cornelius and his household, which had been narrated in chapters 10 and 11.[11] After the death of Herod, the narrator turns attention to Saul/Paul, who remains the protagonist until the end. The rescue of Peter from prison thus completes the Petrine half of Acts; the rescue of Hector's corpse and his burial, of course, concludes the *Iliad*.

One detail in Acts not only is distinctive, it functions as a flag to the reader to recall *Iliad* 24. Ancient authors often alerted their readers to the imitation of a particular antecedent by means of significant names. This obviously was the case in the parody of the scene in the *Alexander Romance* discussed in chapter 13. There the author fingered the antecedent by using the names Hermes, Eumelus, and Stranga. Luke did so with the name Rhoda, "Rose."[12] It points to Cassandra; not to the Cassandra myth as a whole but to a single Homeric line. *Iliad* 24.699 is unique in relating Cassandra to Aphrodite: "Cassandra, similar to golden Aphrodite." Dio Chrysostom had this line in mind when reminding his readers that Homer said Cassandra was "no less beautiful than Aphrodite."[13] The goddess of love, in turn, was closely identified with the rose, a signature for her in art.[14] Her relationship to the rose appears already in *Iliad* 23, where the poet says that she warded off decay by "anointing Hector's body with oil, ambrosial oil of roses [ῥοδόεντι]."[15] Homer's description of Aphrodite's protective rose oil apparently inspired the creation of unusual terracotta oil flasks in the form of a goddess often found in graves.[16] Statues of Aphrodite sometimes show her with a flask of rose oil.[17]

According to Euripides, Aphrodite threw over her hair "roses in odorous wreaths."[18] Achilles Tatius called the rose the "invitation to Aphrodite."[19] We also have evidence that, "braiding wreaths of roses plucked whenever they wish from Aphrodite's gardens, lovers hang them in every bridal chamber."[20] Other witnesses to Aphrodite and roses abound.[21] For example, Pausanius states that Elis was home to a sanctuary of the Graces with statues of the goddess holding a rose and a branch of myrtle. "The reason for their holding these things may be guessed to be this. The rose and the myrtle are sacred to Aphrodite and connected with the story of Adonis, while the Graces are of all deities the nearest related to Aphrodite."[22] The connection with Adonis is this: as he died, Adonis's spilt blood sprang up as a rose, or, in one variant, Aphrodite pricked herself on a thorn of a white rose bush and her blood turned the roses red. Philostratus wrote a lover, "The roses, borne on their leaves as on wings, have made haste to come to you. Receive them kindly, either as mementoes of Adonis or as tincture of Aphrodite."[23] In light of this common identification of the rose with Aphrodite, Rhoda's name and her inability to persuade others alert the reader to view her as an ersatz Cassandra, "peer to golden Aphrodite," the goddess of roses.

The final criterion is interpretability, especially evidence of emulation or improvement on the model. The tale in the *Iliad* ends with the tragic burial of Hector's corpse. The tale in Acts ends with rejoicing at Mary's house that their prayers for Peter's release had been answered.

If this reading of Acts 12:1–17 is correct, its implications for reading all of Acts are enormous. Luke expected his more perceptive readers to recognize his stories as retold tales from Homer. With respect to Acts 12, his purpose was not in the least historical; it was almost entirely literary and theological. This particular example, however, is extraordinary insofar as the name Rhoda assumes the reader should be able to relate her to Cassandra through a unique association in ancient Greek literature: "Cassandra, peer to golden Aphrodite." Luke's expectations of Homeric competence in his readers shows how poorly we moderns are equipped to appreciate the intertextual playfulness of ancient texts.

Conclusion

The composition of Acts surely was a complex interplay between historical memory, legends, popular preaching, and literary creativity. Even though the four cases treated in this book seem to imitate tales from the *Iliad,* some of them also contain traits that suggest the presence of historical memory and tradition. For example, behind Acts 1:15–26 almost certainly lurks information about the death of Judas; otherwise, it would be difficult to explain the similarities between Luke's account and Matt 27:1–10. Even though Luke seems to have modeled Peter's prison break after *Iliad* 24, he also knew traditions about the deaths of James and Agrippa I. Paul's farewell speech to the Ephesian elders is riddled with typically Pauline expressions and concerns, making it likely that Luke had read several of the epistles.

In fact, the preface to the Gospel of Luke seems to imply that the author set out to compose a history of sorts, and conservative scholars have sought to defend his reliability. Many form critics, too, have supposed that he intended to write a history, even if his credulous sources were not up to the task. Luke's literary achievement thus is viewed as little more than assembling, arranging, and editing traditions into a meaningful tale. This volume, on the other hand, argues that Luke created each of these stories as fictions to imitate or emulate famous stories in the *Iliad* and without the benefit of preexisting traditions. He was by no means a credulous editor of tradition but a sophisticated author; it is we, his readers, who have been naïve. He not only wrote up stories; he made up stories in the interest of advancing his understanding of the good news of Jesus Christ.

Scholars routinely attribute to pre-Lucan tradition the four tales discussed in this book. The most common assessment of the selection of Matthias to replace Judas in Acts 1:15–26 is to view it as a Jerusalem legend. Scholars usually attribute Acts 10:1–11:18 to a Caesarean legend about the conversion of the first gentile and the founding of an ethnically diverse church there. Even though Acts 12:1–17, Peter's second prison escape, may not be historical, commentators view it as a primitive Palestinian tale that may have been informed by prison escapes in popular Greek religion, as in the cult of Dionysus. Finally, virtually all scholars hold that Paul's famous farewell to the Ephesian elders in Acts 20:17–38 resulted from Luke's reshaping characteristic Pauline vocabulary and expressions into a final testament modeled after Jewish examples.

But each of these narratives has potential parallels in Homer's *Iliad*, and to understand the relationship between them, this book tested them with six criteria that might point to mimesis. The first criterion is accessibility, the physical availability of the model. Insofar as each of the proposed examples comes from the *Iliad*, the most famous and widely available book in antiquity, the satisfaction of this criterion is certain.

Analogy is the second criterion; it asks whether other ancient authors imitated the same story. Only one proposed Homeric model lacks an analogous imitation (the casting of lots for an opponent for Hector), but all the others were frequent mimetic targets. The lying dream to Agamemnon and the portent of the serpent and sparrows served as models for the author of the *Odyssey*, Aeschylus, Herodotus, Vergil, Lucan, Statius, Silius Italicus, Philostratus, and Nonnus. Priam's rescue of Hector's corpse informed the author of the *Odyssey*, Apollonius Rhodius, Artapanus, Vergil, Pseudo-Callisthenes, Nonnus, and several Christian texts, including the Gospel of Mark and the *Acts of Andrew*. Hector's farewell to Andromache inspired imitations by the author of the *Odyssey*, Aristophanes, Sophocles, Herodotus, Xenophon, Plato, Apollonius Rhodius, Chariton, Vergil, and Silius Italicus. Imitations of Hector's prayer for Astyanax appear in Sophocles, Chariton, Vergil, and Silius Italicus. This list of imitations is by no means comprehensive, but it suffices to demonstrate that Luke's alleged imitations had ancient analogies.

Density is the third criterion, and order is the fourth. They evaluate the volume of parallels between two works and their relative sequencing. Chapters 5, 8, 11, and 15 contain columns that list parallel motifs between the Homeric and Lucan stories, and the Appendix presents many of these parallels in the original languages. To repeat these columns here is superfluous. Not only are the lists of possible shared motifs extensive, the parallels for the most part occur in the same sequence in both works. In most cases, the imitations are more extensive than in their mimetic siblings.

The fifth and most decisive criterion is distinctive traits, the presence in both the model and proposed imitation of unusual words, phrases, names, or motifs that lock the two texts together in an interpretive dance. For example, the casting of lots in Acts 1 contains Homeric vocabulary found nowhere else in the New Testament. The very fact that the casting of lots for Ajax in *Iliad* 7 has no other imitations demonstrates the distinctiveness of it and Acts 1:15–26. The visions of Cornelius and Peter share several unusual traits with *Iliad* 2: the location of the visions near the sea, the temporal correspondence of the vision and portent, the interpretation of the animals in the portent with ethnic groups, and the nearly verbatim repetitions of the visions to others.

The most distinctive trait shared by Peter's escape and Priam's is the return of the hero to his loved ones. In the epic, "Cassandra, similar to golden Aphrodite," recognizes Priam, Idaeus, and Hector's corpse in the distance and announces their arrival to the Trojans, and the throng at the gate prevents Priam's entrance into the city. In Acts Rhoda ("Rose," the flower sacred to Aphrodite), recognizes Peter's voice, tells those inside that Peter has escaped, but is not believed; Peter is left outside the gate knocking, like Priam at the gates of Troy.

Paul's farewell to the Ephesian elders shares with *Iliad* 6 its unusual setting and timing. Both Paul and Hector are targets of violence who are eager to meet their fates. In each case this eagerness causes them to say their farewells away from the home of their loved ones. Hector bid Andromache farewell at the gates of Troy; Paul bid farewell to the elders not at Ephesus but at Miletus. Furthermore, each hero said farewell long before his death, unlike the typical final testament. This timing of the farewell allows both authors to intensify the pathos of their subsequent narratives. Those who would deny Luke's imitation of the epic must somehow explain the appearance of such distinctive similarities.

The final criterion is interpretability, the ability of any comparison to shed light on the proposed imitation. Perhaps the most compelling example is the light that *Iliad* 2 sheds on the visions of Cornelius and Peter. Agamemnon, famous for his arrogance, slept when Oneiros came to him, and the dream sent by Zeus was mendacious. Cornelius, on the other hand, was awake and praying when the angel came to him, and he treated the apostle with humility, as though Peter were a deity. Furthermore, the message of the angel was true and salvific. Oneiros instructed Agamemnon to fight against the Trojans, and the imitative dreams to Xerxes, Pompey, Turnus, Etiocles, and Hannibal likewise insisted that they lead their troops to wars that would be fatal to many of them. The visions of Cornelius and Peter, on the other hand, overcome the differences between Jews and gentiles, between East and West.

Emulation is least visible in Acts 12. There is no apparent criticism of the activities of Hermes, Priam, or Cassandra in the activities of the angel, Peter, and Rhoda. If any emulation exists, it probably pertains to the outcome of the events. Priam escaped Achilles, but on his return he had to bury his son and await the fall of Troy. Peter, on the other hand, not only escaped Herod, his return to the believers assembled at Mary's home produced joy. Not long afterward, God took his revenge on Herod's body.

Luke's emulation of the epic is clearer in the case of Paul's farewell. Hector's heroism consisted in his courage at war, and his prayer for his son was that he, too, would excel at killing his enemies and hauling off the spoils. But Paul's heroism consisted in providing "what was beneficial"; he "desired of no one silver or gold or clothing." His prayer for the elders was that they, too, care for the weak. Zeus refused to honor the prayer for Astyanax, but the reader of Acts is to assume that God honored Paul's prayer for the elders.

The study of mimesis of Greek poetry in the New Testament is quite recent, but it encounters some of the same challenges that have vexed research on the influence of the Hebrew Bible and other Jewish texts — influence that is present in these texts every bit as much, and often more transparently, as the influence of Homer. Was the influence conscious or unconscious? In many cases, one might argue that an author was so thoroughly steeped in the Hebrew Bible or Homeric epic that he or she imitated unconsciously.

In cases where an author may be borrowing consciously, does he or she do so covertly or overtly? An author may not care whether any reader detects the presence of the model. One may imitate for the sheer pleasure of reshaping beloved literature to express one's own ideas. Imitating a successful model often facilitated the composition of a narrative, so rhetoricians coached aspiring authors to disguise mimesis to avoid charges of plagiarism or pedantic aping. Such occulting sometimes involved eclecticism, the use of two, three, even four or five models. Surviving school exercises, rhetorical handbooks, and ancient literary criticism discuss mimesis in detail and demonstrate the significant role imitation and emulation played in ancient education.

In other cases, authors broadcast their imitations by supplying intertextual flags to alert readers to the presence of mimesis or emulation. This is the most sophisticated use of mimesis, and most of the imitations studied in this book, pagan or Christian, fall into this category. Unless the reader recognizes the model, he or she will fail to see the emulation. Unfortunately, the flags or markers often are so subtle and culturally specific that contemporary readers may miss them. What was overt to them often is covert to us.

If the author imitated overtly, did he or she expect every reader to detect it? Some texts, like the *Aeneid,* make the imitation so obvious that even the uninitiated might hear Homeric echoes, but blatant imitations are the exception, in part because they can be trite. In most cases, imitations disguise a rewarding sensus plenior — a fuller meaning below the surface, somewhat like allegory — that is intended for the more sophisticated. Discovering a clever, obscure twist on a popular tale often produces a smile, as though in the cryptic allusion the author has winked. Hellenistic and Roman intellectuals thought that the Homeric epics themselves were peppered with allegories.[1] Similarly, Jews and Christians read their scriptures for deeper meanings: Philo and Origen are but the most famous examples. If ancient readers relished the discovery of the arcane, it is not surprising to learn that they also could write with deeper meanings implied. New Testament scholars long have argued that subtle allusions to Jewish scriptures may trigger profound intertextual interpretations.

Similarly, the *Acts of Andrew* christianized Greek mythology by presenting its characters as improved counterparts to pagan gods and heroes, many of whom were notorious for their moral lapses. An ersatz Ares throws down his arms, an ersatz Zeus stops chasing women, and an ersatz Aphrodite embraces chastity. Every major character finds an analogy in Greek epic, tragedy, or philosophy. But the work also succeeds as an intriguing tale if one reads it merely for its surface meanings. The author supplies his own postscript to the work, which makes a distinction between two types of readers: the hermeneutical haves and have-nots.

> Hereabouts I should make an end of the blessed tales, acts, and mysteries difficult — or should I say impossible — to express. Let this stroke of the pen end it. I will pray first for myself, that I heard the things that were said just as they had been said, both the obvious and also the obscure, comprehensible only to the intellect. Then I will pray for all who are convinced by what was said, that they may have fellowship with each other, as God opens the ears of the listeners, to make comprehensible all his gifts in Christ Jesus our Lord, to whom, together with the Father, be glory, honor, and power with the all-holy and good and live-giving Spirit, now and always, forever and ever, amen.

It is one thing to be "convinced by what was said," but another to have God "open the ears of the listeners" to receive "*all* his gifts." Our relative ignorance of the epics allows most of us to hear only "the obvious," not the "obscure, comprehensible only to the intellect."

If an author imitated overtly, to what end did he or she do so? The answer to this question will be unique to each case and the options are nearly endless, as specialists in intertextuality rightly observe. In some cases, for example, authors may wish to demonstrate virtuosity at the expense of their models; others may imitate to provide their works with authority derived from recognized classics; others may imitate to ridicule, attack, parody, or satirize their targets. Gérard

Genette speaks of intertextual "transvaluation," the strategic replacement of the values of the targeted text with new ones.[2] Several imitations proposed in this book fit this description. The visions of Cornelius and Peter transvalue the primitive theology and ethnic strife of the epic. God does not lie, and Greeks and barbarians no longer need to fight. Lots select Ajax for combat; lots select Matthias for witnessing to the resurrection. Hector prayed that his son might grow strong to kill and pillage; Paul prayed that the elders might be strong like him to help the weak.

If the orientation of this book is correct, its theological implications are profound. Contemporary theologians often ascribe authority to the narratives of the New Testament by dint of their continuity with the traditions of the early Christian movement. From this perspective, the Gospels and Acts are products of a linear, if complex, process of oral and written composition that might be read both critically and appreciatively. Even if they may not record historical events, they record the hopes, ideals, preaching, and practices from the history of the early Church. However, if we accept that Luke, for example, composed many of his narratives without traditions to inform him, this view must be modified. He no doubt had access to traditions and sources, but they by no means determined the shape of his narrative. Like most of his literary contemporaries, he was in control of his own composition, including the creation of stories as alternatives to the dominant religious narratives of his culture. Ancient evangelism was, to a large extent, a *mythomachia*, a battle among competing fictions. Luke was engaged in a literary battle on at least two fronts: Jewish scriptures in the rear, and Greek poetry up ahead. The principal virtues of his compositions reside not in his linear continuity with historical events or traditions but in his strategic transformation of ancient narratives.

This book began with an ancient question: "Who would claim that the writing of prose is not reliant on the Homeric poems?"[3] Surely Philodemus would be surprised to learn that for two millennia scholars almost universally have denied any such influence on the New Testament. Does the New Testament imitate Homer? For me the answer is a resounding Yes! One cannot discount the parallels presented here as coincidental or trivial. Furthermore, if Luke imitates classical poetry here, it certainly is possible that he and other early Christian authors do so elsewhere. Perhaps it is now time to ask a more comprehensive and challenging question: *How much* of the New Testament imitates Homer?

Appendix
Greek and Latin Parallels

Introduction

1 Kings 17:10–24 (LXX)	Luke 7:11–16
καὶ ἀνέστη καὶ <u>ἐπορεύθη εἰς</u> Σαρεπτα	<u>καὶ ἐγένετο</u> ἐν τῷ ἑξῆς <u>ἐπορεύθη εἰς</u> πόλιν καλουμένην Ναΐν, καὶ συνεπορεύοντο αὐτῷ οἱ μαθηταὶ αὐτοῦ καὶ ὄχλος πολύς.
καὶ ἦλθεν εἰς τὸν πυλῶνα <u>τῆς πόλεως,</u> <u>καὶ ἰδοὺ</u> ἐκεῖ γυνὴ χήρα συνέλεγεν ξύλα. . . .	ὡς δὲ ἤγγισεν <u>τῇ πύλῃ τῆς πόλεως,</u> <u>καὶ ἰδοὺ</u> ἐξεκομίζετο τεθνηκὼς μονογενὴς <u>υἱὸς</u> τῇ μητρὶ αὐτοῦ καὶ αὐτὴ ἦν χήρα, καὶ ὄχλος τῆς πόλεως ἱκανὸς ἦν σὺν αὐτῇ. καὶ ἰδὼν αὐτήν ὁ κύριος ἐσπλαγχνίσθη ἐπ' αὐτῇ
<u>καὶ εἶπεν</u> Ηλιου <u>πρὸς τὴν γυναῖκα ·</u> δός μοι τὸν <u>υἱόν</u> σου. καὶ ἔλαβεν αὐτὸν ἐκ τοῦ κόλπου αὐτῆς καὶ ἀνήνεγκεν αὐτὸν εἰς τὸ ὑπερῷον, ἐν ᾧ αὐτὸς ἐκάθητο ἐκεῖ, καὶ ἐκοίμισεν αὐτὸν <u>ἐπὶ τῆς κλίνης</u> αὐτοῦ. . . .	<u>καὶ εἶπεν αὐτῇ ·</u> μὴ κλαῖε. καὶ προσελθὼν ἥψατο <u>τῆς σοροῦ,</u> οἱ δὲ βαστάζοντες ἔστησαν,

καὶ ἐνεφύσησεν τῷ παιδαρίῳ τρὶς καὶ
ἐπεκαλέσατο τὸν κύριον
καὶ εἶπεν· κύριε ὁ θεός μου,   καὶ εἶπεν· νεανίσκε, σοὶ λέγω, ἐγέρθητι.
ἐπιστραφήτω δὴ ἡ ψυχὴ τοῦ
παιδαρίου τούτου εἰς αὐτόν.
καὶ ἐγένετο οὕτως,
καὶ ἀνεβόησεν τὸ παιδάριον.   καὶ ἀνεκάθισεν ὁ νεκρὸς
                                      καὶ ἤρξατο λαλεῖν,
καὶ κατήγαγεν αὐτὸν ἀπὸ τοῦ ὑπερῴου
εἰς τὸν οἶκον
καὶ ἔδωκεν αὐτὸν τῇ μητρὶ αὐτοῦ. . . .   καὶ ἔδωκεν αὐτὸν τῇ μητρὶ αὐτοῦ.
                                        ἔλαβεν δὲ φόβος πάντας

καὶ εἶπεν ἡ γυνὴ πρὸς Ηλιου   καὶ ἐδόξαζον τὸν θεὸν λέγοντες
ἰδοὺ ἔγνωκα ὅτι ἄνθρωπος θεοῦ εἶ σὺ   ὅτι προφήτης μέγας ἠγέρθη ἐν ἡμῖν
καὶ ῥῆμα κυρίου ἐν στόματί σου   καὶ ὅτι ἐπεσκέψατο ὁ θεὸς
ἀληθινόν.   τὸν λαὸν αὐτοῦ.

Chapter 3

Iliad 2.18–21
τὸν δὲ κίχανεν εὕδοντ᾽ ἐν κλισίῃ,
περὶ δ᾽ ἀμβρόσιος κέχυθ᾽ ὕπνος.
στῆ δ᾽ ἄρ᾽ ὑπὲρ κεφαλῆς Νηληΐῳ
υἷι ἐοικώς, Νέστορι, τόν ῥα μάλιστα
γερόντων τῖ᾽ Ἀγαμέμνων.

Aeneid 7.413–16 and 419
tectis hic Turnus in altis iam mediam nigra
carpebat nocte quietem.
Allecto torvam faciem et furialia membra
exuit, in voltus sese transformat anilis. . . .
fit Calybe Iunonis anus templique sacerdos.

Iliad 2.22–25
τῷ μιν ἐεισάμενος
προσεφώνεε θεῖος ὄνειρος·
εὕδεις, Ἀτρέος υἱὲ δαΐφρονος
ἱπποδάμοιο; οὐ χρὴ παννύχιον εὕδειν
βουληφόρον ἄνδρα, ᾧ λαοί τ᾽
ἐπιτετράφαται καὶ τόσσα μέμηλε.

Aeneid 7.420–22
et iuveni ante oculos
his se cum vocibus offert:
Turne, tot incassum fusos patiere labores,
et tua Dardaniis transcribi sceptra colonis?

Iliad 2.28–30
θωρῆξαί σε κέλευσε κάρη κομόωντας
Ἀχαιοὺς πανσυδίῃ· νῦν γάρ κεν
ἕλοις πόλιν εὐρυάγυιαν Τρώων·

Aeneid 7.429–31
Quare age et armari pubem portisque moveri
laetus in arma para, et Phrygios . . .
duces pictasque exure carinas.

Iliad 2.16 and 18–19
βῆ δ᾽ ἄρ᾽ ὄνειρος, ἐπεὶ τὸν μῦθον
ἄκουσε . . .
βῆ δ᾽ ἄρ᾽ ἐπ᾽ Ἀτρεΐδην Ἀγαμέμνονα·

Thebaid 2.89–90 and 93–94
Nox ea, cum tacita volucer Cyllenius aura
regis Echionii stratis adlapsus . . .
habet ille soporem.

τὸν δὲ κίχανεν εὕδοντ᾽ ἐν κλισίῃ,
περὶ δ᾽ ἀμβρόσιος κέχυθ᾽ ὕπνος.

Iliad 2.20–21
στῆ δ᾽ ἄρ᾽ ὑπὲρ κεφαλῆς Νηληΐῳ
υἷι ἐοικώς, Νέστορι, τόν ῥα μάλιστα
γερόντων τῖ᾽ Ἀγαμέμνων·

Iliad 2.22–25
τῷ μιν ἐεισάμενος προσεφώνεε θεῖος
ὄνειρος· εὕδεις, Ἀτρέος υἱὲ δαΐφρονος
ἱπποδάμοιο; οὐ χρὴ παννύχιον εὕδειν
βουληφόρον ἄνδρα, ᾧ λαοί τ᾽
ἐπιτετράφαται καὶ τόσσα μέμηλε.

Iliad 2.35
ὣς ἄρα φωνήσας
ἀπεβήσετο, τὸν δ᾽ ἔλιπ᾽ αὐτοῦ ...

Iliad 2.305–19

ἡμεῖς δ᾽ ἀμφὶ περὶ κρήνην ἱεροὺς
κατὰ βωμοὺς ἔρδομεν ἀθανάτοισι
τεληέσσας ἑκατόμβας, καλῇ ὑπὸ
πλατανίστῳ, ὅθεν ῥέεν ἀγλαὸν ὕδωρ·
ἔνθ᾽ ἐφάνη μέγα σῆμα· δράκων
ἐπὶ νῶτα δαφοινός, σμερδαλέος,
τόν ῥ᾽ αὐτὸς Ὀλύμπιος ἧκε φόωσδε,
βωμοῦ ὑπαΐξας πρός ῥα πλατάνιστον
ὄρουσεν. ἔνθα δ᾽ ἔσαν στρουθοῖο
νεοσσοί, νήπια τέκνα, ὄζῳ ἐπ᾽
ἀκροτάτῳ, πετάλοις ὑποπεπτηῶτες,
ὀκτώ, ἀτὰρ μήτηρ ἐνάτη ἦν,
ἣ τέκε τέκνα.
ἔνθ᾽ ὅ γε τοὺς ἐλεεινὰ κατήσθιε
τετριγῶτας· μήτηρ δ᾽ ἀμφιποτᾶτο
ὀδυρομένη φίλα τέκνα·
τὴν δ᾽ ἐλελιξάμενος πτέρυγος
λάβεν
ἀμφιαχυῖαν.

tunc senior quae iussus agit.

Thebaid 2.94–97
neu false videri
noctis imago queat, longaevi vatis opacos
Tiresiae vultus vocemque et vellera nota
induitur.

Thebaid 2.101–4
visus fatorum expromere voces:
Non somni tibi tempus, iners,
qui nocte sub alta, germani secure, iaces:
ingentia dudum acta vocant
rerumque graves, ignave, paratus.

Thebaid 2.120
Dixit,
et abscedens ...

Aeneid 2.199–207, 212–17, 222, and 225–27
Hic aliud maius miseris multoque tremendum
obicitur magis atque improvida pectora turbat.
Laocoon, ductus Neptuno sorte sacerdos,
sollemnis taurum ingentem mactabat ad aras.
ecce autem gemini a Tenedo tranquilla per alta
(horresco referens) immensis orbibus angues
incumbunt pelago pariterque ad litora tendunt:
pectora quorum inter fluctus arrecta
iubaeque sanguineae superant undas. ...

illi agmine certo Laocoonta petunt;
et primum parva duorum corpora natorum
serpens amplexus uterque implicat
et miseros morsu depascitur artus;
post ipsum, auxilio subeuntem ac tela ferentem,
corripiunt spirisque ligant ingentibus. ...
clamores simul horrendos ad sidera tollit ...

αὐτὰρ ἐπεὶ κατὰ τέκν᾽ ἔφαγε
στρουθοῖο καὶ αὐτήν,
τὸν μὲν ἀΐζηλον θῆκεν θεός,
ὅς περ ἔφηνε· λᾶαν γάρ μιν
ἔθηκε Κρόνου πάϊς ἀγκυλομήτεω.

at gemini lapsu delubra ad summa dracones

effugiunt saevaeque petunt Tritonidis arcem,
sub pedibusque deae clipeique sub orbe
teguntur.

Iliad 2.2–6
Δία δ᾽ οὐκ ἔχε νήδυμος ὕπνος,
ἀλλ᾽ ὅ γε μερμήριζε κατὰ φρένα
ὡς Ἀχιλῆα τιμήσῃ, ὀλέσῃ δὲ πολέας
ἐπὶ νηυσὶν Ἀχαιῶν.
ἥδε δέ οἱ κατὰ θυμὸν ἀρίστη φαίνετο
βουλή, πέμψαι ἐπ᾽ Ἀτρείδῃ
Ἀγαμέμνονι οὖλον ὄνειρον.

Punica 3.163–67
Tum pater omnipotens, gentem exercere
periclis Dardaniam et fama saevorum tollere
ad astra bellorum meditans
priscosque referre labores,

praecipitat consulta viri segnemque quietem
terret et immissa rumpit formidine somnos.

Iliad 2.16–18
βῆ δ᾽ ἄρ ὄνειρος, ἐπεὶ τὸν μῦθον
ἄκουσε . . .
βῆ δ᾽ ἄρ᾽ ἐπ᾽ Ἀτρείδην Ἀγαμέμνονα·

Punica 3.168–69
Iamque per humentem noctis Cyllenius
umbram aligero lapsu portabat
iussa parentis.

Iliad 2.18–19 and 22–25
τὸν δὲ κίχανεν εὕδοντ᾽ ἐν κλισίῃ,
περὶ δ᾽ ἀμβρόσιος κέχυθ᾽ ὕπνος. . . .
προσεφώνεε θεῖος ὄνειρος·
εὕδεις, Ἀτρέος υἱὲ δαΐφρονος
ἱπποδάμοιο; οὐ χρὴ παννύχιον εὕδειν
βουληφόρον ἄνδρα, ᾧ λαοί τ᾽
ἐπιτετράφαται καὶ τόσσα μέμηλε.

Punica 3.170–74
Nec mora: mulcentem securo membra
sopore aggreditur iuvenem
ac monitis incessit amaris:
Turpe duci totam somno consumere noctem,
o rector Libyae: vigili stant bella magistro.

Iliad 2.35–36
ὣς ἄρα φωνήσας
ἀπεβήσετο, τὸν δ᾽ ἔλιπ᾽ αὐτοῦ
τὰ φρονέοντ᾽ ἀνὰ θυμὸν ἃ ῥ᾽ οὐ
τελέεσθαι ἔμελλον.

Punica 3.214–16

His aegrum stimulis liquere deusque
soporque. it membris gelidus sudor,
laetoque pavore promissa evolvit
somni.

Chapter 4

Iliad 2.17–26

καρπαλίμως δ᾽ ἵκανε
θοὰς ἐπὶ νῆας Ἀχαιῶν,

Acts 10:3–4a and 30–31
εἶδεν ἐν ὁράματι φανερῶς
ὡσεὶ περὶ ὥραν ἐνάτην τῆς ἡμέρας
ἄγγελον τοῦ θεοῦ εἰσελθόντα

βῆ δ' ἄρ' ἐπ' Ἀτρείδην Ἀγαμέμνονα·

πρὸς αὐτὸν
[When Cornelius retells the tale, he says:
ἀπὸ τετάρτης ἡμέρας μέχρι ταύτης
τῆς ὥρας ἤμην τὴν ἐνάτην

τὸν δὲ κίχανεν εὕδοντ' ἐν κλισίῃ, ...
στῆ δ' ἄρ' ὑπὲρ κεφαλῆς
Νηληΐῳ υἷι ἐοικώς, Νέστορι, ...
προσεφώνεε θεῖος ὄνειρος·
εὕδεις, Ἀτρέος υἱέ ...; οὐ χρὴ
παννύχιον εὕδειν βουληφόρον ἄνδρα,
ᾧ λαοί τ' ἐπιτετράφαται
καὶ τόσσα μέμηλε.
νῦν δ' ἐμέθεν ξύνες ὦκα·
Διὸς δέ τοι ἄγγελός εἰμι.

προσευχόμενος ἐν τῷ οἴκῳ μου,
καὶ ἰδοὺ ἀνὴρ ἔστη ἐνώπιόν μου
ἐν ἐσθῆτι λαμπρᾷ.]
καὶ εἰπόντα αὐτῷ·
Κορνήλιε. ὁ δὲ ἀτενίσας αὐτῷ
καὶ ἔμφοβος γενόμενος εἶπεν·
τί ἐστιν, κύριε;

Iliad 2.26–27
Διὸς δέ τοι ἄγγελός εἰμι,
ὃς σεῦ ἄνευθεν ἐὼν μέγα
κήδεται ἠδ' ἐλεαίρει.

Acts 10:4b (cf. 31)

αἱ προσευχαί σου
καὶ ἐλεημοσύναι σου ἀνέβησαν εἰς
μνημόσυνον ἔμπροσθεν τοῦ θεοῦ.

Iliad 2.35
ὣς ἄρα φωνήσας ἀπεβήσετο ...
[Cf. Agamemnon's version of the angel's
departure in 2:70–71: ὣς ὁ μὲν εἰπὼν
ᾤχετ' ἀποπτάμενος, ἐμὲ δὲ γλυκὺς
ὕπνος ἀνῆκεν.]

Acts 10:7
ὡς δὲ ἀπῆλθεν ὁ ἄγγελος
ὁ λαλῶν αὐτῷ, φωνήσας δύο
τῶν οἰκετῶν καὶ στρατιώτην εὐσεβῆ
τῶν προσκαρτερούντων αὐτῷ.

Iliad 2.303–8
ἐς Αὐλίδα νῆες Ἀχαιῶν ἠγερέθοντο
κακὰ Πριάμῳ καὶ Τρωσὶ φέρουσαι·
ἡμεῖς δ' ἀμφὶ περὶ κρήνην
ἱεροὺς κατὰ βωμοὺς ἔρδομεν
ἀθανάτοισι τελήεσσας ἑκατόμβας,
καλῇ ὑπὸ πλατανίστῳ, ὅθεν ῥέεν
ἀγλαὸν ὕδωρ· ἔνθ' ἐφάνη μέγα σῆμα.

Acts 10:9b–10

ἀνέβη Πέτρος ἐπὶ τὸ δῶμα
προσεύξασθαι περὶ ὥραν ἕκτην.
ἐγένετο δὲ πρόσπεινος καὶ
ἤθελεν γεύσασθαι. παρασκευαζόντων δὲ
αὐτῶν, ἐγένετο ἐπ' αὐτὸν ἔκστασις.

Iliad 2.320
ἡμεῖς δ' ἑσταότες θαυμάζομεν
οἷον ἐτύχθη.

Acts 10:17a and 19a
διηπόρει ὁ Πέτρος
τί ἂν εἴη τὸ ὅραμα ὃ εἶδεν. ...
τοῦ δὲ Πέτρου διενθυμουμένου
περὶ τοῦ ὁράματος ...

Iliad 2.56–60 and 63–67
κλῦτε, φίλοι· θεῖός μοι ἐνύπνιον
ἦλθεν ὄνειρος ἀμβροσίην διὰ νύκτα·
μάλιστα δὲ Νέστορι δίῳ
εἶδός τε μέγεθός τε φυήν τ’
ἄγχιστα ἐῴκει.
στῆ δ’ ἄρ’ ὑπὲρ κεφαλῆς

καί με πρὸς μῦθον ἔειπεν·
εὔδεις, Ἀτρέος υἱέ…;
Διὸς δέ τοι ἄγγελός εἰμι,
ὃς σεῦ ἄνευθεν ἐὼν μέγα
κήδεται ἠδ’ ἐλεαίρει·

θωρῆξαί σε κέλευσε κάρη κομόωντας
Ἀχαιοὺς πανσυδίη· νῦν γάρ κεν
ἕλοις πόλιν εὐρυάγυιαν Τρώων.

Acts 10:30b–32
ἀπὸ τετάρτης ἡμέρας μέχρι ταύτης
τῆς ὥρας ἤμην τὴν ἐνάτην
προσευχόμενος ἐν τῷ οἴκῳ μου,

καὶ ἰδοὺ ἀνὴρ ἔστη ἐνώπιόν μου
ἐν ἐσθῆτι λαμπρᾷ
καὶ φησίν·
Κορνήλιε,

εἰσηκούσθη σου ἡ προσευχὴ
καὶ αἱ ἐλεημοσύναι σου ἐμνήσθησαν
ἐνώπιον τοῦ θεοῦ.
πέμψον οὖν εἰς Ἰόππην
καὶ μετακάλεσαι Σίμωνα ὅς ἐπικαλεῖται
Πέτρος, οὗτος ξενίζεται ἐν οἰκίᾳ
Σίμωνος βυρσέως παρὰ θάλασσαν.

Iliad 2.333–35
ὣς ἔφατ’, Ἀργεῖοι δὲ μέγ’ ἴαχον,
ἀμφὶ δὲ νῆες σμερδαλέον κονάβησαν
ἀϋσάντων ὑπ’ Ἀχαιῶν, μῦθον
ἐπαινήσαντες Ὀδυσσῆος θείοιο.

Acts 11:18
ἀκούσαντες δὲ ταῦτα ἡσύχασαν

καὶ ἐδόξασαν τὸν θεὸν λέγοντες·
ἄρα καὶ τοῖς ἔθνεσιν ὁ θεὸς τὴν
μετάνοιαν εἰς ζωὴν ἔδωκεν.

Chapter 7

Iliad 6.485–89
ἔπος τ’ ἔφατ’ ἔκ τ’ ὀνόμαζε·
δαιμονίη, μή μοί τι λίην ἀκαχίζεο
θυμῷ·
οὐ γάρ τίς μ’ ὑπὲρ αἶσαν ἀνὴρ Ἄϊδι
προϊάψει· μοῖραν δ’ οὔ τινά φημι
πεφυγμένον ἔμμεναι ἀνδρῶν,
οὐ κακόν, οὐδὲ μὲν ἐσθλόν,
ἐπὴν τὰ πρῶτα γένηται.

Acts 21:13–14
τότε ἀπεκρίθη ὁ Παῦλος·
τί ποιεῖτε κλαίοντες καὶ
συνθρύπτοντές μου τὴν καρδίαν;
ἐγὼ γὰρ οὐ μόνον δεθῆναι ἀλλὰ καὶ
ἀποθανεῖν εἰς Ἰερουσαλὴμ ἑτοίμως….
ἡσυχάσαμεν εἰπόντες·
τοῦ κυρίου τὸ θέλημα γινέσθω.

Iliad 6.440–46
τὴν δ’ αὖτε προσέειπε…
ἀλλὰ μάλ’ αἰνῶς αἰδέομαι Τρῶας

Acts 20:18–21
εἶπεν αὐτοῖς·
ὑμεῖς ἐπίστασθε… πῶς μεθ’ ὑμῶν…

καὶ Τρῳάδας ἑλκεσιπέπλους, αἴ κε
κακὸς ὣς νόσφιν <u>ἀλυσκάζω</u> πολέμοιο·
οὐδέ με θυμὸς ἄνωγεν,
ἐπεὶ μάθον ἔμμεναι ἐσθλὸς αἰεὶ
<u>καὶ πρώτοισι μετὰ Τρώεσσι μάχεσθαι,</u>
<u>ἀρνύμενος πατρός</u> τε μέγα κλέος
<u>ἠδ᾽</u> ἐμὸν αὐτοῦ.

ἐγενόμην, . . . <u>ὡς</u>
<u>οὐδὲν</u> ὑπεστειλάμην τῶν <u>συμφερόντων</u>

τοῦ μὴ <u>ἀναγγεῖλαι ὑμῖν</u> <u>καὶ διδάξαι</u>
<u>ὑμᾶς δημοσίᾳ</u> καὶ κατ᾽ οἴκους,
διαμαρτυρόμενος Ἰουδαίοις τε
<u>καὶ</u> Ἕλλησιν τὴν εἰς θεὸν μετάνοιαν
καὶ πίστιν εἰς τὸν κύριον ἡμῶν Ἰησοῦν.

Iliad 6.361–62 and 367–68
ἤδη γάρ μοι θυμὸς ἐπέσσυται
ὄφρ᾽ ἐπαμύνω Τρώεσσ᾽ . . .
<u>οὐ γὰρ οἶδ᾽ εἰ ἔτι</u> σφιν ὑπότροπος
ἵξομαι αὖτις, ἢ ἤδη μ᾽ ὑπὸ χερσὶ
θεοὶ δαμόωσιν Ἀχαιῶν.

Acts 20:22–23
καὶ νῦν ἰδοὺ δεδεμένος ἐγὼ τῷ
πνεύματι πορεύομαι εἰς Ἰερουσαλὴμ
τὰ ἐν αὐτῇ συναντήσοντά μοι <u>μὴ εἰδώς,</u>
πλὴν ὅτι τὸ πνεῦμα τὸ ἅγιον κατὰ πόλιν
διαμαρτύρεταί μοι λέγον ὅτι
<u>δεσμὰ καὶ θλίψεις με μένουσιν.</u>

Iliad 6.447–49
<u>εὖ γὰρ ἐγὼ τόδε οἶδα</u> κατὰ φρένα
καὶ κατὰ θυμόν· ἔσσεται ἦμαρ
ὅτ᾽ ἄν ποτ᾽ ὀλώλῃ Ἴλιος ἱρὴ καὶ
Πρίαμος καὶ λαὸς ἐϋμμελίω Πριάμοιο.

Acts 20:25
<u>καὶ νῦν ἰδοὺ ἐγὼ οἶδα ὅτι</u>
οὐκέτι ὄψεσθε τὸ πρόσωπόν μου
ὑμεῖς πάντες ἐν οἷς διῆλθον
κηρύσσων τὴν βασιλείαν.

Iliad 6.490–93
<u>τὰ σ᾽ αὐτῆς ἔργα κόμιζε,</u> ἱστόν τ᾽
ἠλακάτην τε, <u>καὶ ἀμφιπόλοισι</u>
κέλευε ἔργον ἐποίχεσθαι·
πόλεμος δ᾽ ἄνδρεσσι μελήσει πᾶσι,
μάλιστα δ᾽ ἐμοί, τοὶ Ἰλίῳ ἐγγεγάασιν.

Acts 20:28
<u>προσέχετε ἑαυτοῖς</u>
<u>καὶ παντὶ τῷ ποιμνίῳ,</u> ἐν ᾧ ὑμᾶς
τὸ πνεῦμα τὸ ἅγιον ἔθετο ἐπισκόπους
ποιμαίνειν τὴν ἐκκλησίαν τοῦ θεοῦ, ἣν
περιεποιήσατο διὰ τοῦ αἵματος τοῦ ἰδίου.

Iliad 6.447–49
<u>εὖ γὰρ ἐγὼ τόδε οἶδα</u> κατὰ φρένα
καὶ κατὰ θυμόν· ἔσσεται ἦμαρ
ὅτ᾽ ἄν ποτ᾽ <u>ὀλώλῃ</u> Ἴλιος ἱρὴ καὶ
Πρίαμος καὶ λαὸς ἐϋμμελίω Πριάμοιο.

Acts 20:29
<u>ἐγὼ οἶδα ὅτι</u>
εἰσελεύσονται <u>μετὰ τὴν ἄφιξίν μου</u>
<u>λύκοι βαρεῖς εἰς ὑμᾶς</u>
<u>μὴ φειδόμενοι τοῦ ποιμνίου.</u>

Iliad 6.459–62
<u>καί ποτέ τις εἴπῃσιν</u> ἰδὼν
κατὰ δάκρυ χέουσαν·
Ἕκτορος ἤδη γυνή, <u>ὃς ἀριστεύεσκε</u>
<u>μάχεσθαι Τρώων ἱπποδάμων,</u>
ὅτε Ἴλιον ἀμφεμάχοντο.
<u>ὥς ποτέ τις ἐρέει·</u>

Ajax 500–504
<u>καί τις πικρὸν πρόσφθεγμα</u>
δεσποτῶν <u>ἐρεῖ λόγοις</u> ἰάπτων·
ἴδετε τὴν ὁμευνέτιν Αἴαντος, <u>ὃς</u>
<u>μέγιστον ἴσχυσε στρατοῦ,</u> οἵας
λατρείας ἀνθ᾽ ὅσου ζήλου τρέφει.
<u>τοιαῦτ᾽ ἐρεῖ τις.</u>

Iliad 6.490–93
τὰ σ' αὐτῆς ἔργα κόμιζε, . . .

πόλεμος δ' ἄνδρεσσι μελήσει πᾶσι,
μάλιστα δ' ἐμοί, τοὶ Ἰλίῳ ἐγγεγάασιν.

Iliad 6.474–75
αὐτὰρ ὅ γ' ὃν φίλον υἱὸν ἐπεὶ κύσε
πῆλέ τε χερσίν,
εἶπεν ἐπευξάμενος Διί τ' ἄλλοισίν
τε θεοῖσιν.

Iliad 6.466 and 474–75
ὣς εἰπὼν οὗ παιδὸς ὀρέξατο
φαίδιμος Ἕκτωρ· . . .
αὐτὰρ ὅ γ' ὃν φίλον υἱὸν ἐπεὶ κύσε
πῆλέ τε χερσίν,
εἶπεν ἐπευξάμενος Διί.

Iliad 6.475–76
εἶπεν ἐπευξάμενος Διί τ' ἄλλοισίν
τε θεοῖσι·
Ζεῦ ἄλλοι τε θεοί,

Iliad 6.474–78 and 7.1–3
αὐτὰρ ὅ γ' ὃν φίλον υἱὸν ἐπεὶ κύσε
πῆλέ τε χερσίν,
εἶπεν ἐπευξάμενος Διί τ' ἄλλοισίν
τε θεοῖσιν·
Ζεῦ ἄλλοι τε θεοί, δότε δὴ
καὶ τόνδε γενέσθαι παῖδ' ἐμόν,
ὡς καὶ ἐγώ περ, ἀριπρεπέα Τρώεσσιν,
ὧδε βίην γ' ἀγαθόν. . . .

καί ποτέ τις εἴποι, πατρός γ' ὅδε
πολλὸν ἀμείνων, ἐκ πολέμου ἀνιόντα·
. . . ὣς εἰπὼν πυλέων ἐξέσσυτο
φαίδιμος Ἕκτωρ,
τῷ δ' ἅμ' Ἀλέξανδρος κί' ἀδελφεός·
ἐν δ' ἄρα θυμῷ ἀμφότεροι μέμασαν
πολεμίζειν ἠδὲ μάχεσθαι.

Acts 20:31
διὸ γρηγορεῖτε
μνημονεύοντες ὅτι τριετίαν νύκτα καὶ
ἡμέραν οὐκ ἐπαυσάμην μετὰ δακρύων
νουθετῶν ἕνα ἕκαστον.

Chaereas and Callirhoe 8.5.15
θεασάμενος δὲ τὸ παιδίον καὶ
πήλας ταῖς χερσίν,
ἀπελεύσῃ ποτέ μοι καὶ σύ, τέκνον,
πρὸς τὴν μητέρα.

Acts 20:36–37
καὶ ταῦτα εἰπὼν θεὶς τὰ γόνατα αὐτοῦ
σὺν πᾶσιν αὐτοῖς προσηύξατο.
ἱκανὸς δὲ κλαυθμὸς ἐγένετο πάντων.
καὶ ἐπιπεσόντες ἐπὶ τὸν τράχηλον
τοῦ Παύλου κατεφίλουν αὐτόν.

Acts 20:32
παρατίθεμαι ὑμᾶς τῷ θεῷ
καὶ τῷ λόγῳ τῆς χάριτος αὐτοῦ.

Aeneid 12.433–36 and 438–43
Ascanium fusis circum complectitur
armis summaque per galeam
delibans oscula fatur:

disce, puer, virtutem
ex me verumque laborem . . .

tu facito, mox cum matura adoleverit
aetas, sis memor et te animo repetentem
exempla tuorum et pater Aeneas et
avunculus excitet Hector.
Haec ubi dicta dedit, portis sese extulit
ingens, telum immane manu quatiens;
simul agmine denso Antheusque
Mnestheusque ruunt.

Iliad 6.476–78

Ζεῦ ἄλλοι τε θεοί,
δότε δὴ καὶ τόνδε γενέσθαι
παῖδ' ἐμόν, ὡς καὶ ἐγώ περ,
ἀριπρεπέα Τρώεσσιν
ὧδε βίην τ' ἀγαθόν.

Acts 20:32
καὶ τὰ νῦν παρατίθεμαι ὑμᾶς
τῷ θεῷ καὶ τῷ λόγῳ τῆς χάριτος αὐτοῦ,
τῷ δυναμένῳ οἰκοδομῆσαι καὶ δοῦναι
τὴν κληρονομίαν
ἐν τοῖς ἡγιασμένοις πᾶσιν.

Iliad 6.474–81
αὐτὰρ ὅ γ' ὃν φίλον υἱὸν ἐπεὶ κύσε
πῆλέ τε χερσίν,
εἶπεν ἐπευξάμενος Διί τ' ἄλλοισίν
τε θεοῖσι·
Ζεῦ ἄλλοι τε θεοί, δότε δὴ'
καὶ τόνδε γενέσθαι παῖδ' ἐμόν,
ὡς καὶ ἐγώ περ, ἀριπρεπέα Τρώεσσιν,
ὧδε βίην γ' ἀγαθόν,
καὶ Ἰλίου ἶφι ἀνάσσειν·
καί ποτέ τις εἴποι, πατρός γ' ὅδε
πολλὸν ἀμείνων, ἐκ πολέμου ἀνιόντα·
φέροι δ' ἔναρα βροτόεντα κτείνας
δήϊον ἄνδρα,
χαρείη δὲ φρένα μήτηρ.

Chaereas and Callirhoe 3.8.7–8
ἀνατείνασα χερσὶ τὸ βρέφος

ὑπὲρ τούτου σοι, φησίν, ὦ δέσποινα,
γινώσκω τὴν χάριν· ...
δὸς δή μοι γενέσθαι τὸν υἱὸν
εὐτυχέστερον μὲν τῶν γονέων,
ὅμοιον δὲ τῷ πάππῳ·
πλεύσειε δὲ καὶ οὗτος ἐπὶ
τριήρους στρατηγικῆς,
καί τις εἴποι, ναυμαχοῦντος αὐτοῦ,
κρείττων Ἑρμοκράτους ὁ ἔκγονος·
ἡσθήσεται μὲν γὰρ καὶ ὁ πάππος
ἔχων τῆς ἀρετῆς διάδοχον,
ἡσθησόμεθα δὲ οἱ γονεῖς αὐτοῦ
καὶ τεθνεῶτες.

Iliad 6.479–80

καί ποτέ τις εἴποι πατρός γ' ὅδε
πολλὸν ἀμείνων, ἐκ πολέμου ἀνιόντα·

Acts 20:35
μνημονεύειν τε τῶν λόγων τοῦ κυρίου
Ἰησοῦ ὅτι αὐτὸς εἶπεν· μακάριόν
ἐστιν μᾶλλον διδόναι ἢ λαμβάνειν.

Iliad 6.500

αἱ μὲν ἔτι ζωὸν γόον Ἕκτορα
ᾧ ἐνὶ οἴκῳ.

Chaereas and Callirhoe 4.1.1
ταύτην μὲν οὖν τὴν νύκτα
Καλλιρόη διῆγεν ἐν θρήνοις,
Χαιρέαν ἔτι ζῶντα πενθοῦσα.

Iliad 6.490 and 495–96
εἰς οἶκον ἰοῦσα ... ἄλοχος δὲ φίλη
οἶκόνδε βεβήκει ...
θαλερὸν κατὰ δάκρυ χέουσα.

Phaedo 60a
ὦ Κρίτων, ... ἀπαγέτω τις αὐτὴν οἴκαδε.
καὶ ἐκείνην μὲν ἀπῆγόν τινες τῶν τοῦ
Κρίτωνος βοῶσάν τε καὶ κοπτομένην.

Iliad 6.498–501
κιχήσατο δ' ἔνδοθι πολλὰς ἀμφιπόλους,
τῇσιν δὲ γόον πάσῃσιν ἐνῶρσεν.
αἱ μὲν ἔτι ζωὸν γόον Ἕκτορα
ᾧ ἐνὶ οἴκῳ·

οὐ γάρ μιν ἔτ' ἔφαντο
ὑπότροπον ἐκ πολέμοιο ἵξεσθαι.

Acts 20:37–38

ἱκανὸς δὲ κλαυθμὸς ἐγένετο πάντων,
καὶ ἐπιπεσόντες ἐπὶ τὸν τράχηλον
τοῦ Παύλου κατεφίλουν αὐτόν,
ὀδυνώμενοι μάλιστα
ἐπὶ τῷ λόγῳ ᾧ εἰρήκει, ὅτι οὐκέτι
μέλλουσιν τὸ πρόσωπον αὐτοῦ θεωρεῖν.

Chapter 8

Iliad 6.466, 474–75, and 498–502
ὣς εἰπὼν οὗ παιδὸς ὀρέξατο
φαίδιμος Ἕκτωρ· . . . αὐτὰρ ὅ γ' ὃν
φίλον υἱὸν ἐπεὶ κύσε πῆλέ τε χερσίν,
εἶπεν ἐπευξάμενος Διί. . . .
κιχήσατο δ' ἔνδοθι πολλὰς ἀμφιπόλους,
τῇσιν δὲ γόον πάσῃσιν ἐνῶρσεν.
αἱ μὲν ἔτι ζωὸν γόον Ἕκτορα
ᾧ ἐνὶ οἴκῳ·

οὐ γάρ μιν ἔτ' ἔφαντο
ὑπότροπον ἐκ πολέμοιο ἵξεσθαι.

Acts 20:36–38
ταῦτα εἰπὼν θεὶς τὰ γόνατα αὐτοῦ
σὺν πᾶσιν αὐτοῖς προσηύξατο.

ἱκανὸς δὲ κλαυθμὸς ἐγένετο πάντων,
καὶ ἐπιπεσόντες ἐπὶ τὸν τράχηλον
τοῦ Παύλου κατεφίλουν αὐτόν,
ὀδυνώμενοι μάλιστα
ἐπὶ τῷ λόγῳ ᾧ εἰρήκει, ὅτι οὐκέτι
μέλλουσιν τὸ πρόσωπον αὐτοῦ θεωρεῖν.
προέπεμπον δὲ αὐτὸν εἰς τὸ πλοῖον.

Chapter 10

Iliad 7.123
Νέστωρ δ' Ἀργείοισιν ἀνίστατο
καὶ μετέειπεν.

Acts 1:15
ἀναστὰς Πέτρος ἐν μέσῳ τῶν ἀδελφῶν
εἶπεν.

Iliad 7.161
οἱ δ' ἐννέα πάντες ἀνέσταν.

Acts 1:23
καὶ ἔστησαν δύο.

Iliad 7.161–69
οἱ δ' ἐννέα πάντες ἀνέσταν·
ὦρτο πολὺ πρῶτος μὲν ἄναξ ἀνδρῶν
Ἀγαμέμνων, τῷ δ' ἐπὶ Τυδείδης
ὦρτο κρατερὸς Διομήδης, τοῖσι δ'
ἐπ' Αἴαντες, θοῦριν ἐπιειμένοι ἀλκήν,
τοῖσι δ' ἐπ' Ἰδομενεὺς καὶ ὀπάων
Ἰδομενῆος, Μηριόνης, ἀτάλαντος

Acts 1:13–14
εἰς τὸ ὑπερῷον ἀνέβησαν οὗ ἦσαν
καταμένοντες· ὅ τε Πέτρος καὶ
Ἰωάννης καὶ Ἰάκωβος καὶ Ἀνδρέας,
Φίλιππος καὶ Θωμᾶς, Βαρθολομαῖος
καὶ Μαθθαῖος, Ἰάκωβος Ἀλφαίου
καὶ Σίμων ὁ ζηλωτὴς καὶ Ἰούδας
Ἰακώβου.

Ἐνυαλίῳ ἀνδρειφόντῃ, τοῖσι δ' ἐπ'
Εὐρύπυλος, Εὐαίμονος ἀγλαὸς υἱός,
ἂν δὲ Θόας Ἀνδραιμονίδης
καὶ δῖος Ὀδυσσεύς·
πάντες ἄρ' οἵ γ' ἔθελον πολεμίζειν
Ἕκτορι δίῳ.

οὗτοι πάντες ἦσαν προσκαρτεροῦντες
ὁμοθυμαδὸν τῇ προσευχῇ.

Iliad 7.175–82
οἱ δὲ κλῆρον ἐσημήναντο ἕκαστος,
ἐν δ' ἔβαλον κυνέῃ Ἀγαμέμνονος
Ἀτρείδαο· λαοὶ δ' ἠρήσαντο,
θεοῖσι δὲ χεῖρας ἀνέσχον. ὧδε δέ τις
εἴπεσκεν ἰδὼν εἰς οὐρανὸν εὐρύν·
Ζεῦ πάτερ,
ἢ Αἴαντα λαχεῖν, ἢ Τυδέος υἱόν, ἢ
αὐτὸν βασιλῆα πολυχρύσοιο Μυκήνης.
. . .

Acts 1:24–26a

καὶ προσευξάμενοι
εἶπαν·
σὺ κύριε καρδιογνῶστα πάντων,
ἀνάδειξον ὃν ἐξελέξω ἐκ τούτων
τῶν δύο ἕνα λαβεῖν τὸν τόπον
τῆς διακονίας ταύτης καὶ ἀποστολῆς,
ἀφ' ἧς παρέβη Ἰούδας
πορευθῆναι εἰς τὸν τόπον τὸν ἴδιον.
καὶ ἔδωκαν κλήρους αὐτοῖς,
καὶ ἔπεσεν ὁ κλῆρος ἐπὶ Μαθθίαν.

πάλλεν δὲ Γερήνιος ἱππότα Νέστωρ,
ἐκ δ' ἔθορε κλῆρος κυνέης,
ὃν ἄρ' ἤθελον αὐτοί, Αἴαντος.

Chapter 12

Iliad 24.343 and 445–46
τῇ τ' ἀνδρῶν ὄμματα θέλγει
ὧν ἐθέλει. . . .
τοῖσι δ' ἐφ' ὕπνον ἔχευε διάκτορος
Ἀργειφόντης πᾶσιν, ἄφαρ δ' ὤϊξε
πύλας καὶ ἀπῶσεν ὀχῆας . . .

Lucian *The Ship* 42
. . . ἐς ὕπνον κατασπᾶν
ὁπόσους ἂν ἐθέλω

καὶ ἅπασαν θύραν προσιόντι μοι
ἀνοίγεσθαι χαλωμένου τοῦ κλείθρου
καὶ τοῦ μοχλοῦ ἀφαιρουμένου.

Chapter 14

Iliad 24.673–74, 678–82, and 689–91
οἱ μὲν ἄρ' ἐν προδόμῳ δόμου αὐτόθι
κοιμήσαντο, κῆρυξ καὶ Πρίαμος. . . .
εὗδον παννύχιοι . . .
ἀλλ' οὐχ Ἑρμείαν ἐριούνιον ὕπνος
ἔμαρπτεν, ὁρμαίνοντ' ἀνὰ θυμὸν

Acts 12:6b–9a
τῇ νυκτὶ ἐκείνῃ
ἦν ὁ Πέτρος κοιμώμενος μεταξὺ δύο
στρατιωτῶν δεδεμένος ἁλύσεσιν δυσὶν

ὅπως Πρίαμον βασιλῆα νηῶν ἐκπέμψειε
λαθὼν ἱεροὺς <u>πυλαωρούς</u>.

                             <u>φύλακές τε πρὸ τῆς θύρας</u>
                             ἐτήρουν τὴν φυλακήν.

στῆ δ’ ἄρ’ ὑπὲρ κεφαλῆς καί μιν   <u>καὶ ἰδοὺ ἄγγελος κυρίου ἐπέστη</u>
                             καὶ φῶς ἔλαμψεν ἐν τῷ οἰκήματι·
                             πατάξας δὲ τὴν πλευρὰν τοῦ Πέτρου
<u>πρὸς μῦθον ἔειπεν</u>· ...   ἤγειρεν αὐτὸν <u>λέγων</u>· ἀνάστα ἐν τάχει.
ὣς ἔφατ’, ἔδδεισεν δ’ ὁ γέρων,   καὶ ἐξέπεσαν αὐτοῦ αἱ ἁλύσεις ἐκ
κήρυκα δ’ ἀνίστη.   τῶν χειρῶν.
                             εἶπεν δὲ ὁ ἄγγελος πρὸς αὐτόν·
ποῖσιν δ’ Ἑρμείας <u>ζεῦξ’</u> ἵππους ζῶσαι καὶ <u>ὑπόδησαι τὰ σανδάλιά σου.</u>
<u>ἡμιόνους</u> τε,   ἐποίησεν δὲ οὕτως. καὶ <u>λέγει</u> αὐτῷ·
ῥίμφα δ’   περιβαλοῦ τὸ ἱμάτιόν σου καὶ
ἄρ’ αὐτὸς <u>ἔλαυνε</u> κατὰ στρατόν. <u>ἀκολούθει</u> μοι. καὶ ἐξελθὼν ἠκολούθει.

Iliad 24.443–47   Acts 12:10–11a
ἀλλ’ ὅτε δὴ πύργους τε νεῶν καὶ
τάφρον <u>ἵκοντο</u>, οἱ δὲ νέον περὶ δόρπα <u>διελθόντες</u> δὲ πρώτην <u>φυλακὴν</u>
<u>φυλακτῆρες</u> πονέοντο,   καὶ δευτέραν
τοῖσι δ’ ἐφ’ ὕπνον ἔχευε
διάκτορος Ἀργεϊφόντης πᾶσιν,
ἄφαρ δ’ <u>ὤϊξε πύλας</u> καὶ ἀπῶσεν ὀχῆας, ἦλθαν ἐπὶ τὴν πύλην τὴν σιδηρᾶν
<u>ἐς δ’ ἄγαγε</u> Πρίαμον.   τὴν φέρουσαν εἰς τὴν πόλιν,
                             ἥτις αὐτομάτη <u>ἠνοίγη</u> αὐτοῖς
                             καὶ ἐξελθόντες <u>προῆλθον</u> ...

Iliad 24.692 and 696–97   Acts 12:10b–11b and 12a
ἀλλ’ ὅτε δὴ πόρον <u>ἷξον</u> ἐϋρρεῖος   καὶ ἐξελθόντες <u>προῆλθον</u> ῥύμην μίαν,
ποταμοῖο, ... Ἑρμείας μὲν ἔπειτ’ καὶ εὐθέως <u>ἀπέστη ὁ ἄγγελος</u>
ἀπέβη πρὸς μακρὸν Ὄλυμπον ... ἀπ’ αὐτοῦ. ...
οἱ δ’ ἐς ἄστυ <u>ἔλων</u> οἰμωγῇ τε   συνιδών τε <u>ἦλθεν ἐπὶ τὴν οἰκίαν</u> ...
στοναχ   ῷˮ   ῳῳῃ

Chapter 15

Iliad 24.697–700 and 703–6   Acts 12:13–14
οὐδέ τις ἄλλος ἔγνω πρόσθ’ ἀνδρῶν <u>κρούσαντος</u> δὲ αὐτοῦ τὴν θύραν
καλλιζώνων τε γυναικῶν, ἀλλ’ ἄρα τοῦ <u>πυλῶνος</u>
<u>Κασσάνδρη</u>, ἰκέλη χρυσέῃ Ἀφροδίτῃ, <u>προσῆλθεν παιδίσκη</u> ὑπακοῦσαι
<u>Πέργαμον εἰσαναβᾶσα</u> φίλον πατέρ’ <u>ὀνόματι</u> Ῥόδη,

εἰσενόησεν. . . .
κώκυσέν τ᾽ ἄρ᾽ ἔπειτα γέγωνέ τε πᾶν
κατὰ ἄστυ·
ὄψεσθε, Τρῶες καὶ Τρῳάδες, Ἕκτορ᾽
ἰόντες, εἴ ποτε καὶ ζώοντι μάχης
ἒκ νοστήσαντι χαίρετ᾽, ἐπεὶ μέγα
χάρμα πόλει τ᾽ ἦν παντί τε δήμῳ.

καὶ ἐπιγνοῦσα τὴν φωνὴν τοῦ Πέτρου
ἀπὸ τῆς χαρᾶς οὐκ ἤνοιξεν τὸν
πυλῶνα, εἰσδραμοῦσα δὲ
ἀπήγγειλεν ἑστάναι τὸν Πέτρον
πρὸ τοῦ πυλῶνος.

Abbreviations

AASF	Annales academiae scientiarum Fennicae
AAWM	Abhandlungen der Akademie der Wissenschaften in Mainz
AB	Anchor Bible
AClass	*Acta Classica*
AJT	*American Journal of Theology*
ALGHJ	Arbeiten zur Literatur und Geschichte des hellenistischen Judentums
ALUN	Annales littéraires de l'Université de Nantes
ANRW	*Aufstieg und Niedergang der römischen Welt*
ASP	American Studies in Papyrology
AUUSGrU	Acta Universitatis Upsaliensis, Studia Graeca Upsaliensia
BAGB	*Bulletin de l'Association G. Budé*
BBB	Bonner biblische Beiträge
BEFAR	Bibliothèque des Ecoles françaises d'Athènes et de Rome
BETL	Bibliotheca ephemeridum theologicarum lovaniensium
BGBE	Beiträge zur Geschichte der biblischen Exegese
Bib	*Biblica*
BICS	*Bulletin of the Institute of Classical Studies of the University of London*
BKP	Beiträge zur klassischen Philologie

BMI	The Bible and Its Modern Interpreters
Budé	Collection des universités de France, publiée sous le patronage de l'Association Guillaume Budé
BWANT	Beitäge zur Wissenschaft von Alten (und Neuen) Testament
BZ	*Biblische Zeitschrift*
BZNW	Beihefte zur Zeitschrift für die neutestamentliche Wissenschaft
CBQ	*Catholic Biblical Quarterly*
CJ	*Classical Journal*
CNT	Commentaire du Nouveau Testament
CP	*Classical Philology*
CW	*Classical World*
EH	Europäische Hochschulschriften
EKKNT	Evangelisch-katholischer Kommentar zum Neuen Testament
ETL	*Ephemerides theologicae lovanienses*
FB	Forschung zur Bibel
FS	Festschrift
FRLANT	Forschungen zu Religion und Literatur des Alten und Neuen Testaments
FUME	*Forschung an der Universität Mannheim und Erbegnisse*
GBLS	Greifswalder Beiträge zur Literatur-und Stilforschung
HTKNT	Herders theologischer Kommentar zum Neuen Testament
HTR	*Harvard Theological Review*
ICC	International Critical Commentary
ICS	*Illinois Classical Studies*
JBL	*Journal of Biblical Literature*
JHC	*Journal of Higher Criticism*
JSNT	*Journal for the Study of the New Testament*
JSNTSup	Journal for the Study of the New Testament Supplements
JTS	*Journal of Theological Studies*
LCL	Loeb Classical Library
LD	Lectio Divina
LIMC	*Lexicon iconographicum mythologiae classicae*
MPG	J.-P. Migne, *Patrologiae cursus completus (series Graeca)*
NCS	Noyes Classical Studies
NR	Noctes Romanae
NovT	*Novum Testamentum*
NRSV	New Revised Standard Version of the Bible
NTD	Das Neue Testament deutsch
NTS	*New Testament Studies*
OBL	Orientalia et biblica lovaniensia

OBT	Overtures to Biblical Theology
ÖTKNT	Ökumenischer Taschenbuchkommentar zum Neuen Testament
PW	Pauly-Wissowa, *Real-Encyclopädie der classischen Alter-tumswissenschaft*
PzB	*Protokolle zur Bibel*
RevQ	*Revue de Qumran*
RB	*Revue biblique*
RHPR	*Revue d'histoire et de philosophie religieuses*
RNT	Regensburger Neues Testament
RSC	*Rivista di studi classici*
RSR	*Revue des sciences religieuses*
RTHP	Recueil de travaux d'histoire et de philologie
RTP	*Revue de théologie et de philosophie*
SAC	Studies in Antiquity and Christianity
SANT	Studien zum Alten und Neuen Testament
SB	Sources bibliques
SBLTT	Society of Biblical Literature Texts and Translations
ScEs	*Science et esprit*
SHAW	Sitzungsberichte der Heidelberger Akademie der Wissenschaften
ST	*Studia theologica*
SUSI	Skrifter Utgivna av Svenska Institutet
TA	Theologische Arbeiten
TAPA	*Transactions of the American Philological Association*
TBAW	Tübinger Beiträge zur Altertumswissenschaft
TCH	Transformation of the Classical Heritage
TLZ	*Theologische Literaturzeitung*
TU	Texte und Untersuchungen zur Geschichte der altchristlichen Literatur
TynBul	*Tyndale Bulletin*
TZ	*Theologische Zeitschrift*
WD	*Wort und Dienst*
WJA	*Würzburger Jahrbücher für die Altertumswissenschaft*
WS	Wiener Studien
WSA	Würzburger Studien zur Altertumswissenschaft
WUNT	Wissenschaftliche Untersuchungen zum Neuen Testament
ZBKNT	Zürcher Bibelkommentar, Neues Testament
ZNW	*Zeitschrift für die neutestamentliche Wissenschaft*

Notes

Introduction

1. Philodemus *On Poetry* 5.30.36–31.2 (Jensen, 67–69).

2. New Haven: Yale University Press, 2000. The most obvious similarities pertain to characterizations. Like Odysseus, Jesus is a wise carpenter who suffers many things and sails on the sea with associates who are foolish, craven, and even treacherous. Like Odysseus, Jesus comes to his "house," the Jerusalem Temple, which has fallen into the hands of his rivals, the Jewish authorities, who, like Penelope's suitors, devour widows' houses. Peter plays a role similar to Eurylochus, Odysseus's second in command; blind Bartimaeus calls to mind the blind seer Tiresias; Judas and Barabbas play roles derived from Melanthius and Irus; the unnamed woman who anoints Jesus for burial resembles Odysseus's nurse Eurycleia ("Renowned-far-and-wide"), who recognized her lord's identity when washing his feet. The youth who fled naked at Jesus' arrest and reappears at his tomb is an ersatz Elpenor, whose soul met Odysseus in Hades. Mark's so-called "Messianic Secret" derives from Odysseus's disguise to keep the suitors in the dark concerning his identity lest they slay him. Jesus, too, sought to silence those who witnessed his great deeds lest word get back to his foes.

Whole episodes seem to have been modeled after the *Odyssey*. I compare Jesus' calling of fishermen to follow him with Athena's summoning a crew; the calming of the sea transforms the tale of Aeolus's bag of winds; the exorcism of the Gerasene demoniac borrows from the stories of Circe and Polyphemus; the beheading of John the Baptist resembles the murder of Agamemnon; the multiplication of loaves and fish for five thousand men and again for four thousand men and women reflects the twin feasts in *Odyssey* 3 and 4, the first of which feeds four thousand five hundred men at the edge of the sea. Jesus walks on water like Hermes and

Athena. The Transfiguration of Jesus before Peter, James, and John is a transform of Odysseus's transfiguration before his son, Telemachus. Odysseus's picaresque entry into the city of the Phaeacians inspired Jesus' entry into Jerusalem. The cleansing of the Temple imitates Odysseus's slaying of the suitors, and the agony at Gethsemane echoes Odysseus's agony during his last night with Circe before going off to Hades.

Mark also borrowed from the *Iliad*. The epic frequently predicts the deaths of its heroes, Achilles and Hector, providing Mark with a possible model for his repeated predictions of Jesus' death. Homer did not narrate the death of Achilles, but Mark found the death of Hector and the rescue of his corpse promising prototypes for his Passion Narrative. Like Hector, Jesus heroically refused wine and felt abandoned by his god. Elijah did not appear to help Jesus just as Deiphobos failed to help Hector. The centurion gloated over Jesus as Achilles had gloated over Hector. Three women lamented Jesus' death, like Hecuba, Andromache, and Helen, who lamented Hector. Joseph of Arimathea plays the role of Priam in courageously rescuing Jesus' corpse at night. Mark did not borrow blindly from the epics; he transformed them to portray Jesus as superior to the likes of Odysseus and Hector. Most notably, unlike the *Iliad*, the earliest gospel is indeed good news: Jesus, unlike Hector, rises from his grave.

I also have published several other studies of the influence of classical Greek poetry on ancient Jewish and Christian writings: *Christianizing Homer: "The Odyssey," Plato, and "The Acts of Andrew"* (New York: Oxford University Press, 1994); "Luke's Eutychus and Homer's Elpenor: Acts 20:7–12 and *Odyssey* 10–12," *JHC* 1 (1994): 5–24; "The Soporific Angel in Acts 12:1–17 and Hermes' Visit to Priam in *Iliad* 24: Luke's Emulation of the Epic," *Forum* n.s. 2.2 (1999): 179–87; "The Shipwrecks of Odysseus and Paul," *NTS* 45 (1999): 88–107; "The Ending of Luke and the Ending of the *Odyssey*," in *For a Later Generation: The Transformation of Tradition in Israel, Early Judaism and Early Christianity*, ed. Randal A. Argall et al. (Harrisburg: Trinity Press International, 2000), 161–68; and "Tobit and the *Odyssey*," in *Mimesis and Intertextuality in Antiquity and Christianity*, ed. Dennis R. MacDonald, SAC (Harrisburg: Trinity Press International, 2001), 11–40.

3. There still exists no authoritative treatment of mimesis in Greco-Roman literature, but the following studies are useful: Peter Hermann, *Wahrheit und Kunst. Geschichtschreibung und Plagiat im klassischen Altertum* (Leipzig: B. G. Teubner, 1911); Eduard Stemplinger, *Das Plagiat in der griechischen Literatur* (Leipzig: B. G. Teubner, 1912; reprint, Hildesheim: Georg Olms Verlag, 1990), 118–21 and 212–15; George Converse Fiske, *Lucilius and Horace: A Study in the Classical Theory of Imitation* (Madison: University of Wisconsin Press, 1920; reprint Westport: Greenwood, 1971); Helen North, "The Use of Poetry in the Training of the Ancient Orator," *Traditio* 8 (1952): 1–33; Richard McKeon, "Literary Criticism and the Concept of Imitation in Antiquity," in *Critics and Criticism*, ed. Ronald Salmon Crane (Chicago: University of Chicago Press, 1952), 147–75; H. Koller, *Die Mimesis in der Antike: Nachahmung, Darstellung, Ausdruck* (Berne: A. Francke, 1954); Donald Lemen Clark, *Rhetoric in Greco-Roman Education* (New York: Columbia University Press, 1957), 144–76; Jacques Bompaire, *Lucien écrivain. Imitation et création*, BEFAR 190 (Paris: Boccard, 1958); Bernard Kytzler, "Imitatio und Aemulatio in der Thebais de Statius," *Hermes* 97 (1969): 209–32; B. P. Reardon, *Courants littéraires grecs des IIe et IIIe siècles après J.-C.*, ALUN 3 (Paris: Belles Lettres, 1971), 3–11; Tomas Hägg, *Narrative Technique in Ancient Greek Romances: Studies of Chariton, Xenophon Ephesius, and Achilles Tatius*, SUSI 8.8

(Uppsala: Almquist & Wikells Boktryckeri, 1971), 306–35; Herbert Juhnke, *Homerisches in römischer Epik flavischer Zeit. Untersuchungen zu Szenennachbildungen und Strukturentsprechungen in Statius' Thebais und Achilleis und in Silius' Punica,* Zetemata 53 (Munich: C. H. Beck, 1972); Hermann Strasburger, *Homer und die Geschichtsschreibung,* SHAW (Heidelberg: C. Winter, 1972); Jan Fredrik Kindstrand, *Homer in der zweiten Sophistik,* AUUSGrU 7 (Uppsala: University of Uppsala, 1973); Hermann Funke, "Homer und seine Leser in der Antike," *FUME* (1976–1977): 26–38; Elaine Fantham, "Imitation and Decline: Rhetorical Theory and Practice in the First Century after Christ," *CP* 73 (1978): 102–16; D. A. Russell, "De imitatione," in *Creative Imitation in Latin Literature,* ed. D. A. West and A. J. Woodman (Cambridge: Cambridge University Press, 1979), 1–16; Georg Nicholaus Knauer, *Die Aeneis und Homer,* 2d ed., Hypomnemata 7 (Göttingen: Vandenhoeck & Ruprecht, 1979); and "Vergil's *Aeneid* and Homer," in *Oxford Readings in Vergil's Aeneid,* ed. S. J. Harrison (Oxford: Oxford University Press, 1990), 390–412; Thomas M. Greene, *The Light in Troy: Imitation and Discovery in Renaissance Poetry* (New Haven: Yale University Press, 1982); G. Williams, "Roman Poets as Literary Historians: Some Aspects of *Imitatio,*" *ICS* 8 (1983): 211–37; Thomas Louis Brodie, "Greco-Roman Imitation of Texts as a Partial Guide to Luke's Use of Sources," in *Luke-Acts: New Perspectives from the Society of Biblical Literature Seminar,* ed. Charles H. Talbert (New York: Crossroad, 1984), 17–46; Virginia Knight, *The Renewal of Epic: Responses to Homer in the Argonautica of Apollonius,* Mnemosyne Sup. 152 (Leiden: E. J. Brill, 1995); Stephen Hinds, *Allusion and Intertext: Dynamics of Appropriation in Roman Poetry* (New York: Cambridge University Press, 1998); Ellen Finkelpearl, *Metamorphosis of Language in Apuleius: A Study of Allusion in the Novel* (Ann Arbor: University of Michigan Press, 1998); and Dennis R. MacDonald, ed., *Mimesis and Intertextuality in Antiquity and Christianity,*" SAC (Harrisburg: Trinity Press International, 2001).

4. Quintilian *Institutio oratoria* 10.2.1.

5. George A. Kennedy, *The Art of Persuasion in Greece* (Princeton: Princeton University Press, 1963), 332.

6. For a defense of this perspective, see especially Gérard Genette, *Palimpsestes. La Littérature au second degré* (Paris: Editions du Seuil, 1982), 450.

7. The popularity of the *Iliad* for ancient Mediterranean cultures is beyond question, but the following works provide useful documentation: John A. Scott, *Homer and His Influence* (Boston: Marshall Jones, 1925); Félix Buffière, *Les Mythes d'Homère et la pensée grecque,* Budé (Paris: Belles Lettres, 1956); Howard Clarke, *Homer's Readers: A Historical Introduction to the "Iliad" and the "Odyssey"* (Newark: University of Delaware Press, 1980); Robert Lamberton, *Homer the Theologian: Neoplatonist Allegorical Reading and the Growth of the Epic Tradition,* TCH 9 (Berkeley: University of California Press, 1986); and *Homer's Ancient Readers: The Hermeneutics of Greek Epic's Earliest Exegetes,* ed. Robert Lamberton and John J. Keaney (Princeton: Princeton University Press, 1992). For uses of Homer among early Christians see Nicole Zeegers-Vander Vorst, *Les Citations des poètes grecs chez les apologistes chrétiens du IIᵉ siècle,* RTHP 4.47 (Leuven: Leuven University Press, 1972); and MacDonald, *Christianizing Homer,* 17–34.

8. On the physical survivals of the *Iliad* see Roger A. Pack, *The Greek and Latin Literary Texts from Greco-Roman Egypt,* 2d ed. (Ann Arbor: University of Michigan Press, 1965).

9. Ps.-Heraclitus *Quaestiones Homericae* 1.5–6.

10. Important treatments of Homeric heroes in art in appear in *LIMC*. The following studies also are useful: Margaret R. Scherer, *The Legends of Troy in Art and Literature* (New York: Phaidon, 1964); Knud Friis Johansen, *The Iliad in Early Greek Art* (Copenhagen: Munksgaard, 1967); Thomas H. Carpenter, *Art and Myth in Ancient Greece: A Handbook* (London: Thames and Hudson, 1991); Susan Woodford, *The Trojan War in Ancient Art* (Ithaca: Cornell University Press, 1993); and Anthony M. Snodgrass, *Homer and the Artists: Text and Picture in Early Greek Art* (New York: Cambridge University Press, 1998).

11. Marion Lausberg, "Lucan und Homer," *ANRW* 2.32.3 (1985), 1578.

12. On Artapanus, see p. 128, and on Tobit, see MacDonald, "Tobit and the *Odyssey*."

13. M. Z. Kopidakis, "Ἰώσηφος ὁμηρίζων," *Hellenika* 37 (1986): 3–25.

14. See the catalogue of these materials in Raffaela Cribiore, *Writing, Teachers, and Students in Graeco-Roman Egypt*, ASP 36 (Atlanta: Scholars Press, 1997).

15. Hinds, *Allusion and Intertext,* 31.

16. Minneapolis: Fortress Press, 2000.

17. Ibid., vii–viii.

18. Ibid., 26.

19. Ibid., 164.

20. Ibid., 61–86.

21. Ibid., 86.

22. Ibid., 182.

23. See, for example, R. Keydell, "Quintus Smyrnaeus und Vergil," *Hermes* 82 (1954): 254–56; and M. Mondino, "Di alcune fonti de Quinto Smirneo: V. Quinto Smirneo e i poeti latini," *RSC* 5 (1957): 229–35.

24. *Consolatio ad Polybium* 11.5; cf. 8.2.

25. *Legacy,* 103. The closest parallel she detects is the catalogue of nations in Acts 2:9–11 and *Aeneid* 6.792–96 and especially 8.722–28.

26. R. J. Tarrant, "Aspects of Virgil's Reception in Antiquity," in *The Cambridge Companion to Virgil,* ed. Charles Martindale (Cambridge: Cambridge University Press, 1997), 56–57.

27. "Vergil in der griechischen Antike," *Klio* 67 (1985): 281–85.

28. *Sibylline Oracles* 11.144–68; translation by John J. Collins, in *The Old Testament Pseudepigrapha,* vol. 1: *Apocalyptic Literature and Testaments,* ed. James H. Charlesworth (Garden City, N.Y.: Doubleday, 1983), 438.

29. Luke 4:25–26; cf. Heb 11:35.

30. On the influence of Elijah narratives on Luke, see Jean-Daniel Dubois, "La Figure d'Elie dans la perspective lucanienne," *RHPR* 53 (1973): 155–76; Jean Martucci, "Les récits de miracle. Influence des récits de l'Ancien Testament sur ceux du Nouveau," *ScEs* 27 (1975): 136–37; Wolfgang Roth, *Hebrew Gospel: Cracking the Code of Mark* (Oak Park: Meyer-Stone Books, 1988), 8 and 38; Markus Öhler, *Elia im Neuen Testament. Untersuchungen zur Bedeutung des alttestamentlichen Propheten im frühen Christentum,* BZNW 88 (Berlin: Walter de Gruyter, 1997), 136–39; and a series of studies by Thomas Louis Brodie, especially "Luke 7,36–50 as an Internalization of 2 Kings 4,1–37: A Study in Luke's Use of Rhetorical Imitation," *Bib* 64 (1983): 457–85; "Greco-Roman Imitation,"17–46; "Towards Unraveling Luke's Use of the Old Testament: Luke 7.11–17 as an *Imitatio* of 1 Kings 17.17–24," *NTS* 32 (1986): 247–67; "The Departure for Jerusalem (Luke 9,51–56)

as a Rhetorical Imitation of Elijah's Departure for the Jordan (2 Kgs 1,1–2,6)," *Bib* 70 (1989): 96–109; and "Luke-Acts as an Imitation and Emulation of the Elijah-Elisha Narratives," in *New Views on Luke and Acts*, ed. Earl Richard (Collegeville, Minn.: Liturgical Press, 1990), 78–85.

31. E.g., Ernst Haenchen, *The Acts of the Apostles: A Commentary*, trans. and ed. B. Noble et al. (Philadelphia: Westminster Press, 1971), 339–40; Jürgen Roloff, *Die Apostelgeschichte übersetzt und erklärt*, 17th ed., NTD 5 (Göttingen: Vandenhoeck & Ruprecht, 1981), 161; and Josef Zmijewski, *Die Apostelgeschichte*, RNT (Regensburg: Pustet, 1994), 403.

32. E.g., Aulus Gellius *Attic Nights* 9.9.1–3.

33. Brodie relates Luke's καὶ ἐγένετο ἐξῆς to 1 Kings 17.17a: καὶ ἐγένετο μετὰ ταῦτα ("Luke's Use," 251).

34. Ibid., 262; see also Félix Gils, *Jésus prophète d'après les évangiles synoptiques*, OBL 2 (Leuven: Leuven University Press, 1957), 26–27, and Martucci, *Récits*, 134–35.

35. 1 Kings 17:10 (LXX): εἰς τὸν πυλῶνα τῆς πόλεως; Luke 7:12: τῇ πύλῃ τῆς πόλεως.

36. François Bovon, *L'Evangile selon saint Luc (1,1–9,50)*, CNT IIIa (Geneva: Labor et Fides, 1991), 350.

37. Brodie, "Luke's Use," 253–54 and 258.

38. Ibid., 256.

39. Bovon, *L'Evangile*, 350.

40. Brodie, "Luke's Use," 259. See also Heinz Schürmann, *Das Lukasevangelium*, 3d ed., HTKNT 3 (Freiburg: Herder, 1984), 400–402.

41. MacDonald, "Ending of Luke."

42. See MacDonald, *Christianizing Homer*.

43. Thomas S. Kuhn masterfully discussed this process in *The Structure of Scientific Revolutions*, 3d ed. (Chicago: University of Chicago Press, 1996).

Chapter 1. Cornelius and Peter

1. Acts 2:17 and 21, citing Joel 3:1–5.

2. Acts 10:34b–35.

3. Acts 11:15.

4. Acts 11:1.

5. Acts 15:8–9.

6. C. K. Barrett, *A Critical and Exegetical Commentary on the Acts of the Apostles*, ICC (Edinburgh, T & T Clark, 1994), 1.495. See also Edgar Haulotte, "Fondation d'une communauté de type universel. Actes 10,1–11,18," *RSR* 58 (1970): 63–64, and Roloff, *Apostelgeschichte*, 164. The importance of Cornelius's conversion did not escape the notice of ancient readers. See the extensive treatment of patristic interpretations in François Bovon, *De vocatione gentium. Histoire de l'interprétation d'Actes 10,1–11,18 dans les six premiers siècles*, BGBE 8 (Tübingen: Mohr [Siebeck], 1967).

7. So also Alfons Weiser, *Die Apostelgeschichte*, 2 vols., ÖTKNT 5 (Gütersloh: Gütersloher Verlagshaus Mohn, 1981), 1.249.

8. Acts 10:1–8.

9. Acts 10:9–16.

10. The following scholars hold to some form of this double, independent tradition theory: Martin Dibelius, *Studies in the Acts of the Apostles*, trans. M. Ling and P. Schubert (New York: Scribner's, 1956), 109–22; Otto Bauernfeind, *Kommentar und Studien zur Apostelgeschichte. Mit einer Einleitung von Martin Hengel*, WUNT 22 (Tübingen: Mohr [Siebeck], 1980), 141–43; Hans Conzelmann, *The Acts of the Apostles: A Commentary on the Acts of the Apostles*, trans. James Limburg, A. Thomas Kraabel, and Donald H. Juel, ed. Eldon J. Epp with Christopher Mathews, Hermeneia (Philadelphia: Fortress Press, 1987), 80; François Bovon, "Tradition et rédaction en Actes 10,1–18," *TZ* 26 (1970): 22–45, Weiser, *Apostelgeschichte*, 262; Zmijewski, *Apostelgeschichte*, 413–16; and Barrett, *Acts*, 493–96, 516, and 535.

11. According to Walter Schmithals, Luke composed these tales to make Peter, not Paul, the apostle to the gentiles (*Die Apostelgeschichte des Lukas*, ZBKNT 3.2 [Zurich: Theologischer Verlag, 1982], 102–4). Beverly Roberts Gaventa argues that Luke created them to emphasize the role of hospitality in the gentile mission (*From Darkness to Light: Aspects of Conversion in the New Testament*, OBT 20 [Philadelphia: Fortress Press, 1986], 107–25). "The narrative that stands in Acts 10:1–11:18 was written entirely by Luke and reflects his concerns at every point" (109). In this context one might also mention a study by Walter T. Wilson, who gives primary credit for the creation of the Cornelius story to Lucan redaction ("Urban Legends: Acts 10:1–11:18 and the Strategies of Greco-Roman Foundation Narratives," *JBL* 120 [2001]: 77–99). "Acts 10:1–11:18 represents Luke's attempt to fashion for Gentile Christianity a foundational myth, one that would have been not only congenial to a hellenized readership but also appropriate to his apologetic, etiological, institutional, and providential aims in writing. As such, it can be effectively compared in terms of form and function with other Greco-Roman myths about community origins" (95).

12. E.g., Haenchen, *Acts*, 361–63. This is the conclusion also of John S. Hanson, "The Dream-Vision Report and Acts 10.1–11.18: A Form-Critical Study" (dissertation, Harvard University, 1978).

13. E.g., Karl Löning, "Die Korneliustradition," *BZ* 18 (1974): 1–19, Roloff, *Apostelgeschichte*, 164–66, and Klaus Haacker, "Dibelius und Cornelius. Ein Beispiel formgeschichtlicher Überlieferungskritik," *BZ* 24 (1980): 234–51.

14. E.g., Achilles Tatius *Leucippe and Clitophon* 4.1, Apuleius *Metamorphoses* 11.3–6 and 13 (cf. 22). See Rosa Söder, *Die apokryphen Apostelgeschichten und die romanhafte Literatur der Antike*, WSA 3 (Darmstadt: Wissenschaftliche Buchgesellschaft, 1969; reprint of 1932 edition), 171–80, Alfred Wikenhauser, "Doppelträume," *Bib* 29 (1948): 100–111, Gaventa, *Darkness*, 109–11, and Hanson, "Dream-Vision Report," esp. 34–50 and 117–24.

15. Joseph A. Fitzmyer, *The Acts of the Apostles: A New Translation with Introduction and Commentary*, AB 31 (New York: Doubleday, 1998), 448.

16. Weiser, *Apostelgeschichte*, 252.

17. Joseph B. Tyson has noted the unusual absence of biblical allusions in the Cornelius story, with the exception of Peter's speech in 10:34–43. "Perhaps it is because Luke knew that his narrative constituted a significant alteration in the authority of scripture that he departed from his usual practice of citing it to justify the Gentile mission" ("The Gentile

Mission and the Authority of Scripture in Acts," *NTS* 33 [1987]: 629). This might well be the case, but I shall argue that Luke's primary model for his complex tale was not biblical but classical.

Chapter 2. Lying Dream and True Portent

1. *Iliad* 2.1–19.

2. William Stuart Messer, *The Dream in Homer and Greek Tragedy* (New York: Columbia University Press, 1918), 3–7; Joachim Hundt, *Der Traumglaube bei Homer,* GBLS 9 (Greifswald: Hans Dallmeyer, 1935), 39–43; and A. H. M. Kessels, *Studies in the Dream in Greek Literature* (Utrecht: HES Publishers, 1978), 7–10. Oneiros is not a dream god per se; that role usually was filled by Hermes, "the nearest approach to a dream divinity in the Homeric poems" (Messer, *Dream in Homer,* 4). After Homer, Hermes won the epithet "dream-sender" (ὀνειροπομπός).

3. *LIMC*, s.v. "Oneiros." See also Euripides *Hecuba* 70–71: "black-winged dreams."

4. *Iliad* 2.16–41.

5. On this point, see Porphyry *Quaestionum Homericarum ad Iliadem* to 2.305–29 and Eustathius *Commentarii ad Homeri Iliadem* to 2.307.

6. *Iliad* 2.76–81.

7. *Iliad* 2.114–15.

8. *Iliad* 2.301–20.

9. *Iliad* 2.321–29.

10. For this interpretation, see the scholia and the detailed symbolic explanation by Porphyry *Quaestionum Homericarum ad Iliadem* to 2.305–29. Eustathius was aware of Porphyry's treatment and agreed with it (*Commentarii ad Homeri Iliadem* to 2.307, p. 183).

11. *Iliad* 2.330–35.

12. *Iliad* 2.419–20.

13. *Iliad* 9.17–22.

14. According to the data assembled by Teresa Morgan in *Literate Education in the Hellenistic and Roman Worlds* (New York: Cambridge University Press, 1998), 308–9.

15. Cribiore, *Writing,* catalog number 299 (*P.Ant.* III 156).

16. Ibid., number 331 (T.Hamb.inv. 736).

17. Ibid., number 259 (*P.Oslo* III 66). A paraphrase of *Iliad* 1 and 2 survives from the Byzantine author Moscopoulos (Eleonora Melandri, "La Parafrasi di M. Moscopulo ad Hom. A-B 493 e la tradizione esegetica e lessiografica dell'Iliade," *Prometheus* 9 [1983]: 177–92).

18. Theon *Progymnasmata* 5.205.10–17 (Walz).

19. *Republic* 2.383a.

20. *Zeus Rants* 40.

21. *Gallus* 8.

22. Aristotle *Poetics* 1461a22. See also Alexander Aphrodisiensis *In Aristotelis sophisticos elenchos commentarius* 34.2–35.8.

23. *Quaestionum Homericarum ad Iliadem* loc. cit.

24. Apud Proclus *Commentary on Plato's Republic* 1.115–17.

25. *Commentary on the Dream of Scipio* 1.7.5, translated by William Harris Stahl, *Macrobius: Commentary on the Dream of Scipio* (New York: Columbia University Press, 1952), 118–19.

26. Justin Martyr *First Apology* 25 and Irenaeus *Adversus haereses* 1.12.

27. *Oratio ad graecos* 21.1.

28. Gregory's Epitome 26 (see MacDonald, *Christianizing Homer*, 185).

29. *Metamorphoses* 12.11–23. Ovid interpreted the serpent as the Greek army and the sparrows as Trojans.

30. *De divinatione* 2.28.63–30.65. Cicero mentions a similar portent as Sulla was sacrificing to the gods. A prophet interpreted the darting of a serpent from the altar as a propitious sign and told Sulla to pursue a battle that he ultimately won (1.33.72). According to Eustathius and his ancient authorities, Calchas interpreted the sparrows sitting atop the tree as the clue to their symbolism. Three natural revolutions determine time: the revolution of the earth is one day; that of the moon, one month; that of the sun, one year. If the birds had been nesting in the trunk, they would symbolize days, if in the lower branches months, in the top branches years (*Commentarii ad Homeri Iliadem* to 2.307).

31. *Contra Celsum* 4.91.

32. *Megara* 17–28.

33. *An Ethiopian Story* 2.22 (J. R. Morgan, in B. P. Reardon, *Collected Ancient Greek Novels* [Berkeley: University of California Press, 1989]). R. W. Garson attributes the image to Heliodorus's use of *Iliad* 2 ("Notes on Some Homeric Echoes in Heliodorus' *Aethiopica*," *AClass* 18 [1975]: 137–40), but according to Máximo Brioso Sánchez the novelist used the earlier imitation in Moschus ("Mosco y Heliodoro. El símil de Etiópicas II, 22,4," *Habis* 17 [1986]: 117–21).

34. *Protrepticus* 10 (74).

35. *Oratio 15. In Maccabaeorum laudem*, MPG 35.925, A-B.

Chapter 3. More Dreams and Portents

1. *De divinatione* 1.24.50.

2. Quintilian 4.2.9: "By the very fact that they are so easy, embellishments from dreams and wonders have lost their authority." According to Seneca the Elder, declaiming against trivial uses of dreams was a rhetorical topos (*Suasoriae* 4.4; cf. *Controversiae* 2.1.33 and Petronius *Satyricon* 10).

3. *Dream in Homer*, 57–58 (Messer's emphasis). Joachim Latacz says much the same ("Funktionen des Traums in der antiken Literatur," *WJA* 10 [1984]: 31).

4. This delineation of motifs is similar to that provided by James F. Morris in " 'Dream Scenes' in Homer: A Study in Variation," *TAPA* 113 (1983): 39–54.

5. E.g., F. Oskar Hey, *Der Traumglaube der Antike. Ein historischer Versuch*, Programm des kgl. Realgymnasiums München 1907–1908 (Munich: F. Staub, 1908), 12–13, and Messer, *Dream in Homer*, 24–31.

6. E.g., Georg Danek, *Epos und Zitat. Studien zu den Quellen der Odyssee*, WS 22 (Vienna: Österreichische Akademie der Wissenschaften, 1998), 1–23.

7. See the misgivings about literary dependence by Hundt (*Traumglaube*, 65. n. 76).

8. *Odyssey* 4.799–802 and 6.13–19.

9. *Iliad* 2.20–25.

10. *Odyssey* 4.803–4.

11. *Odyssey* 6.21–25; cf. *Iliad* 2.795. Compare *Odyssey* 6.24: τῇ μιν ἐεισάμενος προσέφη γλαυκῶπις Ἀθήνη, and *Iliad* 2.22: τ ῷ μιν ἐεισάμενος προσεφώνεε θεῖος ὄνειρος.

12. *Odyssey* 4.805–7.

13. *Iliad* 2.26–27 and 30–31.

14. *Odyssey* 4.812–13 and 825.

15. *Odyssey* 6.36–40.

16. *Iliad* 2.35.

17. *Odyssey* 4.838–39.

18. *Odyssey* 6.41–42.

19. *Odyssey* 4.839–41.

20. *Odyssey* 6.48–65.

21. For the most part, dreams in the tragedies do not strictly follow the Homeric pattern, though their function is similar. Echoes of the lying dream are audible also in Apollonius *Argonautica* 3.616–32 and 4.1347–61 and perhaps Plutarch *Alexander* 18. Plutarch probably had *Iliad* 2 in mind also when composing the dream to Agesilaus: a voice told him that he alone, like Agamemnon, was general of all of the Greek forces, leading them against the armies of Asia, and even sailing off from Aulis. Like Agamemnon, he was to offer in sacrifice his own daughter, something he refused to do (*Agesilaus* 6.4).

22. See Plutarch *Pompey* 68.2, Florus 2.13.45, Julius Obsequens 65a; cf. Appian *Civil War* 2.68. On the complex connection with Livy, see W. Rutz, "Die Träume des Pompeius in Lucans Pharsalia," *Hermes* 91 (1963): 335–37.

23. See especially Lausberg, "Lucan," 1574–80. On mimesis in Latin poetry see especially Williams, "Roman Poets," 211–37.

24. Lausberg, "Lucan," 1574.

25. *Bellum civile* 7.7–8. Ovid's paraphrase of the lying dream to Agamemnon uses a similar expression: *deceptus imagine somni* (*Metamorphoses* 13.216).

26. For a discussion of this imitation see Knauer, *Aeneis und Homer*, 236–37, and "Vergil and Homer," *ANRW* 2.32.2 (1981): 883 ("This dream scene [in the *Iliad*] has in fact served as pattern from the dream scene with Allecto and Turnus"). The most thorough treatment of dreams in the *Aeneid* is Hans Rudolf Steiner, *Der Traum in der Aeneis*, NR 5 (Bern: Paul Haupt, 1952); he discusses the dream of Turnus in 62–66 and compares it with *Iliad* 2 in 64–65. Useful as well is Clyde Murley, "The Use of Messenger Gods by Vergil and Homer," *Vergilius* 3 (1939): 3–11.

27. *Aeneid* 7.312–16; cf. *Iliad* 2.13–14, where Homer says Hera "bent [ἐπέγναμψεν]" the minds of the Olympians.

28. *Aeneid* 7.339.

29. *Aeneid* 7.408–9.

30. *Aeneid* 7.331.

31. *Aeneid* 7.408, 476, and 561.

32. *Aeneid* 7.413–16 and 419; see the Appendix.

33. *Aeneid* 7.420–22; see the Appendix.

34. *Aeneid* 7.427–28.

35. *Aeneid* 7.429–31; see the Appendix.

36. *Aeneid* 7.432.

37. *Aeneid* 7.458–59.

38. *Aeneid* 7.445–55.

39. Juhnke demonstrates that Statius borrowed directly from Homer for his dream in *Thebaid* 2 (*Homerisches*, 65–67). In addition to Juhnke's authoritative treatment, see Kytzler, "Imitatio und Aemulatio," 209–32.

40. *Thebaid* 1.241–43.

41. *Thebaid* 1.298.

42. *Thebaid* 2.89–90 and 93–94; see the Appendix. Statius actually devoted much of the opening of the poem to Mercury's journey; see also 1.303–11 and 2.1–80.

43. *Thebaid* 2.94–97; see the Appendix.

44. *Thebaid* 2.101–4; see the Appendix.

45. *Thebaid* 2.115–16.

46. *Thebaid* 2.116–17.

47. *Thebaid* 2.120; see the Appendix.

48. *Thebaid* 2.125–27.

49. Adele J. Haft, "τὰ δὴ νῦν πάντα τελεῖται: Prophecy and Recollection in the Assemblies of *Iliad* 2 and *Odyssey* 2," *Arethusa* 25 (1992): 224. It should be noted that Haft argues for a more complex and interactive relationship between the two epics. Richard B. Rutherford is more confident that *Odyssey* 2 imitates *Iliad* 2 ("From the *Iliad* to the *Odyssey*," *BICS* 38 [1991–93]: 44). Danek, however, refuses to decide on the mechanics of the parallels: "conscious imitation; style of the poet himself; traditional style" (*Epos und Zitat*, 75).

50. *Odyssey* 2.146–47.

51. *Odyssey* 2.155–56.

52. *Odyssey* 2.165–66. Compare also the description of Halitherses in 2.157–160 with that of Calchas in *Iliad* 1.68–73. *Odyssey* 2.160 and *Iliad* 1.73 are identical.

53. *Odyssey* 2.174–76.

54. *Iliad* 2.330 and *Odyssey* 2.176.

55. *Agamemnon* 104–59. For an explanation of the transformation of the serpent-sparrow portent to the eagles-hare, see Richard Seaford, "Homer and Tragic Sacrifice," *TAPA* 119 (1989): 87–95. The "great sign" of the "red serpent" in Rev. 12:1–6 could be an imitation of the same scene. The serpent stands before a pregnant woman waiting for her to bear a child so that he can devour it. According to Photius, Alexander of Myndos claimed that the serpent that ate the sparrows once had fought with Heracles against the Nemean lion (*Bibliotheca* 190.147b.27).

56. *Life of Apollonius of Tyana* 1.22.

57. Similarly, Vergil recounts the traditional Roman portent of Aeneas and the white sow with a litter of thirty sucklings, with each suckling representing a year (*Aeneid* 8.40–48). On the origin of this portent see Steiner, *Traum*, 71–72 and 103–4.

58. *Dionysiaca* 25.7–10.

59. *Dionysiaca* 25.4–6.

60. The parallels between *Iliad* 2 and Vergil's account of Laocoön are well known. See especially the detailed comparison of Adele J. Haft in "Odysseus' Wrath and Grief in the *Iliad*: Agamemnon, the Ithacan King, and the Sack of Troy in Books 2, 4, and 14," *CJ* 85 (1990): 107–9. Haft uses the parallels to argue that Homer already knew of the Laocoön

episode and modeled the death of Democoön in *Iliad* 4 after it. Vergil clearly knew of Laocoön from epic tradition; see H. Kleinknecht, "Laokoon," *Hermes* 79 (1944): 66–111.

61. *Aeneid* 2.199–207, 212–17, 222, and 225–27; see the Appendix.

62. "The story of the dream can come only from the lips of the dreamer, and this fact introduces that element of uncertainty about the dream . . . which must be confirmed by the direct omen" (Messer, *Dream in Homer,* 68).

63. Ibid., 67. Messer argues that the combination of the dream and the portent first appeared in Aeschylus.

64. "The analogy with the dream of Agamemnon . . . has often been pointed out" (Reginald Walter Macan, *Herodotus. The Seventh, Eighth, and Ninth Books,* vol. 1, pt. 1 [London: Macmillan, 1908], 22). According to Hundt, the dream in Herodotus 7.12 displays "distinct Homeric influence" (*Traumglaube,* 42). See also Hey, *Traumglaube,* 17–18; Ludwig Huber, "Herodots Homerverständnis," in *Synusia,* FS Wolfgang Schadewaldt, ed. Hellmut Flashar and Konrad Gaiser (Pfullingen: Neske, 1965), 38, and especially H. A. Gärtner's superb treatment of the dreams and their indebtedness to *Iliad* 2 ("Les Rêves de Xerxès et d'Artaban chez Hérodote," *Ktéma* 8 [1983]: 11–18). On Herodotus and Homer generally see Michèle Giraudeau, "L'Héritage épique chez Hérodote," *BAGB* (1984): 4–13.

65. *History* 7.12. Here I part company with Peter Frisch, who thinks Herodotus actually had access to a Persian source (*Die Träume bei Herodot,* BKP 27 [Meisenheim: Anton Hain, 1968], 14–15).

66. *History* 7.18.

67. *History* 7.12, 14, and 17.

68. *History* 7.18.

69. *History* 7.13.

70. *History* 7.15.

71. *History* 7.18.

72. Adolf Köhnken argues that Herodotus imitated the dream to Agamemnon for the first three dreams and composed the fourth dream as a sign of confirmation, but he does not relate it to the serpent-sparrow portent ("Der dritte Traum des Xerxes bei Herodot," *Hermes* 116 [1988]: 24–40).

73. *History* 7.47.

74. *De divinatione* 1.48–49. See also Valerius Maximus 1.7.

75. Livy 21.22.7–9.

76. Polybius despised these superstitious, pseudo-historical explanations of Hannibal's decision (3.48).

77. See Juhnke's treatment in *Homerisches,* 197–98. See also Hundt, *Traumglaube,* 54 n. 41.

78. *Punica* 3.163–67; see the Appendix.

79. *Punica* 3.168–69; see the Appendix.

80. *Punica* 3.170–74; see the Appendix.

81. *Punica* 3.181.

82. *Punica* 3.179–81.

83. *Punica* 3.182.

84. *Punica* 3.198–201.

85. *Punica* 3.214–16; see the Appendix.

86. Other examples of dreams followed by portents or oracles include: Aeschylus *Persians* 176–214 (where after a dream the mother of Xerxes sees a hawk slay an eagle at the altar of Helios), *Prometheus Bound* 637–73, Plutarch *Alexander* 26.3–6, and *Cimon* 18.

Chapter 4. The Visions of Cornelius and Peter

1. Acts 10:1–2. For our purposes one need not decide the relationship of so-called God-fearers to the synagogue.

2. Acts 10:22. Commentators rightly note the similarities between this centurion and Luke's redactional presentation of another in his version of Q's healing of the centurion's son. Only in Luke does one find Jewish advocates referring to the soldier as "worthy. . . . For he loves our ethnos, and he himself built our synagogue" (7:3–5). The similarities suggest that Luke himself was responsible also for the glowing depiction of Cornelius in Acts 10:1–2.

3. Acts 10:24 and 11:14.

4. Acts 10:27.

5. *Iliad* 8.238–42.

6. "Dass Kornelius der 'italischen Kohorte' zugehört haben soll, ist historisch falsch" (Roloff, *Apostelgeschichte*, 168). The *Cohors II miliaria Italica civium Romanorum voluntariorum* was not stationed in Judea until 69 C.E.

7. *Scipio's Dream* 2.1.

8. *Commentary on the Dream of Scipio* 1.3.14–15 (Stahl's translation). Artemidorus quotes Nestor's statement in *Iliad* 2.80–82 and adds: "What he means is that if any common Achaean soldier had mentioned the dream, we would have thought, not that the speaker was a liar, but rather that the dream itself was a lie" (*Interpretation of Dreams* 1.2; the translation is that of Robert J. White, *The Interpretation of Dreams* = *Oneirocritica by Artemidorus*, NCS [Park Ridge, NJ: Noyes Press, 1975]).

9. Valerius Maximus discussed several dreams in ancient literature, most of which appeared to military officers (1.7).

10. The Appendix presents these parallels and others in this chapter in Greek.

11. *Odyssey* 4.803 (στῆ) and 6.21 (στῆ), and Herodotus 7.12 (ἐπιστάντα), 14 (ἐπιστάν), and 17 (ὑπερστάν).

12. Haenchen, *Acts*, 346. Barrett rightly notes that the reference to the ninth hour (3 P.M.) makes it clear that "the vision is not to be thought of as a nocturnal dream" (*Acts*, 502). See also Heliodorus *Aethiopica* 3.11 and 8.11 on visions being more trustworthy than dreams.

13. Cf. *Odyssey* 4.804.

14. Ancient scholia distinguish between daytime and nighttime dreams, and "a daytime vision is more likely to be true" (Roseph Russo in *A Commentary on Homer's Odyssey*, vol. 3: *Books XVII–XXIV*, ed. Alfred Heubeck et al. [Oxford: Oxford University Press, 1988–1992], 3.102).

15. This expression is Jewish; see Lev 6:8, Ps 141:2, Sirach 35:16–17, and Tobit 12:12. F. F. Bruce likens Cornelius's prayers and alms ascending to God to "the smoke of a sacrifice" (*The Book of the Acts*, 2d ed. [Grand Rapids: William B. Eerdmans, 1990], 254).

16. The expression of divine favor also is sincere in *Odyssey* 4.805–7.

17. Acts 10:5–6.

18. Acts 11:14.

19. This construction (στρατιώτην εὐσεβῆ τῶν προσκαρτερούντων αὐτῷ) is similar to Homer's description of Nestor, "whom Agamemnon esteemed most among his elders" (τόν ῥα μάλιστα γερόντων τῖ᾽ Ἀγαμέμνων; *Iliad* 2.21).

20. Praying on a roof has parallels in Jewish texts (Barrett, *Acts,* 504), but the location is unusual, especially in the heat of noon. The location, hour, and hunger conspire to explain Peter's ecstasy, but the location outside also allows for him to see the vessel descending from heaven.

21. Barrett, *Acts,* 505.

22. The list of animals resembles lists of animals in Gen 1:24 (minus birds) and 6:20, Lev 11:46–47, and Rom 1:23. The inclusion of all types of animals but fish has prompted some exegetes to view the descending sheet as a metaphorical Noah's ark insofar as it saved all such creatures from the flood before the Mosaic legislations concerning clean and unclean animals (see discussion in Zmijewski, *Apostelgeschichte,* 420).

23. Acts 10:11–16. The word translated "slay" is θῦσον; θύειν is usually associated with sacrifices. Barrett: "Peter is called upon to perform a religious act, which as such will be completed by eating" (*Acts,* 507). Peter's refusal to eat, which has no parallel in the portent at Aulis, may be been influenced by a similar refusal in Ezek 4:9–15, esp. 14.

24. *Odyssey* 2.155–56.

25. Acts 10:9.

26. Acts 10:17.

27. Acts 10:19.

28. Acts 11:11.

29. Acts 10:20 and 22. The phrase translated here "making no distinction" is μηδὲν διακρινόμενος, which can also mean simply "without hesitation." Luke has Peter repeat the expression in 11:12, but it is Peter's reflection on the episode in Acts 15:9 that tilts the translation: God "made no distinction between us [Jews] and them [the gentiles] by purifying their hearts by faith." Barrett thus paraphrases the occurrence in 10:20 appropriately: "Go, without letting the distinction between Jew and Gentile perplex your mind" (*Acts,* 511).

30. Acts 10:24.

31. Bovon, *Vocatione,* 92–194, esp. 93–118.

32. E.g., Roloff, *Apostelgeschichte,* 170.

33. Acts 10:15 and 19–20.

34. Acts 10:22.

35. Acts 10:28.

36. Acts 10:48. Notice also that Peter "entertained [ἐξένισεν]" the gentile emissaries over night at the house of Simon (10:23).

37. Acts 11:3.

38. This explanation is similar to that offered by Gaventa, for whom the theme of hospitality binds the vision and its interpretation together (*Darkness,* 107–22).

39. See also the discussion on pp. 34–42.

40. *Iliad* 2.50–52 and 55–56.

41. *Iliad* 2.52.

42. Roloff, *Apostelgeschichte*, 171.

43. E.g., Zmijewski, *Apostelgeschichte*, 424.

44. See also *Iliad* 3.120, 7.312, 11.251, 18.251, and 23.36.

45. *Iliad* 1.91; cf. 2.82. On Agamemnon's hubris, see also 1.202–5.

46. Acts 10:33, Fitzmyer's rendering of σύ τε καλῶς ἐποίησας παραγενόμενος (*Acts*, 458).

47. Bovon, *Vocatione*, 50–51.

48. There is no formula introducing the speech in most texts of the epic, but for line 55 the Hellenistic philologian Zenodotus recorded a variant consisting of two lines, the second of which is τοῖσι δ' ἀνιστάμενος μετέφη κρείων Ἀγαμέμνων, "mighty Agamemnon rose up and spoke to them." This variant modestly resembles the introduction to Cornelius's speech in Acts 10:30a: καὶ ὁ Κορνήλιος ἔφη, "And Cornelius said . . ."

49. Acts 10:34–35.

50. *Iliad* 2.301–2.

51. *Iliad* 2.91–92.

52. *Iliad* 2.333–35.

53. *Iliad* 2.394–95.

54. Acts 11:1–3.

55. Acts 11:11.

Chapter 5. Local Legend or Homeric Imitation?

1. Gaventa argues that the reference to Simon's house near the sea "appears to be super-fluous" but actually is important—not the reference to the sea but to the house, which is relevant to the theme of hospitality (*Darkness*, 113).

Luke described the descending container as a huge sheet or sail (ὀθόνην μεγάλην). In Homer ὀθόνη refers to linen cloth (*Iliad* 3.141 and 18.595 and *Odyssey* 7.107), but it later referred, among other things, to sails. In favor of relating it to sails is the statement that it had four corners by which it apparently was taken back into heaven. This seems to be how a scribe responsible for a Western variant took it: "a container tied on four corners like a bright sail [τέσσαρσιν ἀρχαῖς δεδεμένον σκεῦός τι ὡς ὀθόνην λαμπράν]."

2. *Iliad* 2.4 and 17; cf. 47 and 91–93.

3. *Iliad* 2.167–210.

4. *Iliad* 2.333–34.

5. In Herodotus the sign of the olive branch bolstered the three dreams that seemed to promise victory to Xerxes and the Persians. The vision of the devastating serpent in Silius Italicus underscored the assurance to Hannibal that he would conquer Rome.

6. On repetition in *Iliad* 2 see G. S. Kirk, *The Iliad: A Commentary*, vol. 1: *Books 1–4* (Cambridge: Cambridge University Press, 1985), 121–22.

7. *History* 7.47.

8. For repetitions in Acts 10–11 see Ronald D. Witherup, "Cornelius Over and Over and Over Again: 'Functional Redundancy' in the Acts of the Apostles," *JSNT* 49 (1993): 45–66. Repetition not only calls attention to the importance of the scene, it increases suspense, allows for significant variations, and contributes to character development. William S. Kurz

emphasizes the differences in narration by an omniscient narrator and a cognitively limited character ("Effects of Variant Narrators in Acts 10–11," *NTS* 42 [1997]: 570–86). See also Edith M. Humphrey, "Collision of Modes? — Vision and Determining Argument in Acts 10:1–11:18," *Semeia* 71 (1995): 65–84.

9. *Iliad* 2.50–83 (the council) and 84–393 (the gathering of the army).

10. Acts 10:28 and 30–32.

11. Acts 11:5–11 and 13–14.

12. Latacz, "Funktionen," 31–34.

13. *Iliad* 2.81

14. *Iliad* 9.9–28.

15. Acts 15:7–9; cf. 14.

16. Many ancient readers of the *Iliad* also blamed Agamemnon for not questioning the truthfulness of the dream and for taking the "now" to mean "this very day." The episode of the lying dream besmirches Agamemnon as well as Zeus (Latacz, "Funktionen," 35).

17. Huber shows how Herodotus understood the Persian War in terms of Homer's depiction of the Trojan War and repeatedly borrowed from the *Iliad* for his presentation of the conflict between Xerxes and the Greeks ("Homerverständnis," esp. 36–40).

18. Jouette M. Bassler argues that Luke's perspective is consistent with Greco-Roman attitudes toward universalism (the inclusion of the marginalized to privileged groups) whereas Paul's is consistent with Jewish apocalyptic (the abolition of ethnic and cultural differences) and therefore more radical ("Luke and Paul on Impartiality," *Bib* [1985]: 546–52).

19. Acts 10:34–35.

Chapter 6. Hector's Farewell to Andromache

1. E.g., Lars Aejmelaeus, *Die Rezeption der Paulusbriefe in der Miletrede (Apg 20.18–35)*, AASF B, 232 (Helsinki: Suomalainen Tiedeakatemia, 1987).

2. The most important studies of the speech as a testament are Johannes Munck, "Discours d'adieu dans le Nouveau Testament et dans la littérature biblique," in *Aux Sources de la tradition chrétienne. Mélanges offerts à M. Goguel* (Neuchâtel: Delachaux & Niestlé, 1950), 155–70; Otto Knoch, *Die "Testamente" des Petrus und Paulus. Die Sicherung der apostolischen Überlieferung in der spätneutestamentlichen Zeit*, SB 62 (Stuttgart: KBW Verlag, 1973); and William S. Kurz, "Luke 22:14–38 and Greco-Roman and Biblical Farewell Addresses," *JBL* 104 (1985): 251–68. The most thorough study of the genre of the speech is that by Hans-Joachim Michel, *Die Abschiedsrede des Paulus an die Kirche, Agp. 20,17–38. Motivgeschichte und theologische Bedeutung*, SANT 35 (Munich: Kösel-Verlag, 1973). On the farewell discourse in Judaism, see Eckhard von Nordheim, *Die Lehre der Alten*, 2 vols., ALGHJ 13 (Leiden: E. J. Brill, 1980); and Anitra Bingham Kolenkow, "Testaments: The Literary Genre 'Testament,' " in *Early Judaism and Its Modern Interpreters*, ed. Robert A. Kraft and George W. E. Nickelsburg, BMI 2 (Atlanta: Scholars Press, 1986), 259–67.

The following studies also merit mention. Some scholars have sought to defend the historical reliability of the speech, noting that it appears in one of the famous "we-sections" that might suggest the speech the author himself — or the author of his source — actually heard (e.g., Colin J. Hemer, "The Speeches of Acts: Part 1: The Ephesian Elders at Miletus," *TynBul* 40 [1989]: 76–85 and 239–59). Others have proposed reliance on a speech attributed to Paul that Luke used as a source (e.g., Thomas L. Budesheim, "Paul's *Abschiedsrede* in the Acts of the Apostles," *HTR* 69 [1976]: 9–30; and Lewis R. Donelson, "Cult Histories and the Sources of Acts," *Bib* 68 [1987]: 1–21). Several interpreters have noted the logical disjunctions in Paul's argument and have sought to make sense of it with structural proposals (e.g., J. Cheryl Exum and Charles H. Talbert, "The Structure of Paul's Speech to the Ephesian Elders [Acts 20:18–35]," *CBQ* 29 [1967]: 233–36; Jan Lambrecht, "Paul's Farewell-Address at Miletus [Acts 20,17–38]," in *Les Actes des apôtres. Tradition, rédaction, théologie,* ed. Jacob Kremer et al., BETL 48 [Leuven: Leuven University Press, 1979], 307–37; Jacques Dupont, "La Construction du discours de Milet," in his *Nouvelles études sur les actes des apôtres,* LD 118 [Paris: Cerf, 1984], 424–45; and John J. Kilgallen, "Paul's Speech to the Ephesian Elders: Its Structure [Acts 20:18–35]," *ETL* 70 [1994]: 112–21). Others have mined it to identify the opponents Luke had in mind or to detect his understanding of apostolic tradition and ecclesiastical office (e.g., H. Schürmann, "Das Testament des Paulus für die Kirche, Apg 20, 18–35," in his *Traditionsgeschichtliche Untersuchungen zu den synoptischen Evangelien. Beiträge* [Düsseldorf: Patmos Verlag, 1968], 310–40; G. W. H. Lampe, " 'Grievous Wolves' [Acts 20:29]," in *Christ and Spirit,* FS. C. F. D Moule, ed. Barnabas Lindars and Stephen S. Smalley [Cambridge: Cambridge University Press, 1973], 253–68; Franz Prast, *Presbyter und Evangelium in nachapostolischer Zeit. Die Abschiedsrede des Paulus in Milet [Apg 20,17–38] im Rahmen der lukanischen Konzeption der Evangeliumsverkündigung,* FB 29 [Stuttgart: Verlag katholisches Bibelwerk, 1979]; P.-R. Tragen, "Les 'Destinataires' du discours de Milet. Une approche du cadre communautaire d'Ac 20,18–35," in *À Cause de l'évangile. Études sur les synoptiques et les Actes* [Paris: Cerf, 1985], 779–98; and Evald Lövestam, "Paul's Address at Miletus [Acts 20:18–35]," *ST* 41 [1987]: 1–10).

3. *Abschiedsrede,* 68–71.

4. Several of these arguments against the testamentary hypothesis were raised by Christoph Burchard, "Paulus in der Apostelgeschichte," *TZ* 12 (1975): 889. Lawrence Wills claims the speech is primarily a sermon ("The Form of the Sermon in Hellenistic Judaism and Early Christianity," *HTR* 77 [1984]: 277–99), while Duane F. Watson views it as an instance of Greek epideictic rhetoric ("Paul's Speech to the Ephesian Elders [Acts 20.17–38]: Epideictic Rhetoric of Farewell," in *Persuasive Artistry: Studies in New Testament Rhetoric in Honor of George A. Kennedy,* ed. Duane F. Watson, JSNTSup 50.1 [Sheffield: JSOT Press, 1991], 184–208).

5. I have not found a single reference to the *Iliad* in scholarship on Paul's farewell address. For example, Michel studiously avoided investigating farewell speeches in Greco-Roman literature as a whole, despite the popularity of the form as early as Plato's account of Socrates' death in the *Phaedo.*

6. *Iliad* 6.87–88.

7. *Iliad* 6.113–15.

8. *Iliad* 6.269–76; cf. 296–311.

9. *Iliad* 6.365–68.

10. *Iliad* 6.403.

11. *Iliad* 6.441–50, and 454–55, and 459–65.

12. *Iliad* 6.466–81.

13. *Iliad* 6.487–502.

14. G. S. Kirk, *The Iliad: A Commentary*, vol. 2: *Books 5–8* (Cambridge: Cambridge University Press, 1990), 219.

15. *Brutus* 23.2–3.

16. *Brutus* 23.3–4, quoting *Iliad* 6.429–30 and 491. It is worth noting that Philo cited three lines from *Hector in Troy* (*Migration of Abraham* 156–57, *Special Laws* 2.6, and *Every Good Man Is Free* 112).

17. See *LIMC*, "Andromache," items 4–25, and "Hektor," items 12–29.

18. *Odyssey* 1.356–63 (cf. 21.350–57), Herodotus's *History* 4.162, Sophocles' *Ajax* 500–557, Aristophanes' *Lysistrata* 534–57, Plato's *Phaedo* 59a–60 and 115a–117d, Xenophon's *Cyropaedia* 6.4.2–11, Apollonius's *Argonautica* 1.292–304 (see also 1.557–58 and 3.793–801), Chariton's *Chaereas and Callirhoe* 3.8, 4.1, and 8.5, Xenophon of Ephesus's *Ephesiaca* 1.10.9–11.1, Heliodorus's *Aethiopica* 1.27–28, Vergil's *Aeneid* 2.671–795, 7.443–44, and 12.436–43 (see also 3.316–19 and 4.304–92), Seneca's *Troades* 438–76 and 767–85, Ovid's *Heroides* 13, and Silius Italicus's *Punica* 3.70–135. Other possible imitations of the scene in Latin poetry include lines by Catullus, Propertius, and Statius. Catullus seems to have had Andromache's tears in mind when describing those of a certain Bernice when her husband left for war (*Poem* 66). Anticipating his death, Propertius addressed his lover with echoes of Hector's speech to Andromache (Propertius 1.19). In the *Thebaid*, Statius sends a weeping Agria to her father, the tyrant Capaneus, with her baby Thessander in her arms, fearing that her husband soon would die in battle (3.678–721).

19. *Ars rhetorica* 1.2.314–15 (Spengel).

Chapter 7. Paul's Farewell to the Ephesian Elders

1. Acts 19:21; cf. 23:11 and 27:24.

2. Acts 21:4.

3. François Bovon sees behind both Acts 20–21 and *Iliad* 6 a common pattern present also in Plato's *Crito*, the Apocryphal Acts of Apostles, and Christian martyrdoms. A noble character goes willingly to his death despite opportunities to avoid it ("Le Saint-esprit, l'église et les relations humaines selon Actes 20,36–21,16," in *Les Actes des apôtres. Traditions, rédaction, théologie*, ed. J. Kremer, BETL 48 [Leuven: Leuven University Press, 1979], 340–51).

4. The Appendix presents these and other parallels in this chapter in Greek.

5. Acts 20:18b–21. According to Michel, Acts 20:18b–21 and 26–27 conform to the testamentary motifs of the speaker's self-presentation as a moral example and declaration of integrity, even though they play a role here more dominant than is usually found in testaments, even in 1 Samuel 12, its closest Jewish analog (*Abschiedsrede*, 69). Nothing in these verses, however, suggests that Paul appealed to his behavior at Ephesus as an example for others, nor is the emphasis on Paul's innocence, though the motif is present. The emphasis is on Paul's courage in the face of persecution.

6. Acts 9:23–24.

7. Acts 9:29.

8. Acts 13:50.

9. Acts 14:2 and 5.

10. Acts 17:5.

11. Acts 17:13.

12. Acts 18:12.

13. Acts 20:3; cf. 23:30.

14. For the Greek parallels see the Appendix.

15. Other scholars have recognized similarities between the opening lines of Paul's speech and 1 Thess 2:1–2. Lars Aejmelaeus, for example, makes a compelling case that Luke actually modeled these verses after that letter (*Rezeption*, 98–112 and 128–32). Even if Aejmelaeus were correct, it would not rule out the influence of the *Iliad* as well. Ancient authors frequently imitated multiple models, taking elements from each in the composition of a superior hybrid. A favorite image for such eclecticism was that of a bee taking nectar from several blossoms to blend them "into one delicious compound that, even though it betrays its origin, yet it nevertheless is clearly a different thing from that whence it came" (Seneca *Epistle* 84.3–5). A comparison of Acts 20:18–21 with 1 Thess 2:1–2 suggests how Luke christianized Hector's speech to Andromache.

Acts 20:18b–19 has no equivalent in *Iliad* 6, and here the parallels with 1 Thessalonians 2 are closest.

1 Thess 2:1–2a	Acts 20:18b–19
For *you yourselves know*, brothers,	*You yourselves know* how *I was* with you
our introduction to you,	the entire time *from the first day*
that *it was* not in vain,	*that I arrived in Asia* —
but, as *you yourselves know*,	serving the Lord with all *lowliness, tears*,
even though *we had suffered earlier and*	and *testings* that came to me through the
were abused . . .	plots of the Jews . . .

Just a few verses later in 1 Thessalonians (2:14–16) Paul complains of Jewish opposition to his preaching to gentiles, yet another parallel to Acts 20:19: "through the plots of the Jews." Despite these similarities there is a significant difference: in 1 Thessalonians Paul used the first person plural, "we," which included himself but also his missionary associates, presumably Silvanus and Timothy (1:1). In Acts, however, Paul uses the first person singular as though he alone had the courage to preach in the face of dangerous opposition. Hector, of course, had used the first person singular when addressing Andromache.

Not all scholars are convinced that Luke imitated 1 Thessalonians here, but all recognize that he successfully gave the speech a Pauline voice. Verses 18–19 are stuffed with typical Pauline expressions, some of which Deutero-Pauline imitators used as well. For "you yourselves know" compare 1 Thess 1:5, 2:5 and 9–12, Gal 4:13, Phil 4:15, and 2 Thess 3:7–8; for "serving the Lord" compare 1 Thess 1:9, Rom 12:11 and 16:18, Col 3:24, and Eph 6:7; cf. Gal 1:10, Rom 1:1, Phil 1:1, Col 4:12, and Eph 6:6; for "lowliness" compare 2 Cor 10:1 and 11:7, Phil 2:3 and 8 and 4:12, and Eph 4:2; for "tears" compare 2 Cor 2:4 and Phil 3:18; for "Jews and Greeks" compare 1 Cor 22 and 24, 10:32, and 12:13, Gal 3:28, Rom 1:16, 2:9 and 10, and 10:12, and Col 3:11. None of these expressions parallels Hector's speech to Andromache.

16. 1 Thess 2:2; cf. 2 Cor 7:4, Phil 1:20, and Phlm 8. Aejmelaeus argues that Luke modeled Acts 20 after this passage in 1 Thessalonians.

1 Thess 2:2b	Acts 20:20–21
In Philippi *we had boldness* in our God *to speak to you* the *gospel of God* with great struggle.	*I did not hold back anything beneficial,* either from *preaching to you* or teaching you in public and from house to house, by testifying both to Jews and to Greeks about *repentance toward God.*

Whether or not Luke had 1 Thessalonians in mind, here again he used characteristic Pauline expressions: "Jews and Greeks," "testifying," "repentance," and above all "faith." For "testifying" compare 1 Thess 2:12 and 4:6, Gal 5:3, Eph 4:17, 1 Tim 5:2, and 2 Tim 2:14 and 4:1; and for "repentance" compare 2 Cor 7:9–10 and 12:21 and Rom 2:4. "Faith," of course, is a dominating concern throughout both Pauline and Deutero-Pauline letters.

17. Eph 3:12 and 6:19–20 and Acts 9:27–28, 13:46, 14:3, 19:8, 26:26, and 28:31; cf. Col 2:15 and 1 Tim 3:13.

18. *Isthmian Odes* 2.39–40.

19. *De falsa legatione* 338. See also Deut 1:17 LXX, Wisd 6:7, Josephus *Vita* 278, *War* 1.518, and *Antiquities* 2.80, and Plutarch *Demetrius* 47.4.

20. *Sacrifices of Abel and Cain* 35.

21. Wilhem Dittenberger, *Sylloge inscriptionum graecarum.* 4th ed. (Hildesheim: Georg Olms, 1960), nn. 547, lines 9–11, and 700, lines 28–29; cf. n. 613, lines 31–34. For other examples of opposition between παρρησία and ὑποστέλλω, see Demosthenes *De falsa legatione* 237 and *First Philippic* 51, Isocrates *Evagoras* 39, and Plutarch *Moralia* 60c. For an excellent discussion of the matter see Jacques Dupont, *Le Discours de Milet. Testament pastoral de Saint Paul (Actes 20, 18–36),* LD 32 (Paris: Cerf, 1962), 58–67.

22. On the two expressions as correlates see Aejmelaeus, *Rezeption,* 105–7.

23. John Chrysostom delivered a sermon on Acts 20:17–21 and interpreted it as a tribute to apostolic courage. "Here he [Paul] reveals his courage, not courage so much as endurance, as though he were saying, 'I suffered severely, but with you.' . . . He posits both love and courage when he says, "I withheld nothing" (*Homily 44 on the Acts of the Apostles,* MPG 60.309; cf. MPG 56.277 and 60.313).

24. According to Michel, these verses express the Jewish testamentary motif of the announcement of death (*Abschiedsrede,* 69). To be sure, the apostle says the elders will never see him again, but he also confesses that he is unsure about the future: "not knowing what will happen to me." Aejmelaeus argues that Luke here again is imitating Paul's epistles, especially 1 Thess 2:8–10, Phil 2:16–17, and Eph 3:6–7. These proposed parallels with the letters have impressed few interpreters, but there can be little doubt that Luke colored the speech from his Pauline palette: "testifying," "chains," "afflictions," "ministry," "gospel," and "grace" are frequent in the Pauline corpus, as are statements of Paul's willingness to die (e.g., 2 Cor 5:1–9, Gal 6:14, and Phil 1:20–26).

25. See Aejmelaeus, *Rezeption,* 116.

26. Wilhelm Metz, "Hektor als der homerischste aller homerischen Helden," *Gymnasium* 97 (1990): 385–404.

27. *Iliad* 6.487–88.

28. *Argonautica* 1.295–96 and 298–300. Herodotus 1.91.1 almost certainly is an imitation of *Iliad* 6.488: "It is impossible for anyone — even a god — to escape one's ordained fate [μοῖραν]." See Huber, "Homerverständnis," 35–36.

29. Hector's command that Andromache return home to her tasks and her maidservants (ἀμφιπόλοισι) finds an echo in Jason's command to his mother, "Remain here, quiet, among your maidservants [ἀμφιπόλοισι]" (*Argonautica* 1.292–304; cf. *Iliad* 6.484–94). Compare also *Argonautica* 1.557–58 and *Iliad* 6.394–403, and *Argonautica* 3.793–801 and *Iliad* 6.459–65.

30. *Punica* 3.133–35 (LCL).

31. Acts 21:14. Hector's statement concerning the inevitability of fate later generated a lively philosophical debate, to which Christian authors joined their voices: Heraclitus frag. 105, Lucian *Apology* 8.19, Ps.-Lucian *Philopatris* 14.8, Plutarch *Consolatio ad Apollonium* 117e–118a, Porphyry *Ad Iliadem* 1.3.10 and 1.104.3, and Eusebius *Praeparatio evangelica* 6.8.2.5 and 6.8.6.5 (quoting the Epicurean Diogenianus). Clement of Alexandria considered the line a favorite of Greek plagiarists (*Stromata* 6.2.22). Demosthenes mentions a public inscription whose last line may allude to *Iliad* 6.488 (*De corona* 289).

32. W. Schadewaldt, "Hector and Andromache," in *Homer: German Scholarship in Translation*, trans. G. M. Wright and P. V. Jones (Oxford: Clarendon Press, 1997), 124–42 and 135. See also Kirk, *Iliad*, 2.220.

33. Acts 20:26–27. Luke twice already had written of responsibility for someone's blood. According to 5:28, the high priest in Jerusalem accused the apostles of blaming Jewish authorities for the blood of Jesus. Acts 18:6 claims that when Jews in Macedonia rejected apostolic preaching with blasphemies, Paul said, "your blood be on your own heads; I am pure." John Chrysostom noted that if Paul had shrunk from his duty, he would have been responsible for their "blood" and might rightly have been condemned as a murderer — worse than a murderer, suggested Chrysostom. A murderer destroys the body; Paul would have destroyed their souls (MPG 50.656).

34. *Iliad* 6.403.

35. Two curiosities in this verse have piqued the curiosity of commentators. First, the elders are now called ἐπίσκοποι, which is here translated as "overseers" but later came to mean "bishops." Scholars have sought to determine how this designation relates to the use of ἐπίσκοπος in Judaism, to the titles elder and deacon, and to later usage. The second peculiarity is the final phrase and its apparent reference to God's blood. Ancient scribes emended the text by changing the church "of God" to the church of "the Lord," or "the Lord and God," or "the Lord Jesus," or "Jesus Christ," or "Christ." Scholars have opined that the word "son" dropped out after the word "own" by confusion: the blood "of God's own [son]." Others have taken the reference to "his own" to be a christological title, "his Own." Still others suggest that Luke crudely incorporated a traditional christological statement into the speech without recognizing what it might then imply about heavenly hemoglobin.

Luke does not make clear how the blood of Jesus rescued "the church of God." If read in light of other New Testament texts, like Heb 9:12 and Rev 1:5–6 and 5:9–10, Jesus' blood would seem an alternative to the blood of animal sacrifices in the temple for the remission of sins. The reference to the new covenant in Jesus' blood in Luke 22:19–20, however, suggests that the blood of Jesus contrasts with the blood of the sacrificed animals at the giving of the Mosaic covenant in Exod 24:5–6.

36. I have followed F. J. Foakes Jackson and Kirsopp Lake in translating the verb περιε-ποιήσατο as "rescued." They state that the use of περιποιέομαι "in the Old and New Testament seems to be prevailingly 'save alive,' or 'rescue from destruction'" as in Luke 17:33, Heb 10:39, and Eph 1:14 (*The Beginnings of Christianity,* Part 1: *The Acts of the Apostles,* 5 vols. [London: Macmillan, 1920–1933; reprint, Grand Rapids: Baker, 1979], 4.261).

37. *Odyssey* 1.356–59; cf. *Iliad* 6.490–93. These lines are repeated almost verbatim in *Odyssey* 21.350–53.

38. Compare *Iliad* 6.495–99 and *Odyssey* 1.360–63 and 21.354–57. For a judicious discussion of the relationship of *Iliad* 6 and *Odyssey* 1, see Danek, *Epos und Zitat,* 61–62.

39. Stephanie West in Heubeck, *Commentary,* 1.120. West athetizes this passage, as did Aristarchus, but the authenticity of the passage does not alter the point made here. Whether created by the *Odyssey* poet or by a later scribe, the passage seems an imitation of *Iliad* 6. See also Rutherford, "From the *Iliad,*" 51.

40. In *Iliad* 6.433–39 Andromache offered Hector advice that, had he followed it, would have prolonged his life.

41. See *Iliad* 6.463, where Hector says someday Andromache will long for a man to save her.

42. *Lysistrata* 534–48 and 556–57; the translation, with alterations, is that of Jeffrey Henderson, *Three Plays by Aristophanes: Staging Women* (New York: Routledge, 1996). See also Quintus Smyrnaeus *Posthomerica* 1.468–69.

43. Henderson, *Three Plays,* 213–14 n. 11.

44. Herodotus *History* 4.162.

45. *Aeneid* 7.443–44.

46. Acts 20:29–31. According to Michel, Acts 20:29–31 instantiate the testamentary motif of prophecies of future events that often include woes (*Abschiedsrede,* 70). Here the fit with Jewish testaments is strongest. 2 Timothy, unquestionably a pseudo-Pauline final testament, gives an extended warning about the future in keeping with the genre (2 Tim 3:1–4:4; cf. 1 Tim 1:3–7, 4:1–7, and 6:3–4, Eph 4:14, and 2 Pet 2:1–3:18). Paul himself warned against those who preached contradictory messages (e.g., Gal 1:6–9 and 5:7–12 and Rom 16:17–18).

Fridolin Keck and Aejmelaeus have demonstrated tantalizing similarities between these verses and Mark 13:21–23, where Jesus warns four disciples of future pseudo-Messiahs and pseudo-prophets (Keck, *Die öffentliche Abschiedsrede Jesu in Lk 20,45–21,36. Eine redaktions-und motivgeschichtliche Untersuchung,* FB 25 [Stuttgart: Verlag Katholisches Bibelwerk, 1973], 161–64; and Aejmelaeus, *Rezeption,* 142–48). Luke obviously knew Mark but did not use these verses in his own version of Jesus' apocalyptic prophecies in Luke 21, possibly reserving them for Acts. Several other scholars have examined Acts 20:29–30 for evidence identifying these opponents with contemporary religious movements (e. g., Schürmann, "Testament des Paulus," 310–40; Lampe, "'Grievous Wolves,'" 253–68; Prast, *Presbyter und Evangelium,* passim; Tragen, "'Destinataires,'" 779–98, and Lövestam, "Paul's Address," 1–10).

47. *Iliad* 6.447–49.

48. E.g., Matt 7:15, *Didache* 16:3 (quite possibly based on Matt 7:15 as was Justin Martyr in *First Apology* 16.13 and *Dialogue with Trypho* 35.3), Ignatius *Philad* 2:1–2, and 2 Clem 5:2–4; cf. John 10:11–12 and Philostratus *Life of Apollonius of Tyana* 8.22. Wolf

tropes in Jewish literature include Ezek 22:27 (LXX), Zeph 3:3 (LXX), 4 Ezra 5:18, and 1 Enoch 89:13–27. For a useful treatment of this ancient metaphor see Dupont, *Discours,* 209–13.

49. *Iliad* 16.156–63 (LCL).

50. *Iliad* 16.352–56 (LCL).

51. E.g., Quintus Smyrnaeus *Posthomerica* 7.504–11, 8.267–72, and 13.44–49, 258–66 (concerning the death of Astyanax) and 133–42. Vergil uses the image of savage wolves in Aeneas's recounting of the fall of Troy, but he applies it to the Trojans, not to the Greeks (*Aeneid* 2.355–60).

52. *Iliad* 6.450, 454–55, and 459–65.

53. *Ajax* 500–504; see the Appendix.

54. *Ajax* 516–19.

55. Lisa B. Hughes, "Vergil's Creusa and *Iliad* 6," *Mnemosyne* 50 (1997): 415 n. 28.

56. Acts 20:32.

57. Luke uses a similar expression with the verb παραδίδωμι in Acts 14:26 and 15:40. See also Jesus' prayer in Luke 23:46: "Father, into your hands I commend [παρατίθεμαι] my spirit" (quoting Ps 31:5).

58. Acts 20:36.

59. E.g., Dupont, *Discours,* 285–86; Prast, *Presbyter und Evangelium,* 149; and Aejmelaeus, *Rezeption,* 166.

60. On this matter I agree with Bruce, *Acts,* 435; Weiser, *Apostelgeschichte,* 568 and 579; Zmijewski, *Apostelgeschichte,* 745–46; Fitzmyer, *Acts,* 675; and Marion L. Soards, *The Speeches in Acts: Their Content, Context, and Concerns* (Louisville: Westminster/John Knox, 1994), 105.

61. Acts 20:32–36, redacted.

62. The analysis of this chain of tradition is the burden of Prast's study, *Presbyter und Evangelium;* see esp. 157–211. See also Michel, *Abschiedsrede,* 73–100.

63. Dupont, *Discours,* 244–50; and Aejmelaeus, *Rezeption,* 157–58.

64. Michel surely is right in viewing this verse as a blessing of the elders in keeping with the literary final testament (*Abschiedsrede,* 70).

65. Aejmelaeus suggests that Luke may have been influenced by 1 Thess 2:13 ("the Logos of God, which also is at work in you who believe"), by 1 Thess 5:11 ("build each other up"), and by Eph 1:18 ("the wealth of the glory of his inheritance to the saints"); cf. Deut 33:3–4. Aejmelaeus also notes that verses 33–34 are strewn with Pauline vocabulary and sentiments (*Rezeption,* 166–75 and 219–24). Especially suggestive are parallels in 1 Thess 2:9–12 and 4:11–12 and 1 Cor 4:11–12; see also Eph 4:28.

66. *Iliad* 6.476–81.

67. Compare *Troades* 767–85 with *Iliad* 6.476–81. See also *Troades* 461–76 where Andromache addresses Astyanax before his death with clear allusions to the Homeric scene. On the influence of Homer's Andromache on later writings, especially on poetry, see Thadeusz Zielinski, "De Andromacha Posthomerica," *Eos* 31 (1928): 1–39.

68. For a superb discussion of this scene as well as Aeneas's farewell to Creusa, see Louis H. Feldman, "Ascanius and Astyanax: A Comparative Study of Virgil and Homer," *CJ* 53 (1957–58): 361–66.

69. *Aeneid* 12.430–31 and 433–34.

70. *Chaereas and Callirhoe* 8.5.15; see the Appendix.

71. Reardon, *Greek Novels*, 119 n. 131.

72. *Ajax* 550–51.

73. *Ajax* 556–57.

74. Compare *Ajax* 550–51.

75. *Aeneid* 12.433–36 and 438–43; see the Appendix.

76. *Punica* 3.70–72 and 75–77; cf. *Iliad* 6.476–81.

77. Richard T. Bruère, "Silius Italicus *Punica* 3,62–162 and 4,763–822," CP 47 (1952): 219.

78. *Iliad* 6.479–81.

79. *Chaereas and Callirhoe* 3.8.7–8; see the Appendix.

80. This saying appears nowhere in the Gospels; a tantalizingly similar saying appears in Thucydides 2.97.4, "where it is said that the Thracians thought it better λαμβάνειν μᾶλλον ἢ διδόναι, therein being opposite to the Persians (who thus must have thought it better διδόναι μᾶλλον ἢ λαμβάνειν), which is virtually the Lucan saying" (Barrett, *Acts*, 983; he also cites other examples).

81. *Ajax* 556–57.

82. *Punica* 3.73–75.

83. *Iliad* 6.487–502.

84. *Odyssey* 1.360 and 362–63; cf. 21.354–57.

85. *Cyropaedia* 6.4.11.

86. *Chaereas and Callirhoe* 4.1.1; see the Appendix. See also the farewells in Xenophon Ephesius *Ephesiaca* 1.10.9–11.1.

87. *Aeneid* 4.388–91.

88. See especially *Aeneid* 4.663–71.

89. *Punica* 3.152–59.

90. *Phaedo* 59a.

91. *Iliad* 6.484. This same verb for laughing appears seven more times in the *Phaedo* (62a, 64a and b, 77c, 84d, 101b, and 115c). The ironic importance of laughter just before Socrates' death may well be an imitation of *Iliad* 6.484.

92. *Phaedo* 60a and *Iliad* 6.400.

93. *Iliad* 6.409–10 and *Phaedo* 60a.

94. *Phaedo* 60a; see the Appendix.

95. See especially *Phaedo* 63e–64, 68c–d, 83e–84b, and 88b. Socrates completes his lengthy dialogue by stating that the wise man who had adorned his soul "with its own proper adornment of self-restraint and justice and courage and freedom and truth, awaits his departure to the other world, ready to go when fate calls him. . . . I am now already, as a tragedian would say, called by fate" (115a). Homer's Hector, too, could have said this.

96. *Phaedo* 115b.

97. *Phaedo* 116a; cf. *Iliad* 6.433.

98. *Phaedo* 117c–e.

99. Acts 20:37–38.

100. Acts 21:11.

Chapter 8. Jewish Testament or Homeric Imitation?

1. According to Michel, because Luke avoided narrating Paul's death, he was free to place the testament anywhere he chose. He chose Miletus because the Aegean was the center of Paul's ministry and his farewell to the elders marked a turning point in the development of the church from the first generation to the postapostolic period, from the authority of the apostle to that of elders/bishops. He did not locate the speech at Ephesus because by his day Gnostics had contaminated that city (*Abschiedsrede*, 75–76).

2. *Iliad* 7.307–10.

3. E.g., Ulrich von Wilamowitz-Moellendorff, *Die Ilias und Homer* (Berlin: Weidmann, 1916), 310–11.

4. Clarke, *Homer's Readers*, 169. See also John A. Scott, "The Parting of Hector and Andromache," *CJ* 9 (1914): 274–77.

5. *Iliad* 6.488–89.

6. Compare *Argonautica* 1.292–93 (ἀμφίπολοι γοάασκον) with *Iliad* 6.499 (ἀμφιπό-λους ... γόον ... ἐνῶρσεν).

7. *Aeneid* 2.671–78.

8. Hughes, "Vergil's Creusa," 418.

9. *Aeneid* 2.771–95.

10. Hughes, "Vergil's Creusa," 418.

11. Juhnke, *Homerisches*, 193–96.

12. Acts 20:16–17.

13. Some scholars thus have suspected Luke's splicing together two sources, a first-person travel narrative from Troas to Miletus and a speech to the elders at Ephesus. Donelson provides a useful note on the history of this interpretation in "Cult Histories," 12 n. 33.

14. *Iliad* 6.360–62.

15. *Iliad* 6.363.

16. *Iliad* 6.390–93.

17. Schadewaldt provides a brilliant interpretation of this unusual choreography in "Hector and Andromache," 131–32. See also Dieter Lohmann, *Die Andromache-Szenen der Ilias. Ansätze und Methoden der Homer-Interpretation*, Spudasmata 42 (Hildesheim: Olms Verlag, 1988).

Hector's ardor to return to the battlefield did not flag after he bade Andromache adieu. Paris finally was ready for the battle and "rushed [σεύατ'] through the city, confident in his quick feet" (6.505). He apologized to Hector for having detained him in his haste [ἐσ-σύμενον] by being so slow (518–19). Book 7 begins by continuing their frenetic return to the battlefield. "So saying, glorious Hector rushed [ἐξέσσυτο] through the gates, and with him went Alexander his brother. And in their hearts both were eager [μέμασαν] to fight and make war" (1–3).

Chapter 9. The Selection of Ajax to Fight Hector

1. *Iliad* 7.123.

2. *Iliad* 7.145.

3. *Iliad* 7.154–56.

4. *Iliad* 7.159–61.

5. *Iliad* 7.194–205.

6. The scene was not popular in art; I know of only one possible example; see *LIMC*, "Aias I," item 18.

Chapter 10. *The Selection of Matthias to Replace Judas*

1. P. W. van der Horst notes the parallel between Acts 1:15–26 and *Iliad* 7, but he does not propose literary imitation ("Hellenistic Parallels to the Acts of the Apostles: 1:1–26," *ZNW* 74 [1983]: 25).

2. The discrepancy between the two reports apparently generated a textual variant in Codex Bezae: after the reference to the women this manuscript adds καὶ τέκνοις, "and children."

3. E.g., Luke 10:25 and Acts 5:34, 11:28, 13:16, 15:7, and 23:9.

4. Acts 1:16–20. I have translated the two biblical texts (Pss 69:26 and 109:8) as though they are a single citation. I do so because verse 16 introduced them as a single text (τὴν γραφήν). Note also the parallel structure of the three third-person-singular imperatives linked by conjunctions (γενηθήτω . . . καὶ μὴ ἔστω, καὶ . . . λαβέτω). Luke had to alter the λάβοι in Ps 109 to λαβέτω to establish the parallelism.

5. See especially the analyses of J. Renié, "L'Election de Matthias (Act. 1, 15–26). Authenticité du récit," *RB* 55 (1948): 43–53; and L. Desautels, "Le Mort de Judas (Mt 27,3–19; Ac 1,15–26)," *ScEs* 38 (1986): 221–39. Acts 1:19a clearly is a Lucan creation; cf. Acts 4:10 and 16, 9:42, 13:38, 28:28, and esp. 19:17.

6. This remains the case even though E. Nellessen has argued that the Hebrew text could be the source of the quotations ("Tradition und Schrift in der Perikope von der Erwählung des Matthias [Apg 1, 15–26]," *BZ* 19 [1975]: 215–18).

7. Because of this blatant anachronism, many scholars have taken vss. 18 and 19 as a Lucan insertion that functions as an address to the reader; the NRSV, for example, puts it in parentheses. By omitting these verses, the citation of the biblical texts in verse 20 stands closer to its introduction in verse 16. See, for example, the arguments of Bruce, *Acts,* 109. R. H. Fuller viewed 16b–19 as "a Thucydidean composition, enabling the author to address the reader" ("The Choice of Matthias," in *Studia Evangelica* 6, ed. Elizabeth A. Livingstone, TU 112 [Berlin: Akademie Verlag, 1973], 142 and 143).

But several details suggest that Luke intended the speech to be a coherent unit. The use of οὗτος μὲν οὖν, "this one then," links it to what precedes. Furthermore, the reference to buying the field is needed to understand the biblical quotation. The distance between the introduction of the Psalm and the quotation can be explained as brackets enclosing a chiasm.

A The Davidic "text had to be fulfilled [ἔδει πληρωθῆναι τὴν γραφήν]" (16–17)

  B Judas "purchased a field [ἐκτήσατο χωρίον]" (18a)

    C He "became prone [πρηνὴς γενόμενος]" and died (18b)

    C¹ "It was known [γνωστὸν ἐγένετο]" (19a)

  B¹ "The field was called [κληθῆναι τὸ χωρίον] . . . 'Field of Blood'" (19b)

A¹ "For it was written [γέγραπται] in the Book of Psalms" (20)

8. The death of Judas has been the subject of much scholarly discussion. In addition to the standard critical commentaries on Acts the following studies merit special attention: J. Rendel Harris, "Did Judas Really Commit Suicide?" *AJT* 6 (1900): 490–513, and "St. Luke's Version of the Death of Judas," *AJT* 18 (1914): 127–31; F. H. Chase, "On πρηνὴς γενόμενος in Acts 1:18," *JTS* 13 (1912): 278–85; Kirsopp Lake, "The Death of Judas," in Foakes Jackson and Kirsopp Lake, *Beginnings,* 5.22–30; Pierre Benoit, "La Mort de Judas," in *Synoptische Studien. Wikenhauser zum siebzigsten Geburtstag dargebracht,* ed. J. Schmid and A. Vögtle (Munich: Karl Zink, 1954), 1–19; Eduard Schweizer, "Zu Apg. 1, 16–22," *TZ* 14 (1958): 46; Jacques Dupont, "La Destinée de Judas prophetisée par David (Actes 1:16–20)," *CBQ* 23 (1961): 41–51; O. Betz, "The Dichotomized Servant and the End of Judas Iscariot: Light on the Dark Passages: Matthew 24,51 and Parallel Acts 1,18," *RevQ* 5 (1965): 43–58; Morton S. Enslin, "How the Story Grew: Judas in Fact and Fiction," *Festschrift to Honor F. Wilbur Gingrich: Lexicographer, Scholar, Teacher, and Committed Christian Layman,* ed. Eugene Howard Barth and Ronald Edwin Cocroft (Leiden: Brill, 1972), 123–41; Max Wilcox, "The Judas-Tradition in Acts 1:15–26," *NTS* 19 (1973): 438–52; Nellessen, "Tradition und Schrift"; Frédéric Manns, "Un Midrash chrétien. Le Récit de la mort de Judas," *RSR* 54 (1980): 197–203; Werner Vogler, *Judas Iskarioth. Untersuchungen zu Tradition und Redaktion von Texten des Neuen Testaments und außerkanonischer Schriften,* TA 11 (Berlin: Evangelische Verlagsanstalt, 1983), 65–70 and 85–89; Desautels, "Mort de Judas"; and Günther Schwarz, *Jesus und Judas. Aramaistische Untersuchungen zur Jesus-Judas-Überlieferung der Evangelien und der Apostelgeschichte,* BWANT 123 (Stuttgart: Kohlhammer, 1988), 197–200.

9. Papias, fragment 3.

10. The other instances all appear in 3 Maccabees (5:43 and 50 and 6:23).

11. Lake, "Death of Judas," 5.27. The Vulgate translates πρηνεῖς with *inflatos.*

12. E.g., J. Rendel Harris, who argued that Luke had as his model the death of the traitor Nadan in the story of Ahikar ("Suicide" and "Death of Judas"). F. H. Chase argued that Luke wrote πρηνὴς γενόμενος but with a particular medical meaning for πρηνής, "swollen," related to the verb πίμπρημι ("On πρηνὴς γενόμενος"). Despite the erudite argumentation, Chase has convinced few interpreters. For arguments against his proposal, see Lake, "Death of Judas," 27–29.

13. *Acts of Thomas* 33.

14. *Iliad* 5.58.

15. *Iliad* 15.543.

16. *Iliad* 16.310–11. The word πρηνής is used of warriors falling to their deaths also in 12.396, 16.413 and 579, and 21.118.

17. *Iliad* 13.616–18.

18. *Iliad* 20.413–14 and 416–18.

19. *Iliad* 4.525–26 and 21.181.

20. *Iliad* 7.145. Homer used the word ὕπτιος with this sense also in *Iliad* 4.522, 7.145 and 271, 11.144, 12.192, 13.548, 15.434 and 647, 16.289, and 17.523.

21. *Commentarii ad Homeri Iliadem,* to 7.145. Readers familiar with Homer might also have seen here an analogy to the death of Patroclus. Apollo, shrouded in mist, sneaked up on the Achaean soldier, "stood behind him, and struck his back and broad shoulders with his

downturned hand" (*Iliad* 16.791–92). The adjective translated here as "downturned" is a compound from πρηνής (καταπρηνεῖ). The god then knocked off this helmet, and the Trojan Euphorbus "cast his sharp spear at short range," striking him "in the back between the shoulders" (806–9). As Patroclus tried to flee, Hector ran up to him, apparently from behind, "cast his spear in the lower back and drove the bronze right through. He fell to the earth with a thud" (819–22). The death of Patroclus may have influenced the *Acts of Andrew and Matthias,* where the Devil walks behind the apostle and tells the crowds to slap his mouth (26).

22. Acts 1:21–22.

23. Cf. Mark 3:13–19, Matt 10:1–4, and Luke 6:12–16.

Chapter 11. Jerusalem Legend or Homeric Imitation?

1. Alfons Weiser, "Die Nachwahl des Matthias (Apg 1,15–26). Zur Rezeption und Deutung urchristlicher Geschichte durch Lukas," in *Zur Geschichte des Urchristentums,* ed. G. Dautzenberg et al. (Freiburg: Herder, 1979), 103. See also Renié, "L'Élection," 43–53; Bauernfeind, *Apostelgeschichte,* 25–27; and Desautels, "Mort de Judas."

2. Proponents of an Aramaic-speaking oral tradition include Ethelbert Stauffer, "Jüdische Erbe im urchristlichen Kirchenrecht," *TLZ* 77 (1952): 201–6; William A. Beardslee, "The Casting of Lots at Qumran and in the Book of Acts," *NovT* 4 (1960–1961): 252; Karl Heinrich Rengstorf, "The Election of Matthias," in *Current Issues in New Testament Interpretation,* ed. W. Klassen and G. F. Snyder (New York: Harper, 1962), 178–92; Roloff, *Apostelgeschichte,* 30; Fuller, "Choice,"146; Fitzmyer, *Acts,* 218; and Zmijewski, *Apostelgeschichte,* 81–82. Advocates for an Aramaic source include C. Masson, "La Reconstitution du collège des Douze. D'après Actes 1:15–26," *RTP* 3 (1955): 193–201; Wilcox, "Judas-Tradition," 452 (who argues that the source had already been translated into Greek before Luke received it); A. Jaubert, "L'Élection de Matthias et le tirage au sort," in *Studia Evangelica* 6, ed. Elizabeth A. Livingstone, TU 112 (Berlin: Akademie Verlag, 1973), 280; Nellessen, "Tradition und Schrift," 211–18, and *Zeugnis für Jesus und das Wort. Exegetische Untersuchungen zum lukanischen Zeugnisbegriff,* BBB 43 (Cologne: Peter Hanstein, 1976), 164–69; Manns, "Midrash chrétien"; and F. Schmidt, "Élection et tirage au sort (1QS vi,13–23 et Ac 1,15–26)," *RHPR* 80 (2000): 105–17. Those who argue for an Aramaic source frequently note a parallel between Acts 1:17 and a Palestinian Targum to Gen 44:18 (Targum D), in which Judah speaks of Benjamin: "he was numbered with us among the tribes . . . and will receive a portion (lot) and share with us in the division of the land" (e.g., Wilcox, "Judas-Tradition," 447–51). See Jacques Dupont's appropriately skeptical treatment of this parallel ("Le Douzième apôtre [Actes 1:15–26]. À propos d'une explication récente," in *The New Testament Age,* ed. W. Weinrich [Macon: Mercer, 1984], 139–45). Advocates for a Greek source include P.-H. Menoud, "Les Additions au groupe des douze apôtres, d'après le livre des Actes," *RHPR* 37 (1957): 71–80; and Weiser, "Nachwahl," 274–80. Nellessen provides a succinct history of scholarship before 1975 (*Zeugnis,* 133–36).

3. Some scholars have made Joseph Barsabbas a brother to Judas Barsabbas in Acts 15:22.

Another Barsabbas Justus appears in the apocryphal *Acts of Paul* as a soldier under Nero in Rome. The origin of this tale might well have been a story told to Papias by the daughters of Philip (Dennis R. MacDonald, *The Legend and the Apostle: The Battle for Paul in Story and Canon* [Philadelphia: Westminster Press, 1983], 24–25, 36–37, and 40–41).

Matthias—often confused with Matthew—appears frequently in Christian apocrypha. For example, the beginning of the *Acts of Andrew* apparently began with a lottery that included Matthias, not a lottery to replace Judas but to parcel out the world among the apostles for evangelizing. Andrew drew Achaea, but Matthias drew Myrmidonia, the land of cannibalistic Myrmidons, the savage troops of Achilles in the *Iliad*. The influence of Acts 1:15–26 on this tradition is transparent. The beginning of the *Acts of Andrew* may no longer exist, but the beginnings of the *Acts of Andrew and Matthias in the City of the Cannibals,* the so-called *Martyrium Andreae prius* seem to witness to it independently, though the precise relationship between these texts remains uncertain.

In addition to the casting of lots for Andrew and Matthias, other apocrypha have the apostles cast lots to send Thomas to India and John to Ephesus (e.g., the the *Acts of Thomas* and the *Acts of John by Prochorus*). The *Acts of Philip* refers twice to apostolic lotteries (Acts 3 and 8). Jean-Daniel Kaestli discusses these and several other examples in "Les Scènes d'attribution des champs de mission et de départ de l'apôtre dans les Actes apocryphes," in *Les Actes apocryphes des apôtres. Christianisme et monde païen,* ed. François Bovon, Publication de la Faculté de Théologie de l'Université de Genève 4 (Geneva: Labor et Fides, 1981), 149–64. Origen, too, cited as tradition a lottery in which John won Asia Minor, Andrew Scythia, and Thomas Parthia (see Eric Junod, "Origène, Eusèbe et la tradition sur la répartition des champs de mission des apôtres [Eusèbe, *HE* III,1,1–3]," in Bovon, *Actes apocryphes,* 233–48; and Dennis R. MacDonald, "Legends of the Apostles," in *Eusebius, Christianity, and Judaism,* ed. Harold W. Attridge and Gohei Hata [Detroit: Wayne State University Press, 1992], 176–78). This passage in Origen suggests that a lottery once may have appeared at the beginning of the *Acts of John,* which would make it the earliest known imitation of Acts 1:15–26. Unfortunately, the beginning of the *Acts of John* no longer exists. Otherwise, the *Acts of Andrew* would be the first, and here the lot sends Matthias off to the land of the Myrmidons, Achilles' savage troops in the *Iliad*.

4. E.g., Gerhard Lohfink, "Der Losvorgang in Apg. 1,26," *BZ* 19 (1975): 247–49; Weiser, "Nachwahl," 99; Roloff, *Apostelgeschichte,* 34; and Zmijewski, *Apostelgeschichte,* 89.

5. "Losung," PW 13 (1927): 1451–1504.

6. Ibid., 1467.

7. Prov 16:33; cf. Isa 34:17.

8. Jonah 1:17. The discovery of sin by lot also appears in Josh 7:10–21 and 1 Sam 14:36–42.

9. For evidence of prayers before lotteries, see Plato *Laws* 6.757e and Lucian *Hermotimus* 40.

10. E.g., Num 26:52–56 and 33:53–54, and Ezek 47:22 and 48:29. According to *Jubilees* 8, the three sons of Noah cast lots to determine their habitations after the flood. Jewish authors expressed fears that foreign armies would parcel out their peoples and lands by lot (Joel 3:3, Obad 11, and Nah 3:10 LXX). A Psalmist complained that his opponents cast lots for his clothing (22:19), a complaint that the Gospel of Mark used to describe the Crucifixion (15:24; cf. Matt 27:35, Luke 23:34, and John 19:24).

11. Josh 18–19; cf. Josephus *Antiquities* 5.81–87.

12. 1 Sam 10:20–24; cf. Josephus *Antiquities* 6.61–65.

13. In some respects, the lapse of the lottery resembles the cessation of divination by the Urim and Thummim, oracular devices used to determine the divine will in ancient Israel. There is no evidence of their use after the reign of King David, and according to Ezra 2:63 and Neh 7:65 it had ceased to exist, though hopes survived that the practice one day might resume. Apparently it never did.

14. Luke 1:8–9 (NRSV). According to Lev 16:8–10, priests presented two animals as scapegoats and cast lots to see which would meet the knife.

15. E.g., Jaubert, "L'Election," 274–80.

16. *Jewish War* 4.153–57.

17. Schmidt, however, argues that the lot at Qumran was an actual lottery, not just a vote ("Election"); cf. Jaubert, "L'Election," 275–76.

18. "Casting of Lots," 249–50. See also Everett Ferguson, "Qumran and Codex D (Acts 1:15–26)," *RevQ* 8 (1972): 75–80.

19. Beardslee, "Casting of Lots," 249.

20. E.g., Thucydides 3.50, Dionysius of Halicarnassus *Roman Antiquities* 7.13.5, and the writings of Isaeus.

21. E.g., Homer *Iliad* 15.187–93, Plato *Gorgias* 523a, and Apollodorus *Library* 1.2.1.

22. For lotteries in horse races see Homer *Iliad* 23.351–57 and its imitations in Pseudo-Callisthenes *Alexander Romance* 1.19 and Nonnus *Dionysiaca* 37.226–35. For going first in contests see *Iliad* 3.314–25 and 23.859–62. For the lottery for Helen, see Diodorus Siculus 4.63.3.6 and Plutarch *Theseus* 31.2–3.

23. Plato *Republic* 10.617d. Not all lotteries were worth winning. Greek mythological monsters occasionally required the sacrifice of children, and cities chose the victims by lot (Plutarch *Theseus* 17,1–3 and 18.1, and Pausanius *Description of Greece* 9.26.7). Cannibals cast lots to see which one of them would provide dinner for the others (Herodotus 3.25 and *Acts of Andrew and Matthias* 22–23). Generals used lots to determine which units would lead the charge into battle and which disobedient soldiers to execute as examples for others (Dionysius of Halicarnassus *Roman Antiquities* 9.50.1.8 and 9.50.7.6, Plutarch *Pericles* 27.2.4, Cassius Dio *Roman History* 56.23.3, and Josephus *Jewish War* 3.97; cf. Esther 3:7 and 9:24). According to Josephus, Jews trapped at Masada cast lots to see which of them had the unspeakable duty of killing nine others before killing themselves (*Jewish War* 7.396). In another passage, Josephus claims that he talked to the troops under his command to determine the order in which they would kill each other to avoid death at the hands of the Romans. Fortune (τύχη) would decide the order. When it turned out that in the end only he and another were left standing ("whether by fortune or the providence of God"), he convinced the other man not to cast lots so that they both could survive (*Jewish War* 3.387–91).

24. E.g., Herodotus 3.80 and 83, Plato *Republic* 561a–b and *Laws* 690c and 744a, and Demosthenes *Letter to Apollonius* 4 (102e). See the discussion of James Wycliffe Headlam, *Election by Lot at Athens*, 2d ed., ed. D. C. MacGregor (Cambridge: Cambridge University Press, 1933).

25. Xenophon *Memorablia* 1.2.9.

26. *Special Laws* 4.151–57; see Jaubert, "L'Election," 277–78. Philostratus gives his own critique of the practice in *Life of Apollonius of Tyana* 5.36.48–50.

27. *Oration* 57.46–50 (1313–14).

28. Cicero *Against Verres* 2.2. 126.

29. 1 Cor 15:5, Q 11:30, and in Mark repeatedly. See the discussion by W. Hornby, "The Twelve and the Phylarchs," *NTS* 32 (1986): 503–27.

30. E.g., Masson, "Reconstitution," 195–200; Rengstorf, "Election"; Wilcox, "Judas-Tradition," 451; Jaubert, "L'Élection," 279; and Nellessen, *Zeugnis,* 136–67.

31. Roloff, *Apostelgeschichte,* 34–36; see Acts 14:4 and 14.

32. E.g., Menoud, "Additions," 78–80; Nellessen, *Zeugnis,* 128–45; Zmijewski, *Apostelgeschichte,* 90–95; and especially Günter Klein, who gives a thorough treatment of the matter, showing how innovative and significant the completion of the Twelve was for Luke (*Die zwölf Apostel. Ursprung und Gehalt einer Idee,* FRLANT n.s. 59 [Göttingen: Vandenhoeck & Ruprecht, 1961], 204–16).

33. Luke 22:30.

34. Many manuscripts of Luke 22:30 in fact mention "twelve thrones."

35. Ps 122:4–5 speaks of thrones in David's Jerusalem where the tribes are judged.

36. Judas's last-minute recantation in Matt 27:3–4 probably is not sufficient penance to requalify him as an eschatological leader, but it does modestly rescue his reputation.

37. Luke 24:9 and 33.

38. Rengstorf argues that Luke used the story to remind the reader that Christ sent the Gospel first to Jews ("Election," 187–92). So also Fitzmyer, *Acts,* 221.

39. Acts 12:1–2.

40. There is, however, an imitation of Nestor's speech and the volunteering of heroes in Apollonius Rhodius *Argonautica* 3.502–75.

Chapter 12. Priam's Escape from Achilles and Its Imitators

1. E.g., Mark 16:1–8, Matt 28:1–8, Luke 24:1–12, John 20.1–13, *Gospel of Peter* 9:34–13:57, *Acts of Paul* 7, *Acts of John* 72–73, *Acts of Andrew and Matthias* 18–19, *Acts of Andrew* Passion 28–32, and *Acts of Thomas* 122 and 151–55.

2. Acts 12:6–10.

3. "Gebet und Wunder. Zwei Abhandlungen zur Religions- und Literaturgeschichte," in *Genethliakon,* FS Wilhelm Schmid, TBAW 5 (Stuttgart: W. Kohlhammer, 1929), 169–464. The study was republished twice, once as a monograph (Stuttgart: W. Kohlhammer, 1929), and again in combination with another study in his *Religionsgeschichtliche Studien* (Darmstadt: Wissenschaftliche Buchgesellschaft, 1968).

4. Ibid., 326–41, esp. 340.

5. *Rettungswunder. Motiv-, traditions- und formkritische Aufarbeitung einer biblischen Gattung,* EH 123 (Frankfurt am Main: Peter Lang, 1979), 493–95.

6. Weinreich and Kratz ignored Priam's escape, even though they discussed the door opening scenes in *Iliad* 5.748–52 and 8.392–96, where the gates of heaven open automatically for Hera, thanks to the influence of the Hours.

7. E.g., Eustathius *Commentarii ad Homeri Iliadem* to 24.343 and *Commentarii ad Homeri Odysseam* to 3.332.

8. Nicholas Richardson, *The Iliad: A Commentary,* vol. 6: *Books 21–24* (Cambridge: Cambridge University Press, 1993), 291.

9. In both one finds a divine council, the sending of messengers to secure the release of someone (Hector in the *Iliad*, Odysseus in the *Odyssey*), the messengers donning magical sandals that whisk them over the sea (Hermes in the *Iliad* and in *Odyssey* 5, and Athena in *Odyssey* 1), taking on a disguise, and then lying about their identities (see Danek, *Epos und Zitat*, 50–53, and Heubeck, *Commentary* 1.87). After delivering their messages the messengers magically disappear. These and other parallels function as links bonding the end of the *Iliad* with the beginning of the *Odyssey*, even though the latter begins with events that took place ten years later. On the relationship of the ending of the *Iliad* and the beginning of the *Odyssey* see Richardson, *Iliad 6*, 21–24.

The poet of the *Odyssey* also modeled the burial of Elpenor in Book 12 after the burial of Hector: cf. *Iliad* 24.201–3 and *Odyssey* 12.16–20. Compare also *Iliad* 24.354–57 with *Odyssey* 10.266–69, *Iliad* 24.346–48 with *Odyssey* 10.274–79, and *Iliad* 24.357 with *Odyssey* 10.481. See Götz Beck, "Beobachtungen zur Kirke-Episode in der Odyssee," *Philologus* 109 (1965): 1–29; Heubeck, *Commentary* 2.58–59, 64, and 68; and MacDonald, *Homeric Epics*, 160.

10. See Karl Deichgräber, *Der letzte Gesang der Ilias*, AAWM (Wiesbaden: Franz Steiner Verlag, 1972), 118–26.

11. Hermes' walking on the water clearly was the model for *Aeneid* 4.219–78. Achilles' relinquishing the corpse informed the return of Pallas's corpse to Evander. The lamentations of the Trojan women echo in the lamentation of Euryalus's mother, and the funeral for Hector (as well as that for Patroclus) provided the model for that of Misenus (*Aeneid* 1.483–87, 6.212–25, 9.465–97, and 11.139–81 and 199–202). See Knauer, "Vergil and Homer," 882.

12. See especially *Thebaid* 12.228–447. The *Acts of Andrew* tells of a lad who died, strangled by a demon. His father "wept profusely" and brought him to Andrew, who healed him. "They led him out to the house with torches and lamps — it was already past nightfall — and brought him inside the house" (GE 14). Several details in the story as well as its placement in the *Acts* point to his youth as an ersatz Hector, now raised from the dead (see *Christianizing Homer*, 128–29). According to Marilyn B. Skinner, the poet Erinna imitated the laments of the Trojan women in mourning the death of her friend ("Briseis, the Trojan Women, and Erinna," *CW* 75 [1982]: 265–69). Josephus seems to have imitated Hecuba's complaint that Priam had lost his senses in deciding to go to Achilles to rescue the corpse. Compare *Iliad* 24.200–202 with *Antiquities* 16.376–80 (Kopidakis, "Ἰώσηφος ὁμηρίζων," 22–23).

13. Quintilian 3.8.53.

14. *Iliad* 24. 18–21 and 66–67.

15. *Iliad* 24.336–37.

16. *Iliad* 24.340–46.

17. *Odyssey* 5.47–48.

18. *Odyssey* 24.1–4. The Phaeacians pour libations to Hermes in hopes of getting a good night's sleep (7.136–38). See also Sophocles *Ajax* 832 and Heliodorus *Aethiopica* 3.5. So closely was Hermes related to sleep that a bedpost was called ἑρμίς; see Eustathius *Commentarii ad Homeri Odysseam* to 8.278. On Hermes' soporific rod see especially Cornutus *De natura deorum* 16.

19. See, for example, *LIMC*, "Achilleus," items. 642, 649, 656, 661, and 680.

20. *Aeneid* 4.242–44. See also Nonnus *Dionysiaca* 20.261–65.

21. *Metamorphoses* 1.715–16 and 11.307–9. On guards miraculously put to sleep, see also Ovid *Metamorphoses* 7.210–14 (of the Golden Fleece) and Statius *Thebaid* 12.307–8 and 447–51, which may have been influenced by *Iliad* 24.

22. *Metamorphoses* 2.818–19; cf. 2.708 and 735–36, 7.210–14, and 8.627.

23. *Iliad* 24.443–48, 453–62, and 468–69.

24. *Iliad* 24.478–79.

25. *Iliad* 24.563–67.

26. *Iliad* 24.347 and *Odyssey* 7.20.

27. *Iliad* 24.429–39 and *Odyssey* 7.22–36.

28. *Iliad* 24.441 and *Odyssey* 7.37–38.

29. *Odyssey* 7.39–42.

30. Compare the following: ὡς ἄρα φωνήσας ἀπέβη γλαυκῶπις Ἀθήνη (*Odyssey* 7.78) and ὡς ἄρα φωνήσας ἀπέβη . . . Ἑρμείας (*Iliad* 24.468–69).

31. *Iliad* 24.471–76 and *Odyssey* 7.135–38.

32. *Odyssey* 7.136–38.

33. *Iliad* 24.477–84 and *Odyssey* 7.139–45.

34. The only difference between the two stories pertains to the need for two beds in the *Iliad*, thus δοιὼ λέχε᾿ for πυκινὸν λέχος in the last line (*Iliad* 24.644–48 and *Odyssey* 7.336–40); cf. 4.296–301, which also may imitate *Iliad* 24.643–49.

35. See Heubeck, *Commentary,* 1.321–22.

36. *The Dream* 28.

37. *The Ship* 42; see the Appendix.

38. *Iliad* 24.677–94.

39. Compare θυρέων . . . ὀχῆες (*Argonautica* 4.41) with ὀχῆα . . . θυράων (*Iliad* 24.566–67); οὐδέ τις ἔγνω τήνγε φυλακτήρων (*Argonautica* 4.48–49) with φυλακτῆρες . . . οὐδέ τις ἔγνω (*Iliad* 24.444 and 692); and λάθε δέ σφεας ὁρμηθεῖσα (*Argonautica* 4.49) with οὐδὲ γὰρ ἄν φυλάκους λάθοι (*Iliad* 24.566).

40. *Dionysiaca* 35.234–36 and 238–41.

41. Compare the following: φυλάκων . . . ὕπνον ἔχευεν . . . πανθελγέι ῥάβδῳ (*Dionysiaca* 35.234–35) with ῥάβδον . . . θέλγει/φυλακτῆρες . . . ὕπνον ἔχευεν (*Iliad* 24.343 and 444–45) and βρισρὴν κληῖδα πυλάων ἠλιβάτων ὤιξε (*Dionysiaca* 35.240–41) with ὤιξε πύλας and μεγάλην κληῖδα θυράων . . . ῷξε (*Iliad* 24.446 and 455–56).

42. Artapanus frag. 3; the translation is that of Carl R. Holladay, *Fragments from Hellenistic Jewish Authors,* vol. 1: *Historians,* SBLTT, Pseudepigrapha Series (Chico: Scholars Press, 1983), 219. For another example of miraculously opening doors in a Jewish text see Josephus *Jewish War* 6.5.3.

43. *Homeric Epics,* 154–61. The right column reproduces Mark 15:42–16:2, virtually every motif of which appears in the paraphrase of *Iliad* Book 24 on the left.

Iliad 24	Mark 15:42–16:2
Priam, king of Troy, set out at night	When it was late, and since it was the day of Preparation, that is, the day before the sabbath, Joseph of Arimathea, a distinguished member of the council, who was also himself waiting expectantly

to rescue the body of his son, Hector,
from his murderer, Achilles.
The journey was dangerous. He entered
Achilles' abode, and asked for the body
of Hector.
Achilles was amazed that Priam dared
to enter his home.
Achilles sent two soldiers to get the
ransom, and summoned maidservants to
"wash and anoint him."

Hector's body had been saved from
desecration.
"Then the maidservants washed and
anointed the body with oil and wrapped
it in a beautiful cape and tunic,
and Achilles himself lifted it
and placed it upon a bier."
[Hector's bones would be placed in an
ossuary, buried in the ground, and covered
with stones.]
[Priam left with the body at night, and
brought it to Troy for a fitting burial.]
Cassandra was the first to see Priam
coming with the bier in the wagon.
Three women led in the lament:
Andromache, Hecuba, and Helen.

After elaborate preparations,
they burned Hector's body at dawn.

for the kingdom of God,

dared to go to Pilate
and asked for the body of Jesus.

Then Pilate was amazed that he might
already be dead;
and summoning the centurion, he asked him
whether he had been dead for some time.
[A woman earlier had anointed Jesus.]
When he learned from the centurion that
he was dead, he granted the body to Joseph.
[Jesus' rapid death and burial saved the
corpse from desecration.]
Then Joseph bought a linen cloth,
and taking down the body, wrapped it
in the linen cloth

and placed it in a tomb that had been
hewn out of the rock.
He then rolled a stone against the door of the
tomb.

Mary Magdalene and Mary the mother of
Joses saw where the body was laid.
When the sabbath was over, Mary
Magdalene, and Mary the mother of James,
and Salome bought spices, so that they
might go and anoint him.
And very early on the first day of the week,
when the sun had risen, they went to the tomb.

I also proposed that the earliest evangelist modeled Jesus' walking on the water after Hermes' flying over the waves in *Iliad* 24 (ibid., 148–53).

44. Matt 28:2–4.

45. Matt 28.12–14. See also *Gospel of Peter* 8.28–11.49.

46. For a fascinating discussion of Matthew's empty tomb narrative and traditions of escape scenes, see Kratz, *Rettungswunder*, 511–41.

47. *Acts of Andrew and Matthias* 19. Other similarities between these texts include Iris's assurance to Priam that he would not be killed and Jesus' assurance of the same to Andrew (cf. *Iliad* 24.181–82 and *Acts of Andrew and Matthias* 18), and the departures of Iris, Hermes, and Jesus (*Iliad* 24.188 and esp. 468: ὡς ἄρα φωνήσας ἐπέβη πρὸς μακρὸν Ὄλυμπον, and *Acts of Andrew and Matthias* 18: καὶ ταῦτα εἰπὼν ὁ σωτὴρ ἐπορεύετο εἰς τοὺς οὐρανούς). See also *Acts of Andrew* Passion 28–32, where a beautiful youth stands before

opened prison doors to allow women access to Andrew incarcerated within. The jailer and the four guards were unable to see them come or go.

48. Notice also that Matthias plays a role that Homer gave to Achilles, that of singing by himself (*Iliad* 9.185–89).

49. For example, the escape from prison in *Acts of John* 72–73 seems to imitate *Acts of Paul* 7, which in turn clearly imitates Acts 12. The opening of prison doors and the sleeping of guards in *Acts of Thomas* 122 and 151–55 probably imitates *Acts of Andrew* Passion 28–32.

Chapter 13. Alexander's Escape from Darius

1. The composition of the *Alexander Romance* is notoriously complex. According to Reinhold Merkelbach, behind the novel lie three sources from the Hellenistic period that the author incorporated into his own fictional account (*Die Quellen des griechischen Alexander-romans*. 2d ed., with Jürgen Trumpf, Zetemata 9 [Munich: Beck, 1977]). Merkelbach attributes the tale of Alexander's escape to the creativity of the novelist himself (127).

2. *Alexander Romance* 2.13, rescension B.

3. *Iliad* 24.181–85.

4. *Iliad* 24.193–94, 200–216, and 287–98.

5. *Alexander Romance* 2.14.

6. *Iliad* 24.263–82.

7. *Iliad* 24.350–51.

8. *Alexander Romance* 2.14. The word used here for wagon is the same Homer used for the wagon of Idaeus. Compare the phrase κτήνη καὶ ἁμάξας with Homer's ἡμιόνους καὶ ἄμαξαν (*Iliad* 24.150 and 179).

9. *Alexander Romance* 2.14.

10. *Iliad* 24.469–71.

11. *Alexander Romance* 2.14.

12. *Alexander Romance* 2.14.

13. *Iliad* 24.483–84; cf. 631–32.

14. *Alexander Romance* 2.14.

15. *Iliad* 24.519 and 565–66, 601, and 618–19.

16. *Iliad* 24.508, 515, and 671–72.

17. *Alexander Romance* 2.15. Hermes was known as a thief; see, for example, *Iliad* 24.24, 71–72, and 109.

18. *Iliad* 24.232–36.

19. *Iliad* 24.651–54.

20. *Iliad* 24.683–88.

21. *Alexander Romance* 2.15.

22. *Iliad* 2.763–69 and 23.288–92 and 373–565. Quintus Smyrnaeus presents Eumelus as a charioteer (*Posthomerica* 4.500–504).

23. See the *Corpus hippiatricorum graecorum*.

24. *Iliad* 22.147–52. Demetrius of Scepsis says he discovered the cold spring but not the hot one (Strabo *Geography* 1.3.17 and 13.1.43). See also the discussion of the Scamander in Athenaeus *Deipnosophistae* 2.14 and Eustathius *Commentarii ad Homeri Iliadem* to

22.148. The author of the *Alexander Romance* mentions the Scamander in 1.42, where Alexander jumps into it to imitate Achilles in *Iliad* 21.

25. *Alexander Romance* 2.16.

Chapter 14. Peter's Escape from Herod

1. Luke's trenchant account of Agrippa's death corresponds in several respects with Josephus *Antiquities* 19.343–52.

2. One finds this form-critical judgment expressed in nearly every scholarly commentary, but the following studies are most explicit: Bauernfeind, *Apostelgeschichte*, 162; Dibelius, *Studies*, 21; August Strobel, "Passa-Symbolik und Passa-Wunder in Act. xii.3ff," *NTS* 4 (1957–58): 212; Jacques Dupont, "Pierre délivré de prison (Ac. 12.1–11)," *Nouvelles études sur les actes des apôtres*, LD 118 (Paris: Cerf, 1984), 330; Haenchen, *Acts*, 390–91; W. Radl, "Befreiung aus dem Gefängnis. Die Darstellung eines biblischen Grundthemas in Apg. 12," *BZ* 27 (1983): 81–86; Roloff, *Apostelgeschichte*, 186–88; Conzelmann, *Acts*, 93; Zmijewski, *Apostelgeschichte*, 457; Jacob Jervell, *Die Apostelgeschichte übersetzt und erklärt*, EKKNT 3 (Göttingen: Vandenhoeck & Ruprecht, 1998), 338; Fitzmyer, *Acts*, 485–86; and Ben Witherington III, *The Acts of the Apostles: A Socio-Rhetorical Commentary* (Grand Rapids: William B. Eerdmans, 1998), 376. Other important treatments include R. Eulenstein, "Die wundersame Befreiung des Petrus aus Todesgefahr, Acta 12,1–23," *WD* 12 (1973): 43–69; Dupont, "Pierre délivré"; Radl, "Befreiung"; and Susan R. Garrett, "Exodus from Bondage: Luke 9:31 and Acts 12:1–24," *CBQ* 53 (1991): 628–43. I have published a briefer version of my analysis of Acts 12 in "Soporific Angel."

3. *Iliad* 24.453–55.

4. *Iliad* 24.565–67.

5. *Iliad* 24.443–46 and 566.

6. Acts 12:6 and 10.

7. Acts 12:4.

8. Acts 12:18–19.

9. On the prayers of the Trojans see *Iliad* 24.281–321 and 327–31.

10. Acts 12:5 and 12.

11. The Appendix presents the parallels in this chapter in Greek.

12. Cf. *Iliad* 10.157–59.

13. E.g., *Odyssey* 5.29, *Homeric Hymn* 4 (to Hermes) 571–72 and 18 (to Hermes) 3, Plato *Cratylus* 408b–c, Euripides *Electra* 461 and *Iphigenia at Aulis* 1302, Apollonius Rhodius *Argonautica* 3.587–88, and Nonnus *Dionysiaca* 3.433, 20.262, and 38.76; of Iris: *Iliad* 24.169 and 173. On Hermes as an angel and a giver of dreams, see especially Cornutus *De natura deorum* 16.

Peter Hofrichter has argued that Luke modeled the appearance of the angel after *Iliad* 24, not the appearance of Hermes to Priam but of Iris to Thetis in lines 77–100. He summarized the parallels as follows:

> Peter finds himself at night in a prison; Thetis is in the dark sea in a cave (Acts 12:4).
> Peter sleeps between two soldiers and is watched by guards; Thetis sits in the midst of
> other sea goddesses (12:5). The angel approaches Peter, strikes him on the side, and

says: "Get up quickly!"—Iris approaches Thetis and says: "Rise up, Thetis!" (12:7). Peter and Thetis both get dressed for their departures (12:8). Both follow the lead of the divine messengers (12:9 and 10). The door opens for the angel and Peter; the waters part for Iris and Thetis (12:11). The believers are gathered at the home of the mother of John Mark; the gathered gods deliberate on Olympus (12:14). Peter and Thetis were both received by a woman: the maid Rhoda opened the door for Peter; Thetis received the cup of welcome from the goddess Hera (12:15). ("Parallele zum 24. Gesang der Ilias in den Engelerscheinungen des lukanischen Doppelwerkes," *PzB* 2 [1993]: 72)

These parallels are impressive and may illumine the composition of Acts 12, but the two appearances of Hermes to Priam are even more compelling.

14. According to *Aeneid* 4, Jupiter (= Zeus) sent Mercury (= Hermes) to Aeneas warning him to leave Carthage as soon as possible. Aeneas was in no danger, but if he stayed in Carthage, he would never fulfill the design of Jupiter to found Rome. Mercury would appear twice to Aeneas, first to initiate the preparations for his departure and second to initiate the departure itself. One will recall that Hermes appeared twice to Priam in *Iliad* 24, first to escort him to Achilles and second to initiate his escape. Mercury's first descent to Aeneas undoubtedly echoes Hermes' first descent to Priam (compare *Iliad* 24. 331–53 and *Aeneid* 4.219–65).

More analogous to Acts 12 is Mercury's second visit to the future founder of Rome in *Aeneid* 4. Aeneas slept on ship when Mercury appeared to him again—this time in a dream and as himself—and asked him, "Son of a goddess, how can you take sleep in this predicament?" (*Aeneid* 4.554–60). Priam slept in Achilles' bivouac when Hermes stood over him—apparently not in disguise—and said, "Old man, you have no concern for harm—the way you are sleeping among your enemies" (*Iliad* 24.683–84). Mercury warned Aeneas of danger and told him to leave at once, just as Hermes had warned Priam. Vergil wrote: "so he spoke [*sic fatus*] and blended into the dark night" (*Aeneid* 4.570). Homer had written: "So he spoke [ὣς ἔφατ']; five lines later one reads that he "went up to high Olympus" (*Iliad* 24.689 and 694). Priam was afraid (ἔδδεισεν) and woke Idaeus from his sleep to make an immediate escape; Aeneas was "struck with terror [*exterritus*]" and awoke his comrades for an immediate departure (*Iliad* 24.689 and *Aeneid* 4.571). Priam thus escaped Achilles; Aeneas escaped Dido. See also *Odyssey* 4.803–4, 6.21 and 41–42, and 15.1–15 and 43–5.

15. Acts 12:10–11.

16. *Iliad* 24.396–97.

17. *Iliad* 24.677–94.

Chapter 15. Hellenistic Legend or Homeric Imitation?

1. *Rettungswunder*, 460 and 470.

2. E.g., Dupont, "Pierre délivré," 330–31; Fitzmyer, *Acts*, 485; and Zmijewski, *Apostelgeschichte*, 459.

3. E.g., Zmijewski, *Apostelgeschichte*, 464.

4. William M. Ramsay saw the details as proof of historical reliability: "We have here personal recollection, narrated to Luke by the maid [Rhoda] herself, and caught up by his

sympathetic and appreciative mind" (*The Bearing of Recent Discovery on the Trustworthiness of the New Testament*, 4th ed. [London: Hodder and Stoughton, 1920], 209).

5. The Appendix presents the parallels in Greek.

6. Scholiasts protested this projection of her clairvoyance; she had gone to the tower merely out of the agony of a daughter and a sister.

7. Apollodorus *Library* 3.12.5. See also Aeschylus *Agamemnon* 1203–12 and Vergil *Aeneid* 2.246–47.

8. *Posthomerica* 12.546.

9. *Posthomerica* 12.555–57.

10. For an alternative assessment of Rhoda's literary role see J. Albert Harrill, "The Dramatic Function of the Running Slave Rhoda (Acts 12.13–16): A Piece of Greco-Roman Comedy," *NTS* 46 (2000): 150–57.

11. Acts 15:7–14.

12. The names Cleopas and Emmaus in Luke 24 seem to point to Eurycleia and Eumaeus, Odysseus's slaves who recognized him from his scar. The name Eutychus, "Lucky," transvalues Homer's "unfortunate" Elpenor in *Odyssey* 10–12. In Acts 16 the name Lydia designates her as a Christian "Lydian woman" or "Maenad," as in Euripides' *Bacchae*.

13. *Orationes* 16.21.

14. See *LIMC*, "Aphrodite," item 816, a coin representing a seated Aphrodite smelling a rose. See also items 1049 and 1323.

15. *Iliad* 23.186–87.

16. See *LIMC*, "Aphrodite," items 72–75.

17. *LIMC*, "Aphrodite," 227 and 696–706.

18. *Medea* 840–41.

19. *Leucippe and Clitophon* 2.1.

20. Himmerius *Declamationes et orationes* 9.229.

21. See, for example, Bacchylides 17.116, Theocritus 10.33, Sappho 2.6–8, Chariton *Chaereas and Callirhoe* 3.2.17, Athenaeus *Deipnosophistae,* 15.30.12 and 37.14, Philostratus *Epistula et dialexeis* 1.4.13, and Nonnus *Dionysiaca* 13.358, 31.210, and 33.56. Aphrodite's affinity to the rose may account for the tradition that she gave birth to the nymph Rhodos, "Rose" (Pindar *Olympian Odes* 7.14; cf. Epimenides frag. 18.1). Rhodes, the "Island of Roses," was home to a temple to the goddess of love whose statue inspired several imitations (see *LIMC*, "Aphrodite," 740). Achilles Tatius tells how Aphrodite transformed a frigid maiden named Rhodopis, "Rosy," into a passionate lover and then into a spring of water where maidens came in memory of the goddess (*Leucippe and Clitophon* 8.12).

22. *Description of Greece* 6.24.7.

23. *Love Letters* 1 (29); cf. 4 (37).

Conclusion

1. See Buffière, *Mythes d'Homère*, and Lamberton, *Homer the Theologian*.

2. *Palimpsestes*.

3. Philodemus *On Poetry* 5.30.36–31.2 (Jensen, 67–69).

Bibliography

Aejmelaeus, Lars. *Die Rezeption der Paulusbriefe in der Miletrede (Apg 20.18–35).* Annales academiae scientiarum Fennicae B, 232. Helsinki: Suomalainen Tiedeakatemia, 1987.

Barrett, C. K. *A Critical and Exegetical Commentary on the Acts of the Apostles.* 2 vols. International Critical Commentary. Edinburgh, T & T Clark, 1994.

Bassler, Jouette M. "Luke and Paul on Impartiality." *Biblica* (1985): 546–52.

Bauernfeind, Otto. *Kommentar und Studien zur Apostelgeschichte. Mit einer Einleitung von Martin Hengel.* Wissenschaftliche Untersuchungen zum Neuen Testament 22. Tübingen: Mohr (Siebeck), 1980.

Beardslee, William A. "The Casting of Lots at Qumran and in the Book of Acts." *Novum Testamentum* 4 (1960–61): 245–52.

Beck, Götz. "Beobachtungen zur Kirke-Episode in der Odyssee." *Philologus* 109 (1965): 1–29.

Benoit, Pierre. "La Mort de Judas." In *Synoptische Studien. Wikenhauser zum siebzigsten Geburtstag dargebracht.* Ed. J. Schmid and A. Vögtle, 1–19. Munich: Karl Zink, 1954.

Betz, O. "The Dichotomized Servant and the End of Judas Iscariot: Light on the Dark Passages: Matthew 24,51 and Parallel Acts 1,18." *Revue de Qumran* 5 (1965): 43–58.

Bompaire, Jacques. *Lucien écrivain. Imitation et création.* Bibliothèque des Ecoles françaises d'Athènes et de Rome 190. Paris: Boccard, 1958.

Bonz, Marianne Palmer. *The Past as Legacy: Luke-Acts and Ancient Epic.* Minneapolis: Fortress Press, 2000.

Bovon, François. *De vocatione gentium. Histoire de l'interprétation d'Actes 10,1–11,18 dans les six premiers siècles.* Beiträge zur Geschichte der biblischen Exegese 8. Tübingen: Mohr (Siebeck), 1967.

———. *L'Evangile selon saint Luc (1,–9,50)*. Commentaire du Nouveau Testament IIIa. Geneva: Labor et Fides, 1991.

———. "Le Saint-esprit, l'église et les relations humaines selon Actes 20,36–21,16." In *Les Actes des apôtres. Traditions, rédaction, théologie*. Ed. J. Kremer, 340–51. Bibliotheca ephemeridum theologicarum lovaniensium 48. Leuven: Leuven University Press, 1979.

———. "Tradition et rédaction en Actes 10,1–18." *Theologische Zeitschrift* 26 (1970): 22–45.

Brioso Sánchez, Máximo. "Mosco y Heliodoro. El símil de Etiópicas II, 22,4." *Habis* 17 (1986): 117–21.

Brodie, Thomas Louis. "The Departure for Jerusalem (Luke 9,51–56) as a Rhetorical Imitation of Elijah's Departure for the Jordan (2 Kgs 1,1–2,6)." *Biblica* 70 (1989): 96–109.

———. "Greco-Roman Imitation of Texts as a Partial Guide to Luke's Use of Sources." In *Luke-Acts: New Perspectives from the Society of Biblical Literature Seminar*. Ed. Charles H. Talbert, 17–46. New York: Crossroad, 1984.

———. "Luke 7,36–50 as an Internalization of 2 Kings 4,1–37: A Study in Luke's Use of Rhetorical Imitation." *Biblica* 64 (1983): 457–85.

———. "Luke-Acts as an Imitation and Emulation of the Elijah-Elisha Narratives." In *New Views on Luke and Acts*. Ed. Earl Richards, 78–85. Collegeville: Liturgical Press, 1990.

———. "Towards Unraveling Luke's Use of the Old Testament: Luke 7.11–17 as an *Imitatio* of 1 Kings 17.17–24." *New Testament Studies* 32 (1986): 247–67.

Bruce, F. F. *The Book of the Acts*. 3d ed. Grand Rapids: William B. Eerdmans, 1990.

Bruère, Richard T. "Silius Italicus *Punica* 3,62–162 and 4,763–822." *Classical Philology* 47 (1952): 219–27.

Budesheim, Thomas L. "Paul's *Abschiedsrede* in the Acts of the Apostles." *Harvard Theological Review* 69 (1976): 9–30.

Buffière, Félix. *Les Mythes d'Homère et la pensée grecque*. Collection des universités de France, publiée sous le patronage de l'Association Guillaume Budé. Paris: Belles Lettres, 1956.

Burchard, Christoph. "Paulus in der Apostelgeschichte." *Theologische Zeitschrift* 12 (1975): 881–95.

Carpenter, Thomas H. *Art and Myth in Ancient Greece: A Handbook*. London: Thames and Hudson, 1991.

Charlesworth, James H. *The Old Testament Pseudepigrapha*. vol. 1: *Apocalyptic Literature and Testaments*. Garden City: Doubleday, 1983.

Chase, F. H. "On πρηνὴς γενόμενος in Acts 1:18." *Journal of Theological Studies* 13 (1912): 278–85.

Clark, Donald Lemen. *Rhetoric in Greco-Roman Education*. New York: Columbia University Press, 1957.

Clarke, Howard. *Homer's Readers: A Historical Introduction to the "Iliad" and the "Odyssey."* Newark: University of Delaware Press, 1980.

Conzelmann, Hans. *The Acts of the Apostles: A Commentary on the Acts of the Apostles*. Trans. James Limburg, A. Thomas Kraabel, and Donald H. Juel. Ed. Eldon J. Epp with Christopher Mathews. Hermeneia. Philadelphia: Fortress Press, 1987.

Cribiore, Raffaela. *Writing, Teachers, and Students in Graeco-Roman Egypt*. American Studies in Papyrology 36. Atlanta: Scholars Press, 1997.

Danek, Georg. *Epos und Zitat. Studien zu den Quellen der Odyssee*. Wiener Studien 22. Wien: Österreichische Akademie der Wissenschaften, 1998.

Deichgräber, Karl. *Der letzte Gesang der Ilias*. Abhandlungen der Akademie der Wissenschaften in Mainz. Wiesbaden: Franz Steiner Verlag, 1972.

Desautels, L. "Le Mort de Judas (Mt 27,3–19; Ac 1,15–26)." *Science et Esprit* 38 (1986): 221–39.

Dibelius, Martin. *Studies in the Acts of the Apostles*. Trans. M. Ling and P. Schubert. Ed. H. Greeven. New York: Charles Scribner's Sons, 1956. (*Aufsätze zur Apostelgeschichte*. Ed. Heinrich Greeven. Forschungen zu Religion und Literatur des Alten und Neuen Testaments, n.s. 42. Göttingen: Vandenhoeck & Ruprecht, 1951.)

Dittenberger, Wilhem. *Sylloge inscriptionum graecarum*. 4th ed. Hildesheim: Georg Olms, 1960.

Donelson, Lewis R. "Cult Histories and the Sources of Acts." *Biblica* 68 (1987): 1–21.

Dubois, Jean-Daniel. "La Figure d'Elie dans la perspective lucanienne." *Revue d'histoire et de philosophie religieuses* 53 (1973): 155–76.

Dupont, Jacques. "La Construction du discours de Milet." In *Nouvelles études sur les actes des apôtres*, 424–45. Lectio Divina 118. Paris: Cerf, 1984.

———. "La Destinée de Judas prophetisée par David (Actes 1:16–20)." *Catholic Biblical Quarterly* 23 (1961): 41–51.

———. *Le Discours de Milet. Testament pastoral de Saint Paul (Actes 20, 18–36)*. Lectio Divina 32. Paris: Cerf, 1962.

———. "Le Douzième apôtre (Actes 1:15–26). À propos d'une explication récente." In *The New Testament Age*. Ed. W. Weinrich, 139–45. Macon: Mercer, 1984.

———. "Pierre délivré de prison (Ac. 12.1–11)." In *Nouvelles études sur les actes des apôtres*, 329–42. Lectio Divina 118. Paris: Cerf, 1984.

Ehrenberg, V. "Losung." *Paulys Real-Encyclopädie der classischen Altertumswissenschaft*. Ed. A. F. Pauly and G. Wissowa. 13.1451–1504.

Enslin, Morton S. "How the Story Grew: Judas in Fact and Fiction." *Festschrift to Honor F. Wilbur Gingrich: Lexicographer, Scholar, Teacher, and Committed Christian Layman*. Ed. Eugene Howard Barth and Ronald Edwin Cocroft, 123–41. Leiden: Brill, 1972.

Eulenstein, R. "Die wundersame Befreiung des Petrus aus Todesgefahr, Acta 12,1–23." *Wort und Dienst* 12 (1973): 43–69.

Exum, J. Cheryl, and Charles H. Talbert. "The Structure of Paul's Speech to the Ephesian Elders (Acts 20:18–35)." *Catholic Biblical Quarterly* 29 (1967): 233–36.

Fantham, Elaine. "Imitation and Decline: Rhetorical Theory and Practice in the First Century after Christ." *Classical Philology* 73 (1978): 102–16.

Feldman, Louis H. "Ascanius and Astyanax: A Comparative Study of Virgil and Homer." *Classical Journal* 53 (1957–58): 361–66.

Ferguson, Everett. "Qumran and Codex D (Acts 1:15–26)." *Revue de Qumran* 8 (1972): 75–80.

Finkelpearl, Ellen. *Metamorphosis of Language in Apuleius: A Study of Allusion in the Novel*. Ann Arbor: University of Michigan Press, 1998.

Fiske, George Converse. *Lucilius and Horace: A Study in the Classical Theory of Imitation*. Madison: University of Wisconsin Press, 1920. Reprint, Westport: Greenwood, 1971.

Fitzmyer, Joseph A. *The Acts of the Apostles: A New Translation with Introduction and Commentary.* Anchor Bible 31. New York: Doubleday, 1998.

Foakes Jackson, F. J., and Kirsopp Lake, eds. *The Beginnings of Christianity.* Part 1: *The Acts of the Apostles.* 5 vols. London: Macmillan, 1920–33; reprint, Grand Rapids: Baker Book House, 1965.

Frisch, Peter. *Die Träume bei Herodot.* Beiträge zur klassischen Philologie 27. Meisenheim: Anton Hain, 1968.

Fuller, R. H. "The Choice of Matthias." In *Studia Evangelica 6.* Ed. Elizabeth A. Livingstone, 140–46. Texte und Untersuchungen zur Geschichte der altchristlichen Literatur 112. Berlin: Akademie Verlag, 1973.

Funke, Hermann. "Homer und seine Leser in der Antike." *Forschung an der Universität Mannheim und Erbegnisse* (1976–77): 26–38.

Gärtner, H. A. "Les Rêves de Xerxès et d'Artaban chez Hérodote." *Ktéma* 8 (1983): 11–18.

Garrett, Susan R. "Exodus from Bondage: Luke 9:31 and Acts 12:1–24." *Catholic Biblical Quarterly* 53 (1991): 628–43.

Garson, R. W. "Notes on Some Homeric Echoes in Heliodorus' *Aethiopica*." *Acta Classica* 18 (1975): 137–40.

Gaventa, Beverly Roberts. *From Darkness to Light: Aspects of Conversion in the New Testament.* Overtures to Biblical Theology 20. Philadelphia: Fortress Press, 1986.

Genette, Gérard. *Palimpsestes. La Littérature au second degré.* Paris: Editions du Seuil, 1982.

Gils, Félix. *Jésus prophète d'après les évangiles synoptiques.* Orientalia et biblica lovaniensia 2. Leuven: Leuven University Press, 1957.

Giraudeau, Michèle. "L'Héritage épique chez Hérodote." *Bulletin de l'Association G. Budé* (1984): 4–13.

Greene, Thomas M. *The Light in Troy: Imitation and Discovery in Renaissance Poetry.* New Haven: Yale University Press, 1982.

Haacker, Klaus. "Dibelius und Cornelius. Ein Beispiel formgeschichtlicher Überlieferungskritik." *Biblische Zeitschrift* 24 (1980): 234–51.

Hägg, Tomas. *Narrative Technique in Ancient Greek Romances: Studies of Chariton, Xenophon Ephesius, and Achilles Tatius.* Skrifter Utgivna av Svenska Institutet: Athen. 8.8. Uppsala: Almquist & Wikells, 1971.

Haenchen, Ernst. *The Acts of the Apostles: A Commentary.* Trans. and ed. B. Noble et al. Philadelphia: Westminster Press, 1971.

Haft, Adele J. "Odysseus' Wrath and Grief in the *Iliad*: Agamemnon, the Ithacan King, and the Sack of Troy in Books 2, 4, and 14." *Classical Journal* 85 (1990): 97–114.

———. "τὰ δὴ νῦν πάντα τελεῖται: Prophecy and Recollection in the Assemblies of *Iliad* 2 and *Odyssey* 2." *Arethusa* 25 (1992): 223–40.

Hanson, John S. "The Dream-Vision Report and Acts 10.1–11.18: A Form-Critical Study." Dissertation, Harvard University, 1978.

Harrill, J. Albert. "The Dramatic Function of the Running Slave Rhoda (Acts 12.13–16): A Piece of Greco-Roman Comedy." *New Testament Studies* 46 (2000): 150–57.

Harris, J. Rendel. "Did Judas Really Commit Suicide?" *American Journal of Theology* 6 (1900): 490–513.

———. "St. Luke's Version of the Death of Judas." *American Journal of Theology* 18 (1914): 127–31.

Haulotte, Edgar. "Fondation d'une communauté de type universel. Actes 10,1–11,18." *Revue des sciences religieuses* 58 (1970): 63–100.

Headlam, James Wycliff. *Election by Lot at Athens.* 2d ed. Ed. D. C. MacGregor. Cambridge: Cambridge University Press, 1933.

Hemer, Colin J. "The Speeches of Acts: part 1: The Ephesian Elders at Miletus." *Tyndale Bulletin* 40 (1989): 76–85 and 239–59.

Henderson, Jeffrey. *Three Plays by Aristophanes: Staging Women.* New York: Routledge, 1996.

Hermann, Peter. *Wahrheit und Kunst. Geschichtschreibung und Plagiat im klassischen Altertum.* Leipzig: B. G. Teubner, 1911.

Heubeck, Alfred, et al. *A Commentary on Homer's Odyssey.* 3 vols. Oxford: Oxford University Press, 1988–92.

Hey, F. Oskar. *Der Traumglaube der Antike. Ein historischer Versuch.* Programm des kgl. Realgymnasiums München 1907–1908. Munich: F. Staub, 1908.

Hinds, Stephen. *Allusion and Intertext: Dynamics of Appropriation in Roman Poetry.* New York: Cambridge University Press, 1998.

Hofrichter, Peter. "Parallele zum 24. Gesang der Ilias in den Engelerscheinungen des lukanischen Doppelwerkes." *Protokolle zur Bibel* 2 (1993): 60–76.

Holladay, Carl R. *Fragments from Hellenistic Jewish Authors.* Vol. 1: *Historians.* Society of Biblical Literature Texts and Translations. Pseudepigrapha Series. Chico: Scholars Press, 1983.

Hornby, W. "The Twelve and the Phylarchs." *New Testament Studies* 32 (1986): 503–27.

Huber, Ludwig. "Herodots Homerverständnis." In *Synusia.* FS Wolgang Schadewaldt. Ed. Hellmut Flashar and Konrad Gaiser, 29–52. Pfullingen: Neske, 1965.

Hughes, Lisa B. "Vergil's Creusa and *Iliad* 6." *Mnemosyne* 50 (1997): 401–23.

Humphrey, Edith M. "Collision of Modes? — Vision and Determining Argument in Acts 10:1–11:18." *Semeia* 71 (1995): 65–84.

Hundt, Joachim. *Der Traumglaube bei Homer.* Greifswalder Beiträge zur Literatur- und Stilforschung 9. Greifswald: Hans Dallmeyer, 1935.

Irmscher, Johannes. "Vergil in der griechischen Antike." *Klio* 67 (1985): 281–85.

Jaubert, A. "L'Election de Matthias et le tirage au sort." In *Studia Evangelica* 6. Ed. Elizabeth A. Livingstone, 274–80. Texte und Untersuchungen zur Geschichte der altchristlichen Literatur 112. Berlin: Akademie Verlag, 1973.

Jervell, Jacob. *Die Apostelgeschichte übersetzt und erklärt.* Evangelisch-katholischer Kommentar zum Neuen Testament 3. Göttingen: Vandenhoeck & Ruprecht, 1998.

Johansen, Knud Friss. *The Iliad in Early Greek Art.* Copenhagen: Munksgaard, 1967.

Juhnke, Herbert. *Homerisches in römischer Epik flavischer Zeit. Untersuchungen zu Szenennachbildungen und Strukturentsprechungen in Statius' Thebais und Achilleis und in Silius' Punica.* Zetemata 53. Munich: Becks, 1972.

Junod, Eric. "Origène, Eusèbe et la tradition sur la répartition des champs de mission des apôtres (Eusèbe, *HE* III,1,1–3)." In *Les Actes apocryphes des apôtres. Christianisme et monde païen.* Ed. François Bovon, 233–48. Publication de la Faculté de Théologie de l'Université de Genève 4. Geneva: Labor et Fides, 1981.

Kaestli, Jean-Daniel. "Les Scènes d'attribution des champs de mission et de départ de l'apôtre dans les Actes apocryphes." In *Les Actes apocryphes des apôtres. Christianisme et monde païen.* Ed. François Bovon, 149–64. Publication de la Faculté de Théologie de l'Université de Genève 4. Geneva: Labor et Fides, 1981.

Keck, Fridolin. *Die öffentliche Abschiedsrede Jesu in Lk 20,45–21,36. Eine redaktions-und motivgeschichtliche Untersuchung,* Forschung zur Bibel 25. Stuttgart: Verlag Katholisches Bibelwerk, 1973.

Kennedy, George A. *The Art of Persuasion in Greece.* Princeton: Princeton University Press, 1963.

Kessels, A. H. M. *Studies in the Dream in Greek Literature.* Utrecht: HES Publishers, 1978.

Keydell, R. "Quintus Smyrnaeus und Vergil." *Hermes* 82 (1954): 254–56.

Kilgallen, John J. "Paul's Speech to the Ephesian Elders: Its Structure (Acts 20:18–35)." *Ephemerides theologicae lovanienses* 70 (1994): 112–121.

Kindstrand, Jan Fredrik. *Homer in der zweiten Sophistik.* Acta Universitatis Upsaliensis. Studia Graeca Upsaliensia 7. Uppsala: University of Uppsala, 1973.

Kirk, G. S. *The Iliad: A Commentary.* Vols. 1–2. Cambridge: Cambridge University Press, 1985–90.

Klein, Günter. *Die zwölf Apostel. Ursprung und Gehalt einer Idee.* Forschungen zu Religion und Literatur des Alten und Neuen Testaments, n.s. 59. Göttingen: Vandenhoeck & Ruprecht, 1961.

Kleinknecht, H. "Laokoon." *Hermes* 79 (1944): 66–111.

Knauer, Georg Nicolaus. *Die Aeneis und Homer.* 2d ed. Hypomnemata 7. Göttingen: Vandenhoeck & Ruprecht, 1979.

——. "Vergil and Homer." *Aufstieg und Niedergang der römischen Welt.* Ed. H. Temporini and W. Haase. 2.32.2.870–918.

——. "Vergil's *Aeneid* and Homer." In *Oxford Readings in Vergil's Aeneid.* Ed. S. J. Harrison, 390–412. Oxford: Oxford University Press, 1990.

Knight, Virginia. *The Renewal of Epic: Responses to Homer in the Argonautica of Apollonius.* Mnemosyne, Supplementum 152. Leiden: E. J. Brill, 1995.

Knoch, Otto. *Die "Testamente" des Petrus und Paulus. Die Sicherung der apostolischen Überlieferung in der spätneutestamentlichen Zeit.* Sources bibliques 62. Stuttgart: KBW Verlag, 1973.

Köhnken, Adolf. "Der dritte Traum des Xerxes bei Herodot." *Hermes* 116 (1988): 24–40.

Kolenkow, Anitra Bingham. "Testaments: The Literary Genre 'Testament.'" In *Early Judaism and Its Modern Interpreters.* Ed. Robert A. Kraft and George W. E. Nickelsburg, 259–67. The Bible and its Modern Interpreters 2. Atlanta: Scholars Press, 1986.

Koller, H. *Die Mimesis in der Antike: Nachahmung, Darstellung, Ausdruck.* Berne: A. Francke, 1954.

Kopidakis, M. Z. "Ἰώσηφος ὁμηρίζων." *Hellenika* 37 (1986): 3–25.

Kratz, Reinhard. *Rettungswunder. Motiv-, traditions- und formkritische Aufarbeitung einer biblischen Gattung.* Europäische Hochschulschriften 123. Frankfurt am Main: Peter Lang, 1979.

Kuhn, Thomas S. *The Structure of Scientific Revolutions.* 3d ed. Chicago: University of Chicago Press, 1996.

Kurz, William S. "Effects of Variant Narrators in Acts 10–11." *New Testament Studies* 42 (1997): 570–86.

———. "Luke 22:14–38 and Greco-Roman and Biblical Farewell Addresses." *Journal of Bibilical Literature* 104 (1985): 251–68.

Kytzler, Bernard, "Imitatio und Aemulatio in der Thebais des Statius." *Hermes* 97 (1969): 209–32.

Lake, Kirsopp. "The Death of Judas." In *The Beginnings of Christianity.* Part 1: *The Acts of the Apostles.* 5 vols. Ed. F. J. Foakes Jackson, and Kirsopp Lake. 5.22–30. London: Macmillan, 1920–33; reprint, Grand Rapids: Baker Book House, 1965.

Lamberton, Robert. *Homer the Theologian: Neoplatonist Allegorical Reading and the Growth of the Epic Tradition.* Transformation of the Classical Heritage 9. Berkeley: University of California Press, 1986.

Lamberton, Robert, and John J. Keaney, eds. *Homer's Ancient Readers: The Hermeneutics of Greek Epic's Earliest Exegetes.* Princeton: Princeton University Press, 1992.

Lambrecht, Jan. "Paul's Farewell-Address at Miletus (Acts 20,17–38)." In *Les Actes des apôtres. Tradition, rédaction, théologie.* Ed. Jacob Kremer et al., 307–37. Bibliotheca ephemeridum theologicarum lovaniensium 48. Leuven: Leuven University Press, 1979.

Lampe, G. W. H. " 'Grievous Wolves' (Acts 20:29)." In *Christ and Spirit.* FS C. F. D. Moule. Ed. Barnabas Lindars and Stephen S. Smalley, 253–68. Cambridge: Cambridge University Press, 1973.

Latacz, Joachim. "Funktionen des Traums in der antiken Literatur." *Würzburger Jahrbücher für die Altertumswissenschaft* 10 (1984): 23–39.

Lausberg, Marion. "Lucan und Homer." *Aufstieg und Niedergang der römischen Welt.* Ed. H. Temporini and W. Haase. 2.32.3.1565–1622.

Löning, Karl. "Die Korneliustradition." *Biblische Zeitschrift* 18 (1974): 1–19.

Lövestam, Evald. "Paul's Address at Miletus (Acts 20:18–35)." *Studia theologica* 41 (1987): 1–10.

Lohfink, Gerhard. "Der Losvorgang in Apg. 1,26." *Biblische Zeitschrift* 19 (1975): 247–49.

Lohmann, Dieter. *Die Andromache-Szenen der Ilias. Ansätze und Methoden der Homer-Interpretation.* Spudasmata 42. Hildesheim: Olms Verlag, 1988.

Macan, Reginald Walter. *Herodotus. The Seventh, Eighth, and Ninth Books.* London: Macmillan, 1908.

MacDonald, Dennis R. *Christianizing Homer: "The Odyssey," Plato, and "The Acts of Andrew."* New York: Oxford University Press, 1994.

———. "The Ending of Luke and the Ending of the *Odyssey.*" In *For a Later Generation: The Transformation of Tradition in Israel, Early Judaism and Early Christianity.* Ed. Randal A. Argall et al., 161–68. Harrisburg: Trinity Press International, 2000.

———. *The Homeric Epics and the Gospel of Mark.* New Haven: Yale University Press, 2000.

———. *The Legend and the Apostle: The Battle for Paul in Story and Canon.* Philadelphia: Westminster Press, 1983.

———. "Legends of the Apostles." In *Eusebius, Christianity, and Judaism.* Ed. Harold W. Attridge and Gohei Hata, 166–79. Detroit: Wayne State University Press, 1992.

———. "Luke's Eutychus and Homer's Elpenor: Acts 20:7–12 and *Odyssey* 10–12." *Journal of Higher Criticism* 1 (1994): 5–24.

——, ed. *Mimesis and Intertextuality in Antiquity and Christianity*. Studies in Antiquity and Christianity. Harrisburg: Trinity Press International, 2001.

——. "The Shipwrecks of Odysseus and Paul." *New Testament Studies* 45 (1999): 88–107.

——."The Soporific Angel in Acts 12:1–17 and Hermes' Visit to Priam in *Iliad* 24: Luke's Emulation of the Epic." *Forum,* n.s. 2.2 (1999): 179–87.

——. "Tobit and the *Odyssey*." In *Mimesis and Intertextuality in Antiquity and Christianity*." Ed. Dennis R. MacDonald, 11–40. Studies in Antiquity and Christianity. Harrisburg: Trinity Press International, 2001.

Manns, Frédéric. "Un Midrash chrétien. Le Récit de la mort de Judas." *Revue des sciences religieuses* 54 (1980): 197–203.

Martucci, Jean. "Les Récits de miracle. Influence des récits de l'Ancient Testament sur ceux du Nouveau." *Science et esprit* 27 (1975): 133–46.

Masson, C. "La Reconstitution du collège des Douze. D'après Actes 1:15–26." *Revue de théologie et de philosophie* 3 (1955): 193–201.

McKeon, Richard. "Literary Criticism and the Concept of Imitation in Antiquity." In *Critics and Criticism*. Ed. Ronald Salmon Crane, 147–75. Chicago: University of Chicago Press, 1952.

Melandri, Eleonora. "La Parafrasi di M. Moscopulo ad Hom. A–B 493 e la tradizione esegetica e lessiografica dell'Iliade." *Prometheus* 9 (1983), 177–92.

Menoud, P.-H. "Les Additions au groupe des douze apôtres, d'après le livre des Actes." *Revue d'histoire et de philosophie religieuses* 37 (1957): 71–80.

Merkelbach, Reinhold. *Die Quellen des griechischen Alexanderromans*. 2d ed., with Jürgen Trumpf. Zetemata 9. Munich: Beck, 1977.

Messer, William Stuart. *The Dream in Homer and Greek Tragedy*. New York: Columbia University Press, 1918.

Metz, Wilhelm. "Hektor als der homerischste aller homerischen Helden." *Gymnasium* 97 (1990): 385–404.

Michel, Hans-Joachim. *Die Abschiedsrede des Paulus an die Kirche, Apg. 20,17–38. Motivgeschichte und theologische Bedeutung*. Studien zum Alten und Neuen Testament 35. Munich: Kösel-Verlag, 1973.

Mondino, M. "Di alcune fonti de Quinto Smirneo: V. Quinto Smirneo e i poeti latini." *Rivista di studi classici* 5 (1957): 229–35.

Morgan, Teresa. *Literate Education in the Hellenistic and Roman Worlds*. New York: Cambridge University Press, 1998.

Morris, James F. " 'Dream Scenes' in Homer: A Study in Variation." *Transactions of the American Philological Association* 113 (1983): 39–54.

Munck, Johannes. "Discours d'adieu dans le Nouveau Testament et dans la littérature biblique." In *Aux Sources de la tradition chrétienne. Mélanges offerts à M. Goguel,* 155–70. Neuchâtel: Delachaux & Niestlé, 1950.

Murley, Clyde. "The Use of Messenger Gods by Vergil and Homer." *Vergilius* 3 (1939): 3–11.

Nellessen, E. "Tradition und Schrift in der Perikope von der Erwählung des Matthias (Apg 1, 15–26)." *Biblische Zeitschrift* 19 (1975): 205–18.

——. *Zeugnis für Jesus und das Wort. Exegetische Untersuchungen zum lukanischen Zeugnisbegriff*. Bonner biblische Beiträge 43. Köln: Peter Hanstein, 1976.

Nordheim, Eckhard von. *Die Lehre der Alten.* 2 vols. Arbeiten zur Literatur und Geschichte des hellenistischen Judentums 13. Leiden: E. J. Brill, 1980.

North, Helen. "The Use of Poetry in the Training of the Ancient Orator." *Traditio* 8 (1952): 1–33.

Öhler, Markus. *Elia im Neuen Testament. Untersuchungen zur Bedeutung des alttestamentlichen Propheten im frühen Christentum.* Beihefte zur Zeitschrift für die neutestamentliche Wissenschaft 88. Berlin: Walter de Gruyter, 1997.

Pack, Roger A. *The Greek and Latin Literary Texts from Greco-Roman Egypt.* 2d ed. Ann Arbor: University of Michigan Press, 1965.

Prast, Franz. *Presbyter und Evangelium in nachapostolischer Zeit. Die Abschiedsrede des Paulus in Milet (Apg 20,17–38) im Rahmen der lukanischen Konzeption der Evangeliumsverkündigung.* Forschung zur Bibel 29. Stuttgart: Verlag katholisches Bibelwerk, 1979.

Radl, W. "Befreiung aus dem Gefängnis. Die Darstellung eines biblischen Grundthemas in Apg. 12." *Biblische Zeitschrift* 27 (1983): 81–96.

Ramsay, William M. *The Bearing of Recent Discovery on the Trustworthiness of the New Testament.* 4th ed. London: Hodder and Stoughton, 1920.

Reardon, B. P. *Collected Ancient Greek Novels.* Berkeley: University of California Press, 1989.

———. *Courants littéraires grecs des IIᵉ et IIIᵉ siècles après J.-C.* Annales littéraires de l'Université de Nantes 3. Paris: Belles Lettres, 1971.

Rengstorf, Karl Heinrich. "The Election of Matthias." In *Current Issues in New Testament Interpretation.* Ed. W. Klassen and G. F. Snyder, 178–92. New York: Harper, 1962.

Renié, J. "L'Election de Mathias (Act. 1,15–26). Authenticité du récit." *Revue biblique* 55 (1948): 43–53.

Richardson, Nicholas. *The Iliad: A Commentary,* vol. 6: *Books 21–24.* Cambridge: Cambridge University Press, 1993.

Roloff, Jürgen. *Die Apostelgeschichte übersetzt und erklärt.* 17th ed. Das Neue Testament deutsch 5. Göttingen: Vandenhoeck & Ruprecht, 1981.

Roth, Wolfgang. *Hebrew Gospel: Cracking the Code of Mark.* Oak Park: Meyer-Stone Books, 1988.

Russell, D. A. "De imitatione." In *Creative Imitation in Latin Literature.* Ed. D. A. West and A. J. Woodman, 1–16. Cambridge: Cambridge University Press, 1979.

Rutherford, Richard B. "From the *Iliad* to the *Odyssey.*" *Bulletin of the Institute of Classical Studies of the University of London* 38 (1991–93): 37–54.

Rutz, W. "Die Träume des Pompeius in Lucans Pharsalia." *Hermes* 91 (1963): 334–45.

Schadewaldt, W. "Hector and Andromache." In *Homer: German Scholarship in Translation.* Trans. G. M. Wright and P. V. Jones, 124–42. Oxford: Clarendon Press, 1997.

Scherer, Margaret R. *The Legends of Troy in Art and Literature.* New York: Phaedon, 1964.

Schmidt, F. "Election et tirage au sort (1QS vi,13–23 et Ac 1,15–26)." *Revue d'histoire et de philosophie religieuses* 80 (2000): 105–17.

Schmithals, Walter. *Die Apostelgeschichte des Lukas.* Zürcher Bibelkommentar, Neues Testament 3.2. Zurich: Theologischer Verlag, 1982.

Schürmann, Heinz. *Das Lukasevangelium.* 3d ed. Herders theologischer Kommentar zum Neuen Testament 3. Freiburg: Herder, 1984.

———. "Das Testament des Paulus für die Kirche, Apg 20, 18–35." In *Traditionsgeschichtliche Untersuchungen zu den synoptischen Evangelien. Beiträge,* 310–40. Düsseldorf: Patmos Verlag, 1968.

Schwarz, G. *Jesus und Judas. Aramaistische Untersuchungen zur Jesus-Judas-Überlieferung der Evangelien und der Apostelgeschichte.* Beiträge zur Wissenschaft vom Alten (und Neuen) Testament 123. Stuttgart: Kohlhammer, 1988.

Schweizer, Eduard. "Zu Apg. 1, 16–22." *Theologische Zeitschrift* 14 (1958): 46.

Scott, John A. *Homer and His Influence.* Boston: Marshall Jones, 1925.

———. "The Parting of Hector and Andromache." *Classical Journal* 9 (1914): 274–77.

Seaford, Richard. "Homer and Tragic Sacrifice." *Transactions of the American Philological Association* 119 (1989): 87–95.

Skinner, Marilyn B. "Briseis, the Trojan Women, and Erinna." *Classical World* 75 (1982): 265–69.

Snodgrass, Anthony M. *Homer and the Artists: Text and Picture in Early Greek Art.* New York: Cambridge University Press, 1998.

Soards, Marion L. *The Speeches in Acts: Their Content, Context, and Concerns.* Louisville: Westminster/John Knox, 1994.

Söder, Rosa. *Die apokryphen Apostlegeschichten und die romanhafte Literatur der Antike.* Würzburger Studien zur Altertumswissenschaft 3. Darmstadt: Wissenschaftliche Buchgesellschaft, 1969. Reprint of 1932 edition.

Stahl, William Harris. *Macrobius: Commentary on the Dream of Scipio.* New York: Columbia University Press, 1952.

Stauffer, Ethelbert. "Jüdische Erbe im urchristlichen Kirchenrecht." *Theologische Literaturzeitung* 77 (1952): 201–6.

Steiner, Hans Rudolf. *Der Traum in der Aeneis.* Noctes Romanae 5. Bern: Paul Haupt, 1952.

Stemplinger, Eduard. *Das Plagiat in der griechischen Literatur.* Leipzig: B. G. Teubner, 1912. Reprint, Hildesheim: Georg Olms Verlag, 1990.

Strasburger, Hermann. *Homer und die Geschichtsschreibung.* Sitzungsberichte der Heidelberger Akademie der Wissenschaften. Philosophisch-historische Klasse. Heidelberg: C. Winter, 1972.

Strobel, August. "Passa-Symbolik und Passa-Wunder in Act. xii.3ff." *New Testament Studies* 4 (1957–58): 210–15.

Tarrant, R. J. "Aspects of Virgil's Reception in Antiquity." In *The Cambridge Companion to Virgil.* Ed. Charles Martindale, 56–72. Cambridge: Cambridge University Press, 1997.

Tragen, P.-R. "Les 'Destinataires' du discours de Milet. Une approche du cadre communautaire d'Ac 20,18–35." In *A Cause de l'évangile. Etudes sur les synoptiques et les Actes,* 779–98. Paris: Cerf, 1985.

Tyson, Joseph B. "The Gentile Mission and the Authority of Scripture in Acts." *New Testament Studies* 33 (1987): 619–31.

van der Horst, P. W. "Hellenistic Parallels to the Acts of the Apostles: 1:1–26." *Zeitschrift für die neutestamentliche Wissenschaft* 74 (1983): 17–26.

Vogler, Werner. *Judas Iskarioth. Untersuchungen zu Tradition und Redaktion von Texten des Neuen Testaments und außerkanonischer Schriften.* Theologische Arbeiten 11. Berlin: Evangelische Verlagsanstalt, 1983.

Watson, Duane F. "Paul's Speech to the Ephesian Elders (Acts 20.17–38): Epideictic Rhetoric of Farewell." In *Persuasive Artistry: Studies in New Testament Rhetoric in Honor of George A. Kennedy.* Ed. Duane F. Watson, 184–208. Journal for the Study of the New Testament Supplements 50.1. Sheffield: JSOT Press, 1991.

Weinreich, Otto. "Gebet und Wunder. Zwei Abhandlungen zur Religions- und Literaturgeschichte." In *Genethliakon*, FS Wilhelm Schmid, 169–464. Tübinger Beiträge zur Altertumswissenschaft 5. Stuttgart: W. Kohlhammer, 1929.

———. *Religionsgeschichtliche Studien.* Darmstadt: Wissenschaftliche Buchgesellschaft, 1968.

Weiser, Alfons. *Die Apostelgeschichte.* 2 vols. Ökumenischer Taschenbuchkommentar zum Neuen Testament 5. Gütersloh: Gütersloher Verlagshaus Mohn, 1981.

———. "Die Nachwahl des Matthias (Apg 1,15–26). Zur Rezeption und Deutung urchristlicher Geschichte durch Lukas." In *Zur Geschichte des Urchristentums.* Ed. G. Dautzenberg et al., 97–110. Freiburg: Herder, 1979.

White, Robert J. *The Interpretation of Dreams = Oneirocritica by Artemidorus.* Noyes Classical Studies. Park Ridge: Noyes Press, 1975.

Wikenhauser, Alfred. "Doppelträume." *Biblica* 29 (1948): 100–111.

Wilamowitz-Moellendorff, Ulrich von. *Die Ilias und Homer.* Berlin: Weidmann, 1916.

Wilcox, Max. "The Judas-Tradition in Acts 1:15–26." *New Testament Studies* 19 (1973): 438–52.

Williams, G. "Roman Poets as Literary Historians: Some Aspects of *Imitatio.*" *Illinois Classical Studies* 8 (1983): 211–37.

Wills, Lawrence. "The Form of the Sermon in Hellenistic Judaism and Early Christianity." *Harvard Theological Review* 77 (1984): 277–99.

Wilson, Walter T. "Urban Legends: Acts 10:1–11:18 and the Strategies of Greco-Roman Foundation Narratives." *Journal of Biblical Literature* 120 (2001): 77–99.

Witherington, Ben, III. *The Acts of the Apostles: A Socio-Rhetorical Commentary.* Grand Rapids: William B. Eerdmans, 1998.

Witherup, Ronald D. "Cornelius Over and Over and Over Again: 'Functional Redundancy' in the Acts of the Apostles." *Journal for the Study of the New Testament* 49 (1993): 45–66.

Woodford, Susan. *The Trojan War in Ancient Art.* Ithaca: Cornell University Press, 1993.

Zeegers-Vander Vorst, Nicole. *Les Citations des poètes grecs chez les apologistes chrétiens du IIᵉ siècle.* Recueil de travaux d'histoire et de philologie 4.47. Leuven: Leuven University Press, 1972.

Zielinski, Thadeusz. "De Andromacha Posthomerica." *Eos* 31 (1928): 1–39.

Zmijewski, Josef. *Die Apostelgeschichte.* Regensburger Neues Testament. Regensburg: Pustet, 1994.

Index